Tapestry 5

Building Web Applications

A step-by-step guide to Java web development with the developer-friendly Apache Tapestry framework

Alexander Kolesnikov

BIRMINGHAM - MUMBAI

Tapestry 5

Building Web Applications

First published: January 2008

Production Reference: 1090108

Published by Packt Publishing Ltd.
32 Lincoln Road
Olton
Birmingham, B27 6PA, UK.

ISBN 978-1-847193-07-0

www.packtpub.com

Cover Image by Nilesh R. Mohite (nilpreet2000@yahoo.co.in)

Credits

Author

Alexander Kolesnikov

Reviewers

Howard Lewis Ship

Massimo Lusetti

Acquisition Editor

Viraj Joshi

Technical Editor

Sarvesh Shanbhag

Editorial Team Leader

Mithil Kulkarni

Project Manager

Abhijeet Deobhakta

Project Coordinator

Abhijeet Deobhakta

Indexer

Monica Ajmera

Proofreader

Angie Butcher

Production Coordinator

Shantanu Zagade

Cover Work

Shantanu Zagade

About the Author

Alexander Kolesnikov is an author and software developer from Greenock, Scotland. He wrote his first program in FORTRAN back in 1979 for a computer that occupied several rooms. He currently works as a Java Web Developer for CIGNA International. A Soviet military researcher in the past, he recently graduated as a Master of Science with Distinction in Enterprise Systems Development from Glasgow Caledonian University and has also gained a number of professional certifications from Sun Microsystems (SCJP, SCWCD, SCBCD). His first book on software development was "Java Drawing With Apache Batik" (BrainySoftware, 2007).

He is interested in many things, ranging from the most recent web technologies to alternative medicine and wishes wholeheartedly that a day was at least three times longer than it is.

I am grateful to the people who made my Tapestry quest happen, and thanks to whom it goes on and on: Howard Lewis Ship, the creator of Tapestry, with special thanks for finding time to review this book; Brian Hainey, my tutor at Glasgow Caledonian, for suggesting Tapestry as a topic for my MSc dissertation; Ian McClure, my manager at CIGNA, who bravely accepted Tapestry as the framework for our next major project, and Viraj Joshi from Packt Publishing whose insightfulness made this book possible.

About the Reviewers

Howard M. Lewis Ship is the creator of Tapestry, and a leading authority on Java development for the enterprise. He's worked at a handful of software and consulting companies in the greater Boston area before becoming an independent consultant in 2003, specializing in Tapestry development and training. Howard now lives in Portland, Oregon with his wife Suzanne, a novelist. Howard has helped review a number of books, and wrote his own book in 2003, Tapestry in Action, covering Tapestry 3. He currently works for Formos Software Development in Vancouver, Washington as a Tapestry Architect and Evangelist.

Massimo Lusetti is a 33 year old IT passionate. He started off playing with Spectrum 80 home computer and having fun with Basic and Z80 registers. Before becoming a Java and Unix addicted developer, he gained some experience with different operating systems. He used OS/2 Warp and Rexx till IBM abandoned it, then started using Linux (1.x version) in 1996, lately in 2000 he discover the BSD world and never looked back.

He started working with Java in 1998 just when Java Swing was released with Java 1.2. Since then he adopted Java for various things—from GUI applications to distributed ones. Besides programming, he developed an interest in Unix programming—particularly in security issues.

In 2000 he founded his own company DataCode SRL which delivers custom software solutions.

Table of Contents

Preface

Tapestry is an open-source framework for creating dynamic, robust, and highly scalable web applications in Java. It divides a web application into a set of pages, each constructed using components. It provides various features such as, allowing the Tapestry framework to assume responsibility for key concerns such as user input validation, localization/internationalization, and exception reporting. It involves creating HTML templates using plain HTML, and combining the templates with small amounts of Java code using (optional) XML descriptor files. Tapestry is designed to handle anything from tiny applications all the way up to massive applications consisting of hundreds of individual pages, developed by large, diverse teams.

What This Book Covers

Chapter 1 looks at the overall features of Tapestry and tells you why Tapestry is special. It talks about the place of Tapestry in the world of Java web development. It also shows the journey from Tapestry 3 to the current Tapestry 5.

Chapter 2 deals with creating a working environment. To develop a Tapestry application, you need to download and install the Java Development Kit (JDK), a project management tool like Maven, and an Integrated Development Environment (IDE) like NetBeans or Eclipse. It also gives a brief description of the procedure to to follow when creating a Tapestry project.

Chapter 3 describes the various features of Tapestry like page templates and page classes, expansions, components, and so on. It actually makes you comfortable working with Tapestry, creating a bare-bones project, handling expansions and components, navigating between pages, and creating and using Application State Objects (ASOs).

Chapter 4 examines some of the components in Tapestry like TextField, PasswordField, Label, PageLink, ActionLink, Loop, If, Output, RadioGroup and Radio, Checkbox, Submit and Select. These are simple components which map almost directly to HTML controls and elements. These are normally used on every page of a Tapestry web application and help you in creating a functionally-rich user interface.

Chapter 5 examines some of the more advanced components such as Grid, BeanEditForm, DateField and FCKEditor. Using these, you can build some functionally-rich user interfaces. You can easily implement repeating patterns like tables and dates on a web page.

Chapter 6 covers that feature of Tapestry 5 which prevents a user to input erroneous data on a web page. This feature, which is called user input validation, not only identifies the erroneous field and marks it in some way, but may also explain why it is erroneous.

Chapter 7 examines internationalization and localization. These are used to make a web application multi-lingual and display it in different locales.

Chapter 8 deals with creating a custom component to enable reusability of code by way of packaging repeating patterns into one single custom component.

Appendix A takes you through the basics of Java for developing web applications. It examines the standard structure of a Java web application, the basics of deployment descriptor and WAR files, and Java enabled services.

Appendix B tells you how to use db4o to create a real data source. It allows you to store even the most complex object structures with ease, while achieving the highest level of performance.

Appendix C gives you some references for obtaining extra information about Tapestry 5 and earlier versions.

Who is This Book for

This book is for those who want to build sophisticated Java web applications quickly and easily. It assumes that the reader is reasonably comfortable with the Java programming language, but no knowledge of web technologies is needed. For experienced Servlet, JSP, or Struts developers, the book will show an alternative way that will allow them to raise their productivity to an incomparable level. With this book you will see that a contemporary component-based framework can be easy to learn and a pleasure to work with.

Conventions

In this book, you will find a number of styles of text that distinguish between different kinds of information. Here are some examples of these styles, and an explanation of their meaning.

There are three styles for code. Code words in text are shown as follows: "A Template must be a well-formed XML document, which means that every element must be either declared as empty or properly closed (say, you can have `<img src=""/>` or `<img src=""></img>`, but not just `<img src="">`), and all attributes' values must be enclosed in quotation marks."

A block of code will be set as follows:

```
package com.packtpub.t5first.pages;
import java.util.Date;
/**
 * Start page of application t5first.
 */
public class Start
{
  public String getCurrentTime()
  {
    Date date = new Date();
    String message = ". Tapestry is cool!";
    return date + message;
  }
}
```

New terms and **important words** are introduced in a bold-type font.

Words that you see on the screen, in menus or dialog boxes for example, appear in our text like this: "Let's add one more piece of information to those that we already collect from the users at the **Registration** page—**Date Of Birth**."

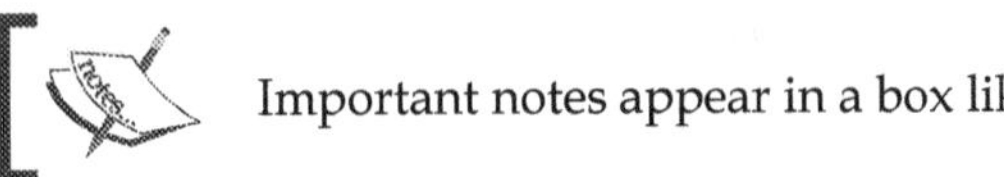

Important notes appear in a box like this.

Reader Feedback

Feedback from our readers is always welcome. Let us know what you think about this book, what you liked or disliked. Reader feedback is important in order for us to develop titles that you get the most out of.

To send us general feedback, simply send an email to feedback@packtpub.com, making sure to mention the book title in the subject of your message.

If there is a book that you need and would like to see us publish, please send us a note in the **SUGGEST A TITLE** form on www.packtpub.com or email suggest@packtpub.com.

If there is a topic that you have expertise in and you are interested in either writing or contributing to a book, see our author guide on www.packtpub.com/authors.

Customer Support

Now that you are the proud owner of a Packt book, we have a number of things to help you to get the most from your purchase.

Downloading the Example Code for the Book

Visit http://www.packtpub.com/support, and select this book from the list of titles to download any example code or extra resources for this book. The files available for download will then be displayed.

The downloadable files contain instructions on how to use them.

Errata

Although we have taken every care to ensure the accuracy of our contents, mistakes do happen. If you find a mistake in one of our books—maybe a mistake in text or code—we would be grateful if you would report this to us. By doing this you can save other readers from frustration, and help to improve subsequent versions of this book. If you find any errata, report them by visiting http://www.packtpub.com/support, selecting your book, clicking on the **Submit Errata** link, and entering the details of your errata. Once your errata are verified, your submission will be accepted and the errata are added to the list of existing errata. The existing errata can be viewed by selecting your title from http://www.packtpub.com/support.

Questions

You can contact us at questions@packtpub.com if you are having a problem with some aspect of the book, and we will do our best to address it.

Foreword

I think we may be on to something here.

You see, Tapestry has been around, in one form or another, for about eight years now. Eight years. A lot can happen in eight years. I've gotten married, relocated across country, written a book, worked for several companies, and consulted at dozens more. I've made many new friends, especially that raucous pirate crew that speaks at the No Fluff Just Stuff software symposiums. I've criss-crossed the country dozens of times, always with a laptop in hand, always tinkering away at the Tapestry source code. Meanwhile, we've seen waves of Java hype and anti-hype, the coming of Ruby and Rails, the growth of the Java language in ways most welcome (and some less so), and the new breed of JVM languages such as Groovy, JRuby and Scala. In fact, the only constants for me over the last eight years have been my wife Suzanne, and Tapestry.

I've been feeling something building. We're in a new age of coding now, an age in which the reach of an individual coder has been greatly extended. There's a universe of Java code libraries waiting to be downloaded and used. Java's cross platform capabilities mean we can develop and test on a personal computer or laptop and then push the exact same binaries to a server for production. If you can't appreciate how wonderful that is, you may be missing the forest for the trees. We've taken Java's strengths for granted and focused on its weaknesses, and too many are waiting with baited breath for The Next Big Thing.

I don't think there's going to be one Next Big Thing. Java's arrival was a Next Big Thing, and though it's unlikely to be the Last Next Big Thing, the rapid rise of Java was a special event, a coincidence of timing that could only happen by riding in the wake of the first introduction of the Internet and the World Wide Web. But I think there's going to be a lot of Next Little Things and we're all free to combine a few of those into our own personal Next Big Thing.

I think Tapestry is destined to be one of the key Next Little Things, one that's going to really change how we all do our jobs. Many a Next Thing is an experiment waiting to be proved valid. Tapestry went through that stage nearly eight years ago, but now benefits from all those years of experience: not just my personal involvement, but the experience of the rest of the Tapestry developers, and the experience of the Tapestry user community. It's got a proven track record for its basic concepts, its governing principles, and its overall approach, even as the code base has been revitalized (ok, rewritten) for Tapestry 5.

But code, design, architecture ... that's all *technology*, and the best technology in the universe doesn't guarantee a win. *Community* is what defines success, a concept well known (if poorly applied) in the open source world, and slowly dawning in the proprietary world. That's where Alexander comes in. Community is best expressed when individuals do ridiculous things for the benefit of others in the community. For example, writing a fourteen (fourteen!) part on-line tutorial about Tapestry 4, and now following up with this book on Tapestry 5.

I think you'll see that Alexander has a real handle on what Tapestry is, and more importantly, how best to use it. Tapestry isn't a Swiss Army knife or even a toolbox; it's an entire workshop for creating web applications in Java. This book is a great guided tour of that workshop, showing where all the bits and pieces are stored and how they can be combined to get things done. Dive in, get smart and start having fun with Tapestry!

Howard M. Lewis Ship

Jan 2, 2008

Portland, Oregon

1
Introduction to Tapestry

Programming for the Web is very rewarding. Your application, once deployed, becomes available to millions of people, and it doesn't matter which the kind of computers they are using. If they have a reasonably new web browser, they have a good chance of being able to fully appreciate your creation, whether they are running Windows, Linux, Mac OS, or UNIX on their workstation or hand held device.

To become a web developer, one would normally need to be intimately familiar with the strange world of HTTP protocol—requests and responses flying across the globe, special places for storing information like session or application context, and so on. In short, one would have to go to a much lower level of software development.

This change of level is especially striking for those who have had some experience with a Rapid Application Development (RAD) environment, like Borland Delphi or Microsoft Visual Basic. When using such an environment, it seems so natural that when a button is pressed on a form the desktop application is immediately ready to do something in response to the user's action and all you need to do as a programmer is to provide some code that will run in response.

However, when it comes to web development, a developer needs to keep in mind a long chain of low level processes that run before and after he or she is able to do something useful in response to a button press on a web page. Is this a GET or a POST request? How do we extract useful information from the request? How do we store this information? How do we create a response?

Working at that level means a lot of time is spent in solving relatively simple problems. As web applications become more and more popular it becomes obvious that a more efficient, higher level approach to web development is needed.

Nowadays, several solutions are offered to solve this problem on different software development platforms. In the world of Java, the most efficient and elegant solution is presented by **Apache Tapestry**. Tapestry is an open-source Java web framework, conceived by Howard Lewis Ship and currently developed by a team of devoted Java pundits from around the world.

Why is Tapestry Special?

Tapestry is an example of a framework that was created keeping the developer in mind.

First of all, its paradigm is very close to that of the RAD environment. A button on the Tapestry page has an event handler method associated with it in a declarative way, and the method is invoked when the button is pressed. The Tapestry web developer doesn't need to remember that the button on the page in a user's web browser and the code of the event handler method on the web server can be thousands miles apart, and doesn't need to care about which communication protocol is being used.

This natural approach makes Tapestry significantly easier to learn than any other web development framework, and it makes the process of development much more efficient. However, there are a number of other attractive features, the combination of which makes Tapestry unique.

Tapestry HTML Templates are Free from Obtrusive Instrumentation

Every web application has to deal with HTML in one or another way. No matter what language is used on the server or what intricate logic is employed to produce the page, what actually gets sent to the user's browser is an HTML page. To make that page dynamic, web applications use some kind of HTML template, or specially prepared chunks of HTML markup, and employ some programming logic to fill that template with dynamically generated data, or manipulate HTML in a desired way.

To make this possible, virtually all web frameworks create a tight mixture of HTML markup and some other kind of code, whether it is Java, PHP, VBScript, JSP tags, JSF, ASP.NET components, or something else. Such an approach has a number of significant disadvantages.

First of all, the more complicated the page design and programming logic, the more difficult it is to weave them together. Second, this tight conglomeration of different kinds of code is extremely difficult to maintain and update. Debugging the programming logic of such a page can be quite a challenge.

Contemporary technologies like Sun's JavaServer Faces or Microsoft's ASP.NET rely on specialized development environments to handle the complexities of mixing a dynamic logic with HTML markup, but design capabilities of such specialized environments are unavoidably limited. As a result, the page design remains quite simplistic and less impressive. Code that is automatically generated by these development environments is usually far from being perfect as it has much duplication and is hard to maintain.

For many applications, it often makes sense to have a special team of designers or to use the services of an external team in order to have a professional looking interface. Unfortunately, in most web technologies the conversion of a thoroughly designed page into an HTML template is a one way procedure. The result becomes incomprehensible for any designer not familiar with programming techniques. So when it comes to a significant change in page design, it might be easier to discard the existing page and start from scratch.

Tapestry solves all these problems in the most elegant way. In Tapestry 3 and 4, templates are valid HTML documents that can be easily read and edited by any designer using a common designer's software, without breaking the logic of the page. In Tapestry 5, templates are XML documents, but they are very close to HTML. With minor reservations, all the advantages of the previous versions apply to them too. The main point is that all versions of Tapestry provide the highest possible level of separation between HTML markup and programming logic.

Custom Components are Very Easy to Create

The use of components allows you to significantly increase the productivity of web development—this is why all the new frameworks, including Tapestry, JavaServer Faces, and ASP.NET are component-based.

However, the choice of core components that come with the framework is always limited, and it is important to give developers an opportunity to create their own custom components. Naturally, such an opportunity is provided by all component-based frameworks, but the level of effort required to create a custom component differs from framework to framework quite significantly.

For instance, to create a custom JavaServer Faces component, the developer needs to know the intricate inner structure of the framework quite well, so this is a task for advanced developers only.

In Tapestry, however, creation of custom components does not require any advanced knowledge, and is perfectly possible for beginners. We will be creating non-trivial custom components in Chapter 8 of this book.

AJAX and DHTML, but No JavaScript Coding

Contemporary web applications are unthinkable without attractive and clever features powered by JavaScript and are commonly known as DHTML and AJAX. However, JavaScript has browser incompatibilities. So Tapestry comes up with a number of components that make the miracles of AJAX available to the application, but, fortunately for developers, all JavaScript is thoroughly hidden inside the framework. AJAX-enabled components are as easy to use as any other Tapestry component, so you can make your application Web 2.0-ready without ever seeing a single line of JavaScript code. Well, at least this is true for the previous version of the framework, 4.1. As of this writing, the AJAX features are currently under development (and will likely be in a finalized state by the time you read this), but it is promised that they will be even more powerful and easier to use than in Tapestry 4.1.

User Input Validation Works Like Magic

User input validation is a must for almost every web application, as users are mere mortals and will always try to submit some erroneous data. A friendly application should clearly explain to the user exactly which piece of input is wrong, but creating an input validation and error reporting subsystem can require quite a lot of work.

Tapestry 4 already had a powerful built-in infrastructure for input validation, but in Tapestry 5 it goes much further. You as a developer will have to do very little, usually simply declaring what exactly you want, while your application will not only clearly mark the erroneous fields, but also automatically display an appropriate message in the language preferred by the current user.

Built-In Internationalization Support

A Java platform itself provides substantial support for internationalization and localization but, in Tapestry we do not need to know the details of that support. We just use a few simple hooks provided by the framework to have our application displayed in as many different languages as we wish.

It is actually quite amazing to see how one mouse click totally changes the language of the application. Everything—text, images, different controls, suddenly begin to speak in a foreign language! It is an impressive feature, considering how little we have to do to enable this flexibility.

Inversion of Control Made Easy

Inversion of Control (IoC) and Dependency Injection are amongst the most popular software development paradigms these days, and they deserve their popularity. In simple terms, Inversion of Control allows developers to save effort and time by allowing some other software to take care of different routine things and provide them services whenever needed.

However, to use the benefits of Inversion of Control in an application, one might need to learn and use an additional framework like Spring. Not in Tapestry though.

Tapestry has an Inversion of Control subsystem of its own, and quite a good one. As a result, Tapestry applications contain very little Java code. All you need to write is business logic while all the infrastructure issues are handled automatically. Aditionally, the Tapestry 5 IoC container additionally provides an opportunity to implement and enforce some of the best design patterns, again, with absolute minimum code serving this purpose.

Spring framework is very popular, and working on a large-scale enterprise application, we often need to make use of some sort of back end, implemented in Spring. Thankfully, Tapestry has a special subsystem for integration with Spring. Using this subsystem in my work, I had an impression that it is easier to use Spring beans in Tapestry than in Spring itself.

More or less the same can be said about integration with another very popular framework, Hibernate. There is a special subsystem in Tapestry responsible for this integration and it is very easy to use.

To summarize, Tapestry is a mature contemporary web development framework with all the features that would be expected from such a framework and with all the power of Java platform to support it. But additionally, Tapestry is based on a unique, developer-friendly paradigm, which makes it especially easy to learn and use.

Is Tapestry the Savior in the World of Java Web Development?

Java technology is traditionally strong on the server side. However, in the last couple of years one might notice some kind of stagnation in the area of Java web development. To explain what I mean, I will need to show you a brief history of Java web development.

In the first stage of web development, it was typical to have some code that a web server could invoke to produce dynamic content. The traditional solution is to have a program written in Perl or C and to invoke it through a CGI interface. The Java solution was different however, and that solution was rather advanced for its time. Java code was running on the server as a **servlet**, a kind of plug-in maintained by a servlet container.

The servlet way was superior because it ensured higher scalability, but perhaps even more importantly from the developer's point of view, a servlet developer could spend more time writing application-specific code, since many of the lower level issues were handled by the servlet container. At that time, Java technology was ahead of the rest of the web development world.

The next generation of web technology was about embedding pieces of code into an HTML page in order to make it dynamic. You can see this approach in JSP, ASP, PHP and ColdFusion.

Again, Java technology was ahead, because JavaServer Pages took special care about separation between the application code and its presentation logic. Ideologically fortified by Model-View-Controller design pattern, this approach culminated in Apache Struts framework.

Basically, a Struts application is a traditional servlet/JSP application, but this framework offered a number of efficient solutions for common problems of web development. Struts developers could avoid reinventing the wheel and reuse existing solutions by modifying them with application-specific code. This significantly increased the efficiency of large-scale web development, and Struts framework became extremely popular, once again ensuring the leading position of Java technologies.

However, around the same time Microsoft came up with an alternative technological solution, ASP.NET. This was a component-based approach which was supported by a sophisticated integrated development environment (IDE), Visual Studio, ASP.NET resembles RAD solutions that brought desktop development to a new level of productivity some years ago. An ASP.NET developer can drop a few components on the page, set their properties in a visual property editor and run the application—all in just a few seconds.

This is when the feeling appeared that the Java approach is not quite the best anymore. ASP.NET was quickly gaining popularity, while the mainstream Java approach was exemplified by a Struts application, not component-based, and was still quite a low-level solution.

The Java world tried to retaliate by creating JavaServer Faces specification. Externally, it resembles ASP.NET, but is built on top of the existing Java-specific solutions.

JSF is supported and promoted by major software vendors like IBM, Oracle, and BEA, and it's implemented in their state-of-the-art commercial IDEs. Its approach was very similar to the Microsoft approach, but somehow JavaServer Faces didn't gain the popularity it was expected to gain. Maybe that is because to create the JSF specification, so many different parties had to come to a compromise.

Or maybe the problem is in the fact that the JavaServer Faces specification is created using existing Java solutions and has inherited their weaknesses. For example, JavaServer Pages technology, used by JSF to render pages, was very sound for its time, but a JSP page can easily become an unintelligible mixture of HTML, standard tags, custom tags, and EL expressions. Also, JSF has some older features from Struts, like its navigation configured in a lengthy XML file. As a result, JSF technology is difficult to comprehend, learn and work.

Or perhaps the problem with JSF is that it mimics so closely the Microsoft solution, while the Java world has its own laws, and something that is good for Microsoft might not be equally good here?

My point is that if we look at Tapestry, the framework that was never supported or promoted by billionaire corporations, we might notice that it can easily compete with the most recent versions of ASP.NET in many respects.

Features like code-behind in ASP.NET that allows the separation of code of the page from its template, is an integral part of Tapestry from the very beginning of the framework. In fact, in Tapestry you cannot just mix code and HTML since all Java code goes into the page class.

In fact, many solutions that are promoted as advanced features of ASP.NET can be found either in the core Tapestry framework or in a library of custom Tapestry components, such as Tacos.

It may well happen that with time, as more people realize the benefits of Tapestry, it might become the model for the next generation of a Java web framework specification.

However, nothing is perfect, and Tapestry has its downsides too. One of them is the fact that the framework's development goes ahead in huge steps, which makes the next version very different from the previous one. To fully appreciate what this means, let's have a look at a brief history of Tapestry.

The Journey of Tapestry from 3 to 5

Tapestry was originally conceived by Howard Lewis Ship around the year 1999, but the early versions of the framework are not widely known.

Tapestry 3 became the first well known version, and I used it for my first Tapestry application that I created in the summer of 2005. Tapestry was a great relief after my experience with servlets and JavaServer Pages. Its approach was very easy for me to understand, maybe because in the past I had plenty of experience with Borland Delphi, a very popular Rapid Application Development environment.

However, some features were not fully implemented in Tapestry 3. Most notably the validation subsystem was somewhat deficient. Also, some obvious components were missing, and I had to create a number of custom components myself (although that wasn't too difficult, frankly speaking). All in all, I was very happy that I had learned Tapestry, and I was going to use it for years.

However, when Tapestry 4 appeared in January 2006, it was so different that I had to learn the framework again. It was not a problem though as Tapestry 4 had streamlined and made many features easier than in the previous version. Most significantly, Tapestry 4 was built on top of Hivemind, another Open Source project created by Howard Lewis Ship. Hivemind made it possible to easily extend and configure Tapestry, but most notably, it allowed users to **inject** anything into the page, as Hivemind was (and is) quite a capable Inversion of Control container. Also, Tapestry introduced a brand new user input validation subsystem, flexible and easy to use.

On a negative note, Tapestry 4 was not compatible with Tapestry 3, and upgrading an application to the new version required a substantial amount of effort.

Tapestry 4.1 became another major step in the development of the framework. It came with Dojo JavaScript toolkit built into it, and as a result it made AJAX functionality easily available to Tapestry developers. It looks like version 4.1 will stay here for a while and allow many people to benefit from using it for building their web applications. It still has a few places where it could be streamlined or enhanced, but, it is a powerful and developer friendly framework.

Very soon however, it became clear that Howard Lewis Ship was working on a completely new, fifth version of Tapestry, and that version was not just a step, but a quantum leap forward. Tapestry 5 was created from scratch, and on one side, it incorporated all the best ideas accumulated by Tapestry developers over the years, while on the other side it got rid of those solutions that proved to be obsolete or inefficient. Needless to say that neither Tapestry 3 nor Tapestry 4 were compatible with Tapestry 5, although their approach was very similar.

Tapestry 5 is a truly contemporary framework. It was specifically designed to be extremely developer friendly. Page classes are now POJOs (Plain Old Java Objects), since they do not need to inherit from any framework-specific classes, and we have more freedom in choosing how to implement them. They are easy to test too. To give Tapestry hints on what we expect from it, we use Java annotations, and the framework adapts to our requirements instead of expecting us to adapt to its rules.

Tapestry 5 comes with new powerful components. Their rich functionality can be easily adjusted for a specific application's needs, and so there will be significantly fewer cases when we need to create custom components. Creating custom components is even easier now than it was before, so our creativity is not limited in any way.

Tapestry 5 is significantly faster than the previous versions too. Not to say that those were slow. Tapestry 3 and Tapestry 4 applications are as fast as any other Java web application. All versions of Tapestry were created with great scalability in mind, which means that Tapestry applications can work under a significant workload—say, thousands of visitors using the application simultaneously.

I am not going to list here all the novelties of Tapestry 5 as we are going to learn them in the course of this book, but I encourage you to visit the Tapestry website (`http://tapestry.apache.org`) and read what the creators of the framework write about the new version. In general, it is significantly easier to learn to work with and efficient too.

It is also stated by its creators that Tapestry 5 will become a stable long-term platform for the future development of the framework. They have taken special care to ensure that the future versions of the framework will be backward compatible.

So it looks like you came to Tapestry just in time!

Summary

Tapestry is a contemporary, feature-rich, component-based, AJAX-enabled Java web framework.

Tapestry was specifically designed to greatly increase the productivity of web development by being user-friendly, easy to understand and learn, and by minimizing the amount of coding. Tapestry 5 incorporates the latest ideas in software development and it is even easier to use, configure and extend than the previous versions. It is also significantly faster.

Tapestry is a perfect tool for any kind of web development—from a personal website to an enterprise-scale solution. Arguably, Tapestry is the future of Java web development.

In the next chapter we are going to create a working environment for Tapestry development, which means that we shall download, install and configure all the necessary pieces of software. After that, we shall create our first Tapestry project—a very simple one, just to make sure that everything works properly.

2

Creating Your Working Environment

To create a working environment for Tapestry development, we need to:

- Download and install the Java Development Kit (JDK), as we are going to do Java development. Chances are, you already have a JDK on your computer, but please check if you've got the correct version.
- Download and install Maven. Maven is a very popular project management tool, and Tapestry 5 projects use this tool extensively for many purposes, from compilation of source code to deploying the complete application to a server. You are not expected to know anything about Maven. All the necessary instructions will be given in this book.
- Download and install an Integrated Development Environment (IDE). There are two excellent free IDEs, NetBeans and Eclipse. NetBeans is easier for beginners, as creating a working environment with it involves fewer moving parts. However, Eclipse is more popular. If you have chosen Eclipse, you will also have to download and install a servlet container. Tomcat is the most popular servlet container, so I will explain how to work with it. NetBeans comes with bundled Tomcat, so you don't have to install a servlet container if you have chosen NetBeans.

As soon as everything is installed, we shall create and run our first Tapestry 5 project and then we shall have a look at what it consists of.

Please note that the approach described here is not the only possible approach. In fact, the official Tapestry 5 tutorial written by Howard Lewis Ship recommends a somewhat different set of tools and describes in great detail how to install them. Refer to `http://tapestry.apache.org/tapestry5/tutorial1/` for further information.

Install a JDK

You might already have a JDK on your computer—say, if you were doing any kind of Java programming before, or if you are running Mac OS X that comes with a preinstalled JDK. Even so, you will need to check the version of the JDK that you have. Tapestry 5 makes an extensive use of annotations, and this feature appeared in the Java language only in version 1.5 (also known as Java 5). So you need to make sure that your version is not older than that.

Fortunately, you can check both things—whether you have a JDK at all, and which version it is—by using just one command. Open the command prompt or a terminal window, and enter the command:

javac -version

Your computer may report something like this:

javac 1.6.0

This means that everything is fine. However, if it responds by saying that there is no such command, or if you see that the version is older than 1.5, then, for a Linux or Windows computer, go to `http://java.sun.com/javase/downloads/index.jsp`, download the latest version of the JDK (not JRE! JRE is a runtime environment, it doesn't contain the tools required for development) and install it following the instructions available on that website.

For Mac, you can get Java 5 update from the Mac OS X Updates page (`http://www.apple.com/downloads/macosx/apple/macosx_updates`). At the time of this writing, the available package for Mac is J2SE 5.0 Release 4, you need to pick the one for your platform, Intel or PPC.

Next, you need to make sure that the required environment variables are set correctly. This will enable other elements of our working configuration to find the JDK successfully. This step is platform-specific. I will give instructions for Windows and Mac OS X. Linux instructions would be very similar to those for Mac, and besides, if you are running Linux, you are probably familiar with the basic technicalities of your distribution.

Configuring the Environment for Windows

First of all, you need to find out where the JDK was installed on your hard drive. Most probably, you will find it at `C:\Program Files\Java`, and the folder name will depend on the version of the JDK, you have installed. It might be something like `C:\Program Files\Java\jdk1.6.0_02`.

We need to do two things:

- Make this folder known to your machine as `JAVA_HOME` environment variable.
- Add its `\bin` subdirectory to the `PATH` environment variable.

On Windows XP, select **Start** | **Control Panel** | **System**, and then select the **Advanced** tab in the **System Properties** dialog.

On Windows Vista, select **Start** | **Control Panel** | **System and Maintenance** | **System**, and then, in the left pane, **Advanced system settings**.

In both cases, you will see a dialog similar to the one shown in the following figure:

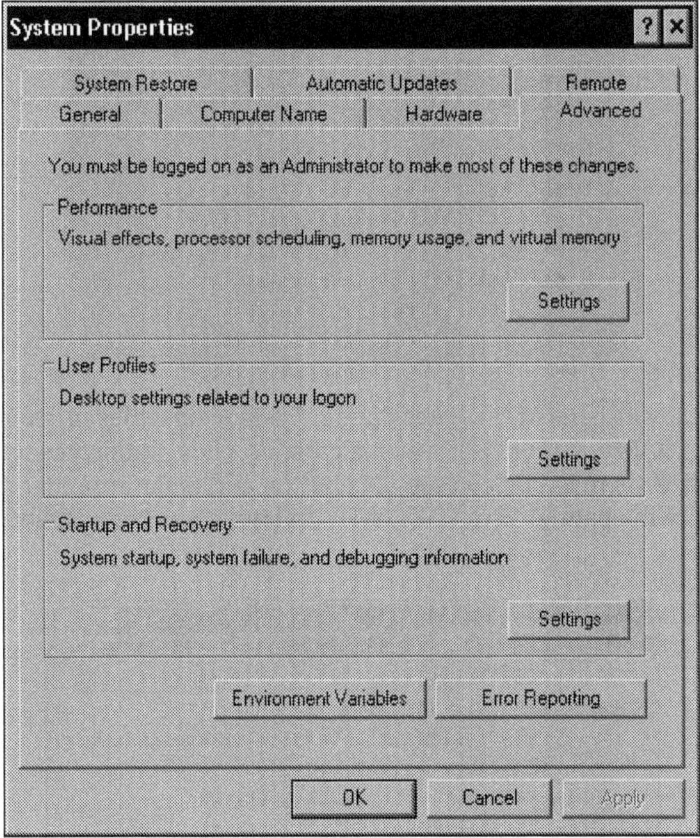

Press the **Environment Variables** button, and you will see the **Environment Variables** dialog, similar to the one shown in the following figure:

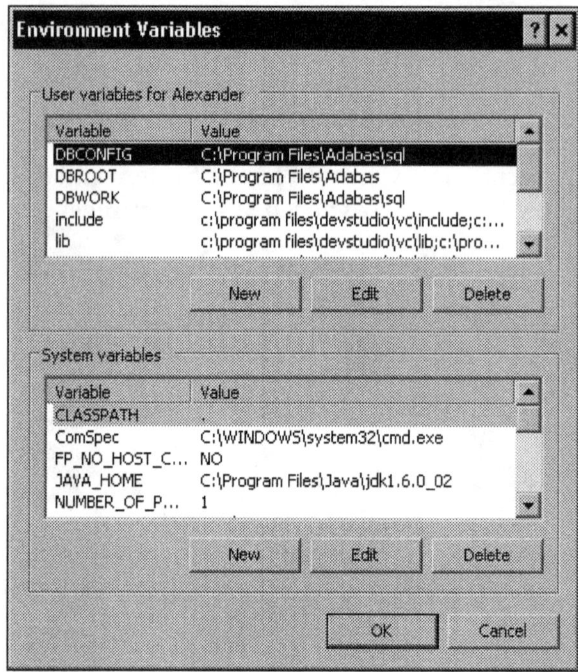

Check if in the lower pane of the latter dialog, **System variables**, there is a variable named **JAVA_HOME**. If there is no such a variable, click on the **New** button below to add it. If there is, click on the **Edit** button and make sure that this variable reflects precisely the path to your JDK folder. In both cases, the result should be similar to this:

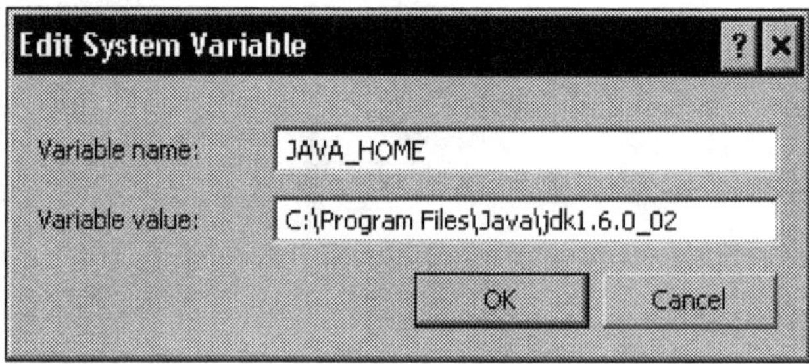

Next, find the **PATH** variable in the same lower pane (the case doesn't matter). Probably, it will already have some value, so you can append the path to the **\bin** subdirectory of the JDK, separating it from the other paths by semicolon, as shown in the following figure:

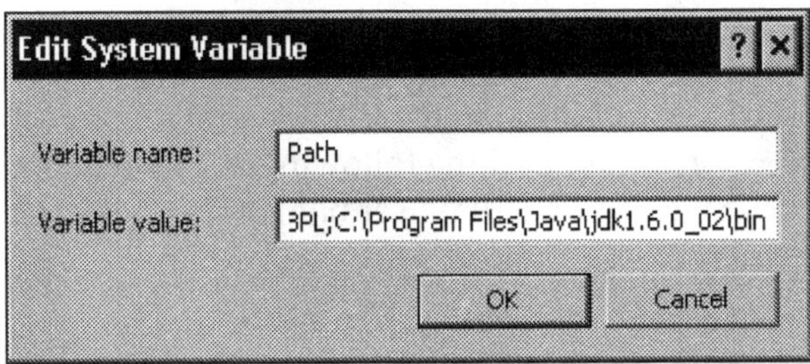

Close all dialogs by pressing OK. If everything was done properly, you should be able now to check the version of **javac**, as explained above.

Configuring environment for Mac OS X

You will need to edit the `.bash_profile` file which is located in your home directory (something like **/Users/YourUserName/.bash_profile**). The dot in front of the file name means that it is a hidden file, so Finder will not display it.

There are different ways to edit this file. The one that I prefer is to use the **TextWrangler** editor that can be downloaded for free from `http://barebones.com/products/textwrangler/`.

Start **TextWrangler** and in the menu select **File | Open Hidden...**, and you will be able to find, open and edit your `.bash_profile` easily.

All you will need to do is to add this single line of code:

```
export JAVA_HOME=/usr
```

This is where Java is installed by default on Mac OS X.

Now everything is ready for the next step, installing Maven.

Install Maven

Please note: you will need to download Maven 2.0.5! The "latest and greatest" version 2.0.7 might not work for you.

You can get Maven 2.0.5 at `http://archive.apache.org/dist/maven/binaries/`. Choose the package that is most convenient for you, like **maven-2.0.5-bin.zip**, download it, unpack and copy the resulting directory to a convenient place on your computer. It can become `/Users/YourUserName/maven-2.0.5` on a Mac or `C:\maven-2.0.5` on a Windows machine.

Finally, add the path to Maven's **bin** directory to the PATH variable of your system. On a Windows machine, the addition to the PATH variable should look like, `C:\maven-2.0.5\bin`. On a Mac, add the following string to `.bash_profile` (but replace **YourUserName** with your actual user name):

```
export PATH=${PATH}:/Users/YourUserName/maven-2.0.5/bin
```

Finally, to check if everything was set up properly, enter the following command:

```
mvn -version
```

The output should be similar to this:

```
Maven version: 2.0.5
```

Now we are ready to use Maven to download and make available everything that is required for a Tapestry project, including all the dependencies.

Create a Skeleton Tapestry project

It is convenient to have a special directory for the project skeletons created by Maven. So please create such a directory (say, *C:\tapestry5\work*) and open the command prompt or a terminal window into it.

Enter the following command (it should be all on one line and is broken into several lines only because it would not fit into the page width otherwise):

```
mvn archetype:create -DarchetypeGroupId=org.apache.tapestry -Darchety
peArtifactId=quickstart -DgroupId=com.packtpub -DartifactId=t5first -
DpackageName=com.packtpub.t5first -Dversion=1.0.0-SNAPSHOT
```

In this command we are asking Maven to do the following:

- `archetype:create`: We ask Maven to create a new project using an existing project template (or *archetype*, as Maven calls it).
- `DarchetypeGroupId=org.apache.tapestry`: This is one of the Tapestry archetypes; now Maven knows in which group of archetypes to look for it.
- `DarchetypeArtifactId=quickstart`: The actual name for the archetype.

- `DgroupId=com.packtpub`: This is a group to which the new project will belong. I have given it the reversed URL of the publisher's website, but you can use any other name if you wish.
- `DartifactId=t5first`: The name for the project itself. Again, use another one if you wish.
- `DpackageName=com.packtpub.t5first`: The package into which the project's Java classes will be placed. It is logically made of the two preceding pieces of information, but not necessarily so.
- `Dversion=1.0.0-SNAPSHOT`: This is not required, but it gives the future application some reasonable version number.

You will need to enter this command every time you want to create a new Tapestry project, but there is no need to memorize it or to type it by hand. One of the ways to simplify things is to have a text file with different versions of this command. You can easily change the details, like package name, and then just copy the command and paste it into the command line. In fact, you do not even need to create such a text file yourself, as I have already created it for you and put it into the code package for this chapter under the `mvn_commands.txt name`.

When the command is entered, Maven begins its work. It downloads all the required files and stores them in a repository on your computer, then creates a skeleton of the Tapestry project. Naturally, you need to be connected to the Internet at this time. The output will look like this:

```
Command Prompt
[INFO] Parameter: package, Value: com.packtpub.t5first
[INFO] Parameter: artifactId, Value: t5first
[INFO] Parameter: basedir, Value: C:\tapestry5\work
[INFO] Parameter: version, Value: 1.0.0-SNAPSHOT
[WARNING] org.apache.velocity.runtime.exception.ReferenceException: reference :
template = archetype-resources/pom.xml [line 14,column 22] : ${tapestry-release-
version} is not a valid reference.
[WARNING] org.apache.velocity.runtime.exception.ReferenceException: reference :
template = archetype-resources/pom.xml [line 90,column 26] : ${tapestry-release-
version} is not a valid reference.
[INFO] ********************* End of debug info from resources from generated POM
 ***********************
[WARNING] org.apache.velocity.runtime.exception.ReferenceException: reference :
template = archetype-resources/src/main/webapp/WEB-INF/Start.html [line 11,colum
n 34] : ${currentTime} is not a valid reference.
[INFO] Archetype created in dir: C:\tapestry5\work\t5first
[INFO] ------------------------------------------------------------------------
[INFO] BUILD SUCCESSFUL
[INFO] ------------------------------------------------------------------------
[INFO] Total time: 2 seconds
[INFO] Finished at: Sat Jul 07 12:03:57 BST 2007
[INFO] Final Memory: 4M/9M
[INFO] ------------------------------------------------------------------------

C:\tapestry5\work>_
```

You can see that there might be some warnings, but that is fine as far as the final message is **BUILD SUCCESSFUL**.

The process will take quite some time, but this is only so for the first project. Creating every next project will take much less time as all the necessary files will be already stored on your computer and there will be no need to download them.

If you now check the contents of the recently created `C:\tapestry5\work` directory, you will find a subdirectory named `\t5first` (or whatever you named the `artifactId` in that long Maven command). In this subdirectory you will already find some files and more subdirectories, but before looking at them in more detail, let's ask Maven to bring together everything that is required for the new project.

At the command prompt, navigate to the new project directory (so that the current directory become `C:\tapestry5\work\t5first`) and enter the following command:

```
mvn package
```

Again, Maven will download a number of files and take a noticeable amount of time, but finally you will see the output as follows:

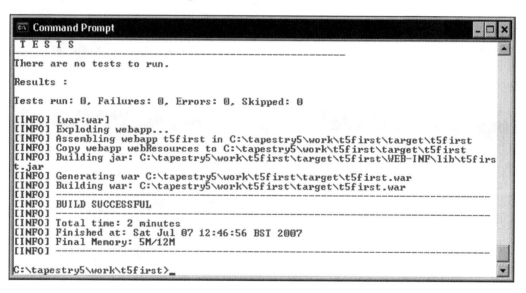

```
Command Prompt
 T E S T S
-------------------------------------------------------
There are no tests to run.

Results :

Tests run: 0, Failures: 0, Errors: 0, Skipped: 0

[INFO] [war:war]
[INFO] Exploding webapp...
[INFO] Assembling webapp t5first in C:\tapestry5\work\t5first\target\t5first
[INFO] Copy webapp webResources to C:\tapestry5\work\t5first\target\t5first
[INFO] Building jar: C:\tapestry5\work\t5first\target\t5first\WEB-INF\lib\t5firs
t.jar
[INFO] Generating war C:\tapestry5\work\t5first\target\t5first.war
[INFO] Building war: C:\tapestry5\work\t5first\target\t5first.war
[INFO] ------------------------------------------------------------------------
[INFO] BUILD SUCCESSFUL
[INFO] ------------------------------------------------------------------------
[INFO] Total time: 2 minutes
[INFO] Finished at: Sat Jul 07 12:46:56 BST 2007
[INFO] Final Memory: 5M/12M
[INFO] ------------------------------------------------------------------------

C:\tapestry5\work\t5first>_
```

This means that the command was executed successfully. Now let's have a look at the contents of the project just created. Refer to the following screenshot:

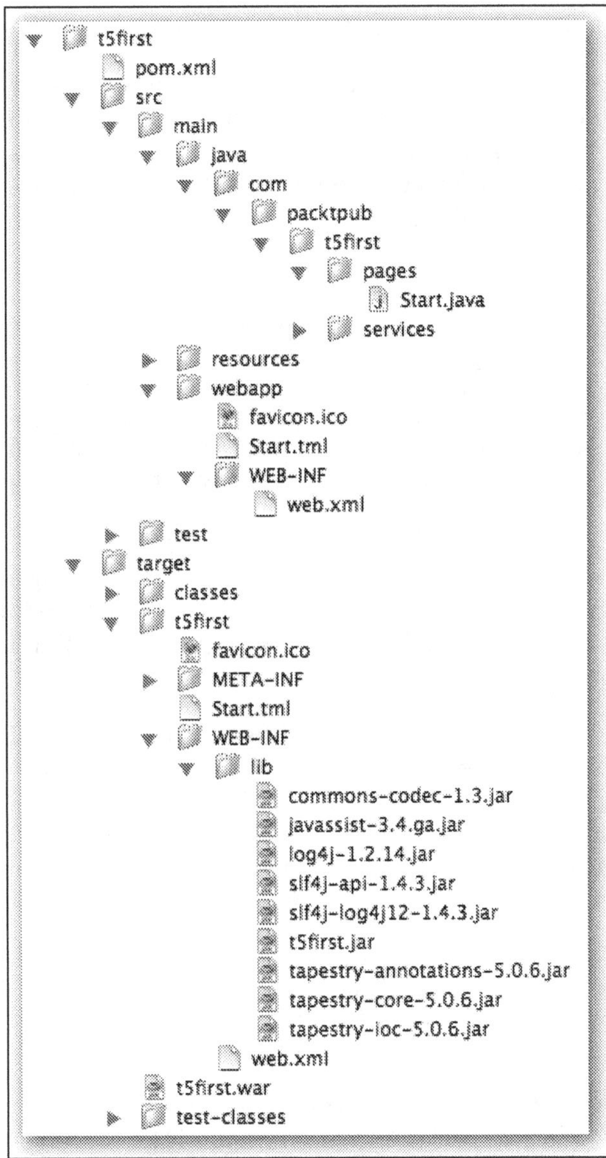

As you can see, there is plenty of everything. Note the items that will be most important for us in the beginning.

First of all, there are two subdirectories under **\t5first**—**\src** and **\target**.

The **\src** subdirectory, as you can guess, contains the source code of the application, including Java files, template files, and the standard deployment descriptor, **web.xml** (if you are new to Java web applications' terminology, please read Appendix A, which provides an overview of the most essential concepts).

Note that there are two files with the name **Start**, but with different extensions. The **Start.java** source file is located in **\main\java** subdirectory, under the structure of subdirectories reflecting its package name (**com.packtpub.t5first.pages**), while the **Start.tml** file is located in the **\main\webapp** subdirectory. These are two parts of the same Tapestry page, and this sort of duality will be discussed properly in the next chapter.

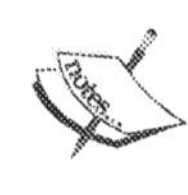

There is actually more than one copy of the **Start.tml** file in the contents of these directories because Maven did its work in two steps. It first created all the necessary files under the **\src** subdirectory and then created the structure of the future application under the **\target** subdirectory. You will follow my logic more easily if you spend some time looking at the picture of the directories, and compare it with the structure you've got on your computer.

Under the **\target** subdirectory, we will find the result of building and packaging the application by Maven. There is already the end product, **t5first.war** file. We can take it and deploy it on a Java-enabled web server (like Tomcat). It has everything required for a Tapestry Web application.

However, there are also the intermediate results of Maven's work. The **\classes** subdirectory contains compiled Java classes, while under **\t5first**, you will find a familiar template file, **Start.tml**, and under **\t5first\WEB-INF**, the deployment descriptor **web.xml**. Most remarkably, the **\t5first\WEB-INF\lib** subdirectory contains all the necessary libraries downloaded for us by Maven from across the Internet. We didn't have to figure out what is required and where to get it.

At this point, we can thank Maven for its service as we are going further. The next step is to start working with the source of the application, building it and deploying to a server. This is where a contemporary IDE will be very helpful.

Please note that if Maven didn't work for you for some reason, the code package for this chapter contains the complete project tree created by Maven, and you can start further work from it.

Install NetBeans

Even if you decided to use Eclipse, I still recommend you to read this section as starting a new project in NetBeans is significantly simpler.

Go to `http://www.netbeans.info/downloads` and download the latest package for your platform. Install it with all the default options. Your working environment is ready.

Now let us use NetBeans to work with the project created for us by Maven.

Start the IDE and in its menu choose **File | New Project...** (or press the second from the left button on the toolbar). You will see the **New Project** dialog opened. In it, select **Web** under **Categories** and **Web Application with Existing Sources** under **Projects**, as shown in the following figure, and click on **Next**:

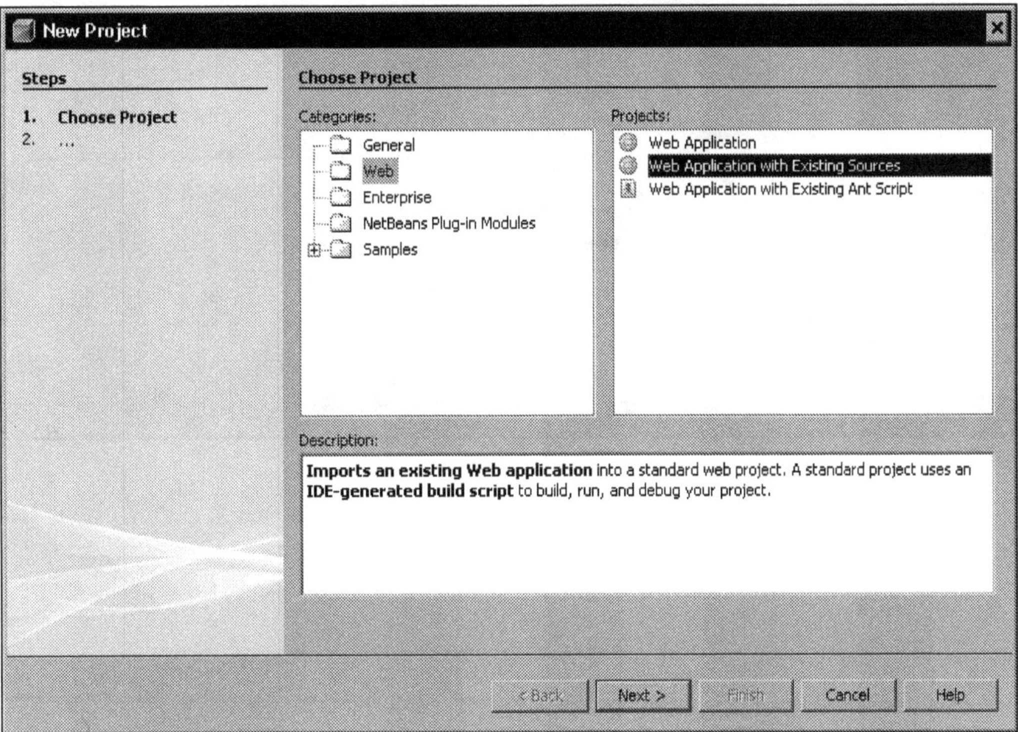

In the next dialog, click on the **Browse...** button next to **Location,** and navigate to the directory of the new project created by Maven (*C:\tapestry5\work\t5first,* if you accepted my choice of naming). Select this directory and press **Open**. Make sure that **Bundled Tomcat** is selected for the server and all the other settings are the same as in the following figure:

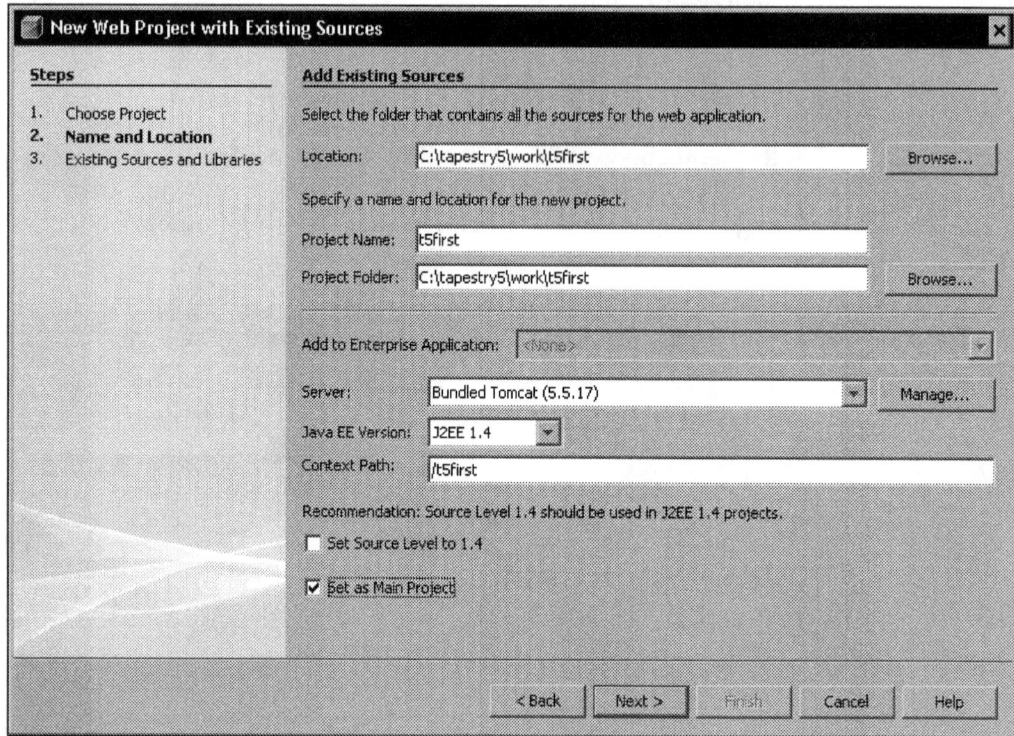

Click on **Next**, to see the following dialog:

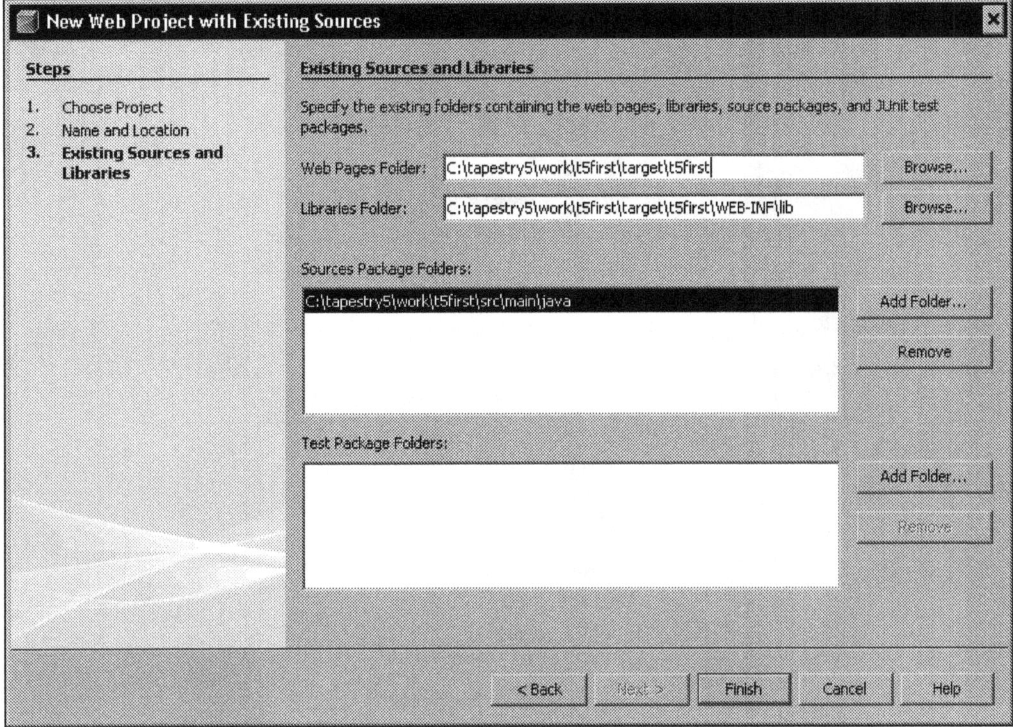

You don't have to change anything as NetBeans should be able to find out all the necessary details automatically. Click on the **Finish** button, and the new NetBeans project will be created for you.

NetBeans structures the project as shown in the following figure:

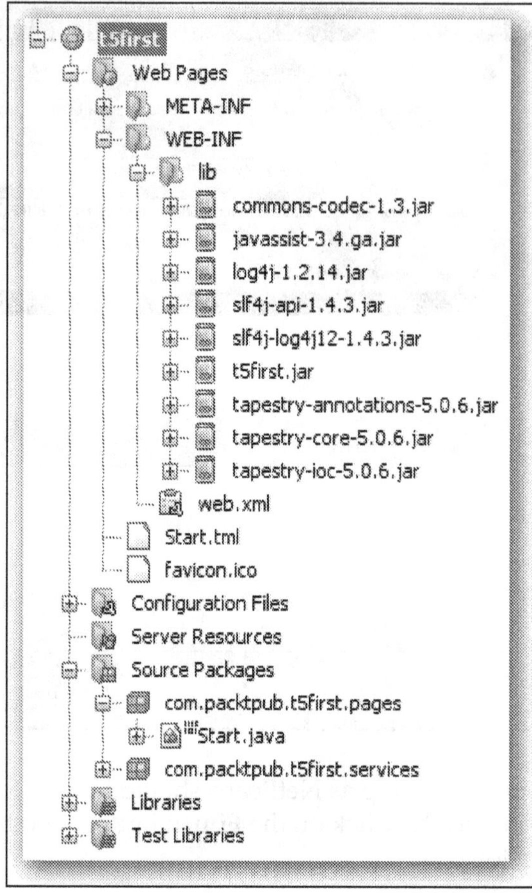

You can see that the structure of the project as recreated by NetBeans is much closer to the structure of a standard Java web application (read Appendix A if you are unsure what this standard structure is).

All the libraries are already in place, and if you want to edit Java classes, their source code can be found in the **Source Packages** folder. However, in this chapter we only need to make sure that working configuration was created successfully, so let's just run the project and see what will happen.

Hit the *F6* key (or press the third from the right button on the toolbar). In the **Output** window you will have to wait for Tomcat startup, but then in a few seconds the default browser's window will open, and in it you will see the Tapestry application running, as shown in the following figure:

Click on the **refresh** link a few times to make sure the page is live, and displays the current time each time after each refresh.

Now let's try to make some changes. Double-click the **Start.java** file in the **Projects** view and it will open in the code editor. You will see that this class contains just one method, `getCurrentTime()` that it returns a `Date`, and this method contains just one line of code. Let's change it to look like this:

```
public String getCurrentTime()
{
  Date date = new Date();
  String message = ". Tapestry is cool!";
  return date + message;
}
```

Save the changes, hit the *F6* key, and you will see that the application reflects the changes you have just made. Let's try another experiment.

Double-click on the **Start.tml** file to open it in the code editor and make some changes to it. For example, change the heading:

```
<h1>t5first Start Page</h1>
```

to:

```
<h1>Tapestry Start Page</h1>
```

Save the file and hit *F6* as before. You will notice this time that the last change is not reflected by the application. This is because NetBeans keeps track of changes in Java files only when we have changed a page template. No Java file was changed, so NetBeans decided that there is actually nothing to update.

The simplest way to deal with this little misconduct is to make some change to a Java file each time you make a change to an HTML file. If there is nothing to change, just add or remove a space somewhere where it doesn't make difference in any Java file. In this case, after pressing *F6*, NetBeans will reload the whole application, including HTML files, and so every change will be picked up.

> The extension of page template files in Tapestry, beginning from version 5.0.6, is *tml*, which is for Tapestry Markup Language. NetBeans doesn't know which editor to use for editing files with such an extension and so it uses a simple text editor. This means that we'll have no syntax highlighting and no other convenient features of advanced NetBeans editors. However, Tapestry template files are XML documents and also they are very close to XHTML files. It will make sense to edit them using either HTML editor or XML editor, and we can easily teach NetBeans which editor to use when dealing with files having *tml* extension.
>
> In NetBeans' menu open **Tools - Options**, and then at the bottom of the dialog that appears press the **Advanced Options** button. In the tree view on the left hand side navigate to **IDE Configuration - System - Object Types**. Then, depending on which editor you prefer to use for page templates, select either **HTML Objects** or **XML Objects**. Then in the **Properties** pane on the right hand side press the small button against **Extensions and MIME Types**, enter *tml* into the **Item** box, press **Add** and then close all dialogs. Now NetBeans will always open page templates in the editor you've chosen.

Now you know enough to start working on a project of your own. I hope you enjoyed dealing with NetBeans. Could it be easier, indeed? But how about debugging an application? Can you believe that debugging a Web application can be not more difficult than debugging a desktop application? Let's try then.

Debugging in NetBeans

Let's return to the `Start.java` file, it is probably still opened in the code editor. Click on the left margin of the code editor against the last line of code (the `return` statement) to place a breakpoint there. The code should look then like this:

```
public class Start
{
        public String getCurrentTime()
        {
            Date date = new Date();
            String message = ". Tapestry is cool!";
            return date + message;
        }
}
```

Press *F5*, or the second button from the right on the toolbar, to debug the project. The application startup will begin as usual, but then it will stop at the breakpoint, so that you can observe the current state of the variables. For this, you can use the **Local Variables** view, as shown below:

Watches | Local Variables | Call Stack

Name	Type	Value
this	Start	#550
date	Date	#551
fastTime	long	1184183121242
cdate		null
Static		
message	String	". Tapestry is cool!"

There are other useful tools available for debugging in NetBeans, but we are not going to look at them in detail for now, as my aim was just to show how easy it can be to debug a Web project in a contemporary IDE.

Press *Ctrl + F5* to allow the application to continue running, and you will see a familiar page opened in the default web browser. Click the **refresh** link, and again, the application will stop at the breakpoint and wait for your further instructions. To complete the debugging session, press *Shift+F5*.

Working with NetBeans is quite easy. Creating a working configuration with Eclipse involves more steps, but, this process is pretty straight-forward too.

Installing Eclipse

Eclipse by itself is a universal platform, starting from which you can create an IDE for just any imaginable purpose using existing building blocks (plug-ins). Sounds exciting, but in fact, we do not want to start building an IDE from scratch, as mutual dependencies between different plug-ins can make this endeavor time and effort consuming.

Instead, I recommend you to download a ready to use package created by Web Tools Platform project, let's call it Eclipse WTP. This package can be downloaded from `http://download.eclipse.org/webtools/downloads/` (look for something like "WTP all-in-one package"). You can download either the latest version 2 or the previous version 1.5, they should be equally good for our purposes, but please note that when testing version 2 on Linux, I got some unexpected behavior from it.

Eclipse WTP has quite a number of benefits over the bare-bones Eclipse, including the following:

- It has source code editors for different Web-related formats, including HTML and XML.
- It is aware of Web and Java EE standard project structures and so can create such projects, import, export them, and so on.
- It has convenient tools for working with servers.
- It makes debugging easy.

In fact, if you had any experience with a commercial Eclipse-based development environment, like Rational Application Developer, you will recognize many of its convenient features in Eclipse WTP.

To install Eclipse WTP, simply unpack the downloaded package and put the resulting directory somewhere on your hard drive (as an example, it can become `C:\eclipse`).

You will also need to decide where you are going to store your Eclipse projects, since, at the first startup Eclipse will ask you to select a directory for this. It can be something like `C:\workspace` in the simplest case.

To run Eclipse, double-click on the `eclipse.exe` file that can be found in the `C:\eclipse` directory (on a Mac, the file name is `Eclipse.app`, you will find it by its nice Eclipse icon).

Unlike NetBeans, Eclipse doesn't have a servlet container bundled with it, so we have to download Tomcat separately.

Installing Tomcat

To install Tomcat, simply download a binary distribution from `http://tomcat.apache.org` and unpack it into some directory, say, `C:\apache-tomcat-6.0`. The most recent version 6 should work fine, but if there are problems, version 5.5 is a very well tested alternative.

Once Tomcat is downloaded, we need to tell Eclipse where we have put it—but that will be done while configuring the project.

Configuring the Project in Eclipse

Start Eclipse and close the **Welcome** screen.

There are different ways of creating a web application from the existing skeleton in Eclipse. However, the one I find the simplest and most convenient is to import the WAR file created for us by Maven.

In the menu, select **File** | **Import...**, and in the dialog that opens select **WAR file**, as shown in the following screenshot, and click on **Next**.

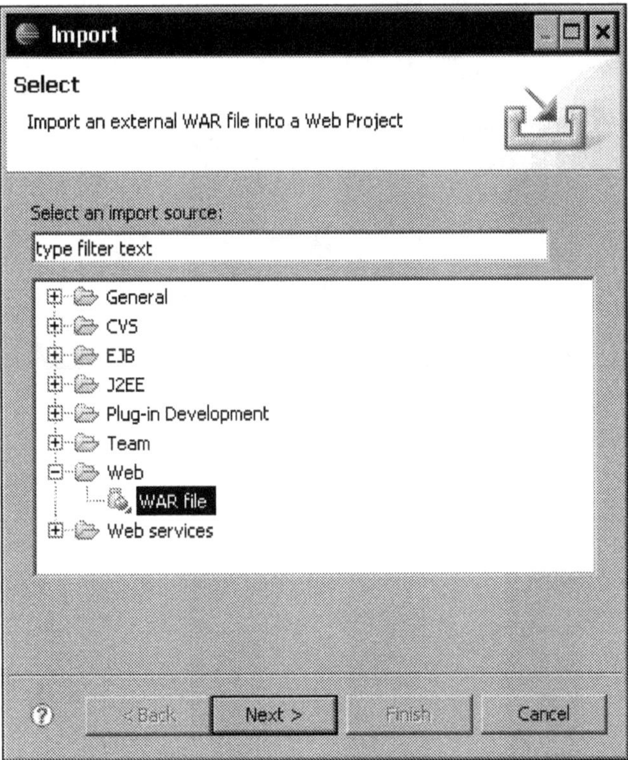

In the next dialog, click on the **Browse...** button next to the **WAR file** text field, navigate to the **t5first.war** file created by Maven and select it.

Press **New...** next to **Target runtime** and in the dialog that opens, select the version of Tomcat that you have installed in the previous section, and click on **Next**. This is shown in the following screenshot:

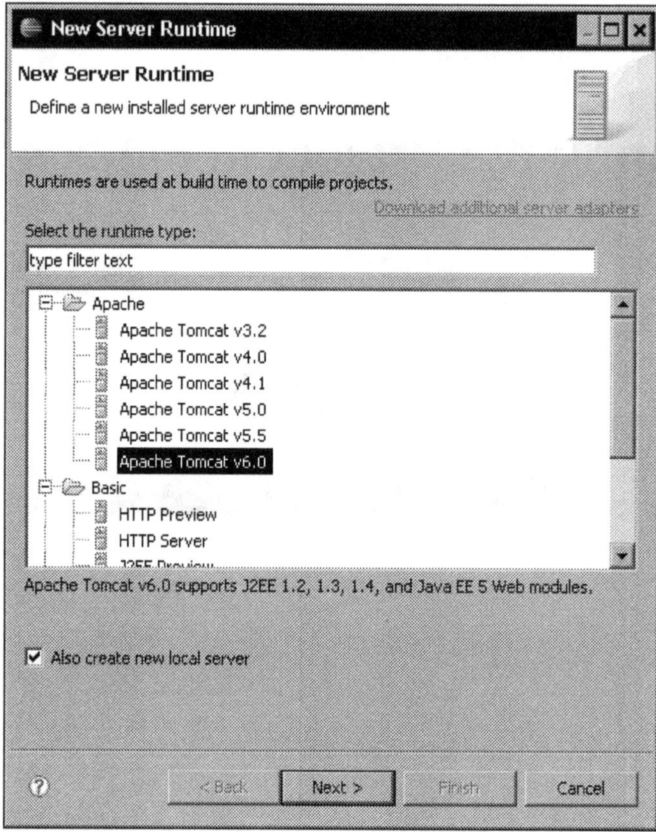

In the next dialog, you need to tell Eclipse where exactly you have installed Tomcat. Click on the **Browse...** button, navigate to the installation directory, select it, and click on **Finish**.

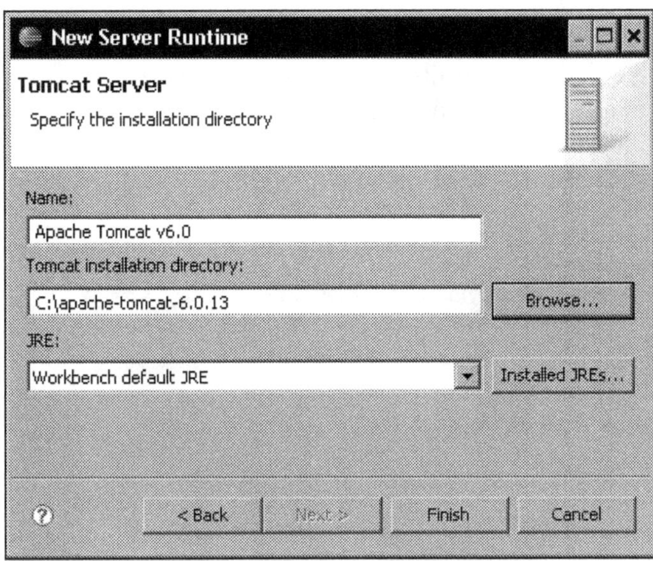

The final result of the server selection should look like this:

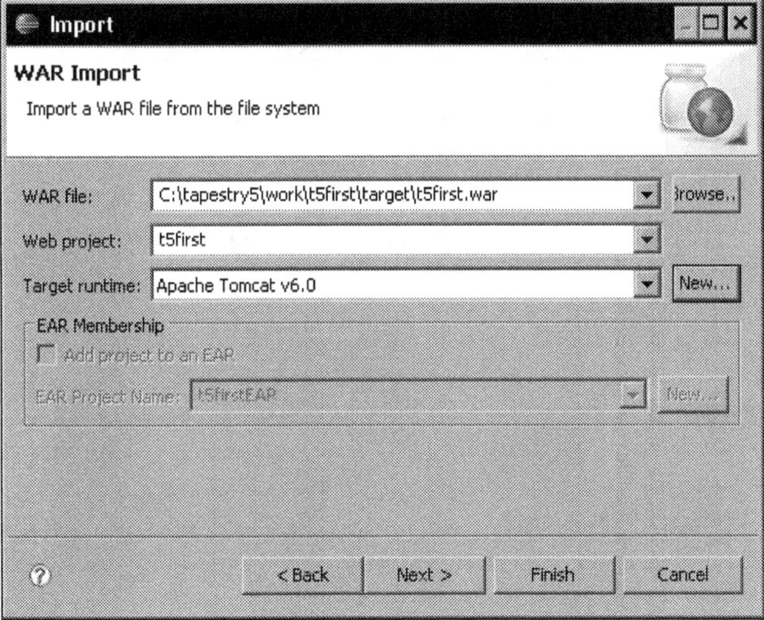

Now click on **Finish**.

Eclipse will create the new project and suggest that you switch to the Java EE perspective, its default perspective for working with Web projects. Let's agree with this.

The project was created successfully, but if you check its structure, shown in the next screenshot, you will notice that one significant element is missing—source files for Java classes used in the project. There are a few different ways how you can get to the existing source files into the project.

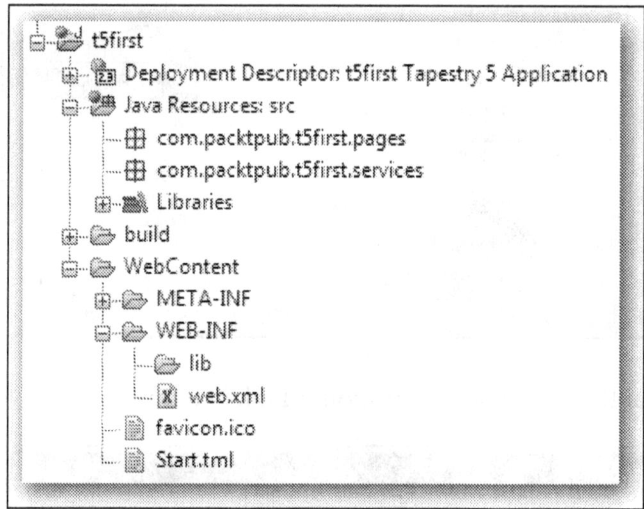

I will describe two of them; choose the one that you prefer.

The first option is to link to the existing source directory. Right-click on the **t5first** project in the **Project Explorer** and in the context menu, select **Properties**. Select **Java Build Path** in the left pane of the dialog which opens and the **Source** tab in the right pane, as shown in the following figure, and click on the **Link Source...** button.

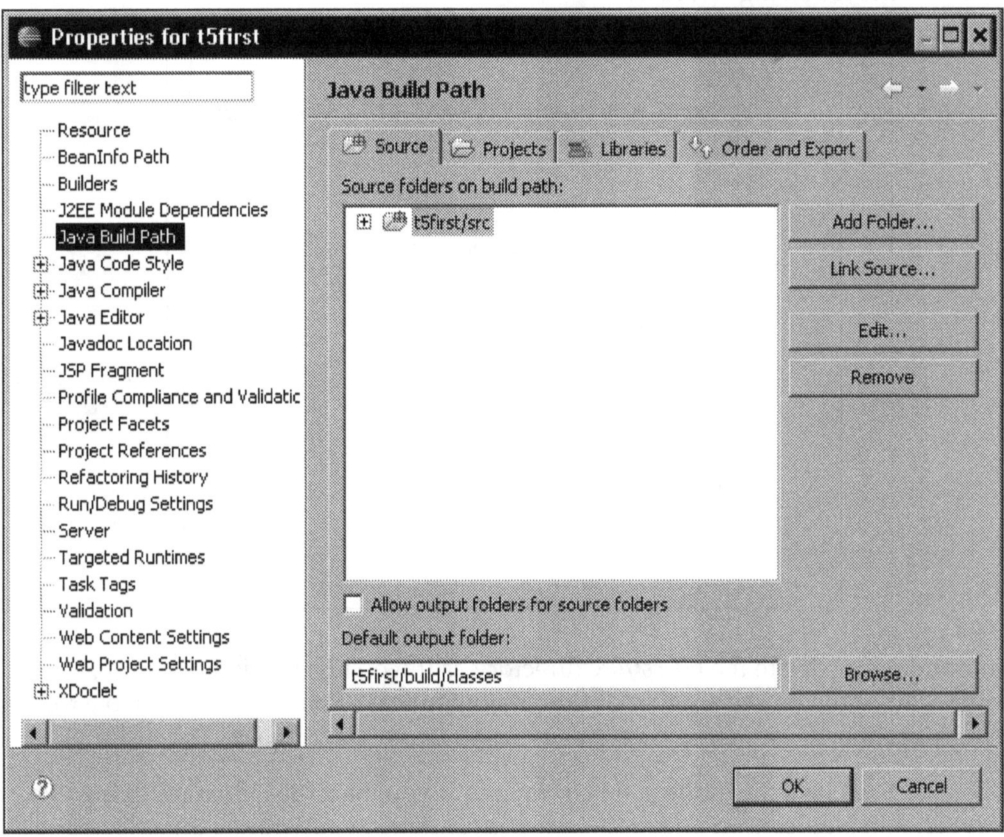

In the next dialog, click on the **Browse...** button and navigate to the directory structure created by Maven as shown previously. Select the **java** subdirectory (its complete path will be perhaps **C:\tapestry5\work\t5first\src\main\java)**. Click on **Finish** and then **OK**. You will see this **java** directory now linked with your project as shown in the following figure:

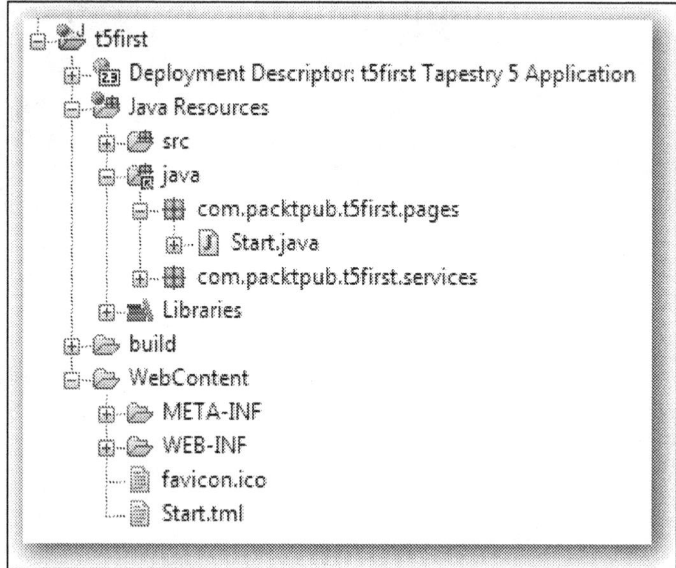

You could now delete the **t5first/src** directory as it won't be needed anymore, but better wait until you see another option of how to make source code available to the application.

Open the **Start.java** file in the code editor, and if you made any changes to it while playing with NetBeans in one of the previous sections, you will see those changes here, as this is exactly the same source file, now linked by Eclipse.

If you do not like the idea of sharing the source code, you can copy it into your Eclipse project instead. Right-click on the **java** directory in **Project Explorer** and click on **Delete**. Confirm your decision in the dialog that opens. Navigate in your file system to the directory structure created by Maven and copy the contents of that **java** subdirectory that we linked previously (these contents should consist of just one **\com** subdirectory, but with more subdirectories and files under it).

Now navigate to your Eclipse workspace, and find the **\t5first** subdirectory containing our new Eclipse project, and then under it the directory named **\src**. Paste the copied **\com** subdirectory into **\src**. Now we need to make sure that Eclipse knows about the addition, for which it is enough to just refresh the project. Click on the project name in **Project Explorer** and press *F5*, or alternatively right-click on the project name and click on **Refresh**. You will see how the code packages have appeared under the Java Resources: **src** folder.

Whichever approach you have chosen to add the source code, let's change the code of the `Start.java` file a little and see how the changes are reflected by the application when we run it. Change the source code to look like this:

```
package com.packtpub.t5first.pages;
import java.util.Date;
/**
 * Start page of application t5first.
 */
public class Start
{
  public String getCurrentTime()
  {
    Date date = new Date();
    String message = ". Tapestry is cool! And Eclipse too!";
    return date + message;
  }
}
```

Right-click on the name of the project in **Project Explorer** and in the context menu select **Run As** | **Run on Server**. The first time you invoke this command, Eclipse will ask you to choose the server. Simply choose the existing server as shown in the next figure, tick the checkbox to always use this server for this project and click on **Finish**.

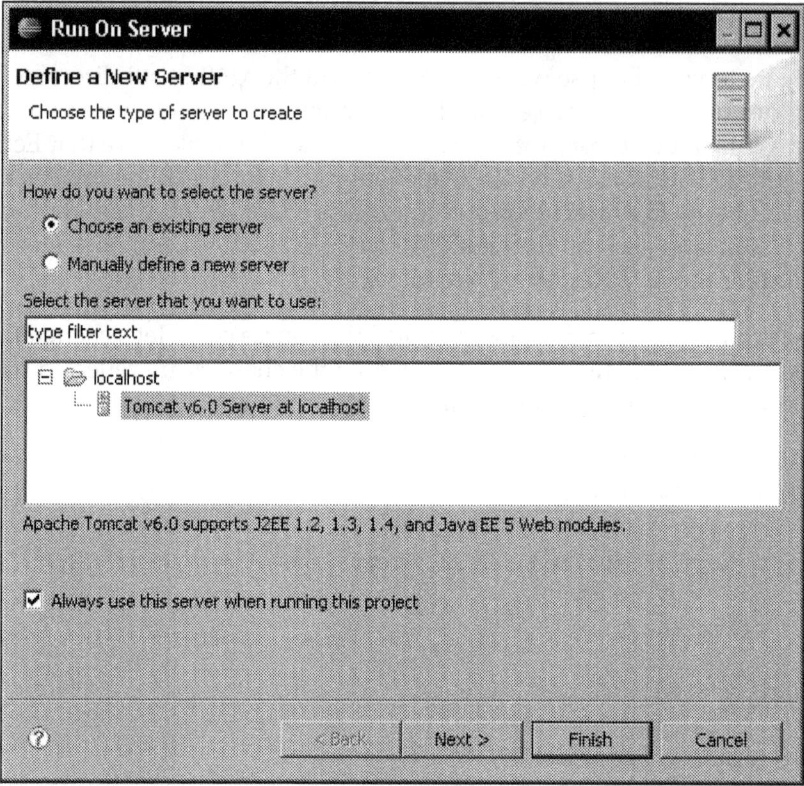

Finally, the application runs in the same way, as it did in NetBeans, although this time it is displayed in the built into Eclipse Web browser rather than an external one. Notice that it does reflect the changes you have done to the code most recently.

Try to make a change to the `Start.java` file, it can be as simple as adding an extra exclamation mark somewhere in the message. Then save the file. If you keep an eye on the server in the servers view at the bottom of the IDE, you will notice that Tomcat will restart the application almost immediately. The console view will output a few lines like these:

```
Jul 10, 2007 8:07:10 AM org.apache.catalina.core.StandardContext reload
INFO: Reloading this Context has started
[INFO] TapestryFilter Startup time: 382 ms to build IoC Registry, 1,893 
ms overall.
```

If you refresh the page in the browser now, you will notice that the change you have just made to the code is almost immediately reflected by the running application without any effort from your side. But is this always true?

Open the **Start.tml** file in the code editor and make some change to its text. For example, replace the current header:

```
<h1>t5first Start Page</h1>
```

with a new one:

```
<h1>My First Tapestry Application</h1>
```

Save the file and reload the page in the browser. You will see that the change you have made is not reflected by the running application, because you have changed an HTML file, and not Java code. Similar to NetBeans, Eclipse doesn't care about changes in HTML files.

One way to update the application in such case is to follow the advice given for NetBeans— make a change, even if it is an insignificant one, to some Java file, and save the file. The application will be then reloaded automatically.

> Similar to NetBeans, Eclipse doesn't know which editor to use for files with a `tml` extension, Tapestry page templates. Let's teach Eclipse to open these files using either HTML or XML editor.
>
> In the menu, open **Window** | **Preferences** and in the tree view on the left hand side navigate to **General** | **Content Types**. On the right hand side, in the **Content types** tree, expand the **Text** node and select the **HTML** item (or **XML** if you prefer). Below, in the **File associations** list box, you will see the list of extensions associated with this file type. Add `*.tml` to them by clicking the **Add...** button. Close all the dialogs by clicking on the **OK** button, and next time, when you open a file with a `tml` extension, it will be opened in an HTML Editor.

Another option is to restart Tomcat. Right-click the running server in the **Servers** view and select **Restart** | **Run**. The server will begin restarting, and you will see some output in the **Console**. Refresh the page in the web browser, as soon as you see a line similar to this:

```
INFO: Server startup in 3986 ms
```

Now you will see that the application reflects all the changes. You can also easily debug the application in Eclipse. Let's see how.

Debugging in Eclipse

Stop Tomcat by pressing the small red square on the right side above the **Servers** view as shown below.

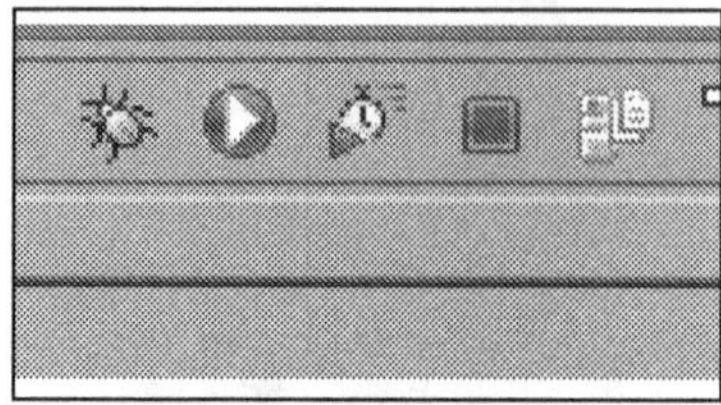

In the **Start.java** file, place a breakpoint against the return statement. For this, double-click on the left margin of the code editor against the desired line. You will see that a small blue circle appears there as shown in the following screenshot:

```
public class Start
{
    public String getCurrentTime()
    {
            Date date = new Date();
            String message = ". Tapestry is cool!";
            return date + message;
    }
}
```

Now click on the small bug icon on the right side above the **Servers** view to start Tomcat in debug mode. Click on the **refresh** link in the web browser. Eclipse will now suggest to switch into a Debugging perspective—accept that. Very soon you will see something similar to what the following figure shows—a rich array of information that you can use to debug the application. Note the **Variables** view at the top right that displays the values of the two currently available variables—**date** and **message**.

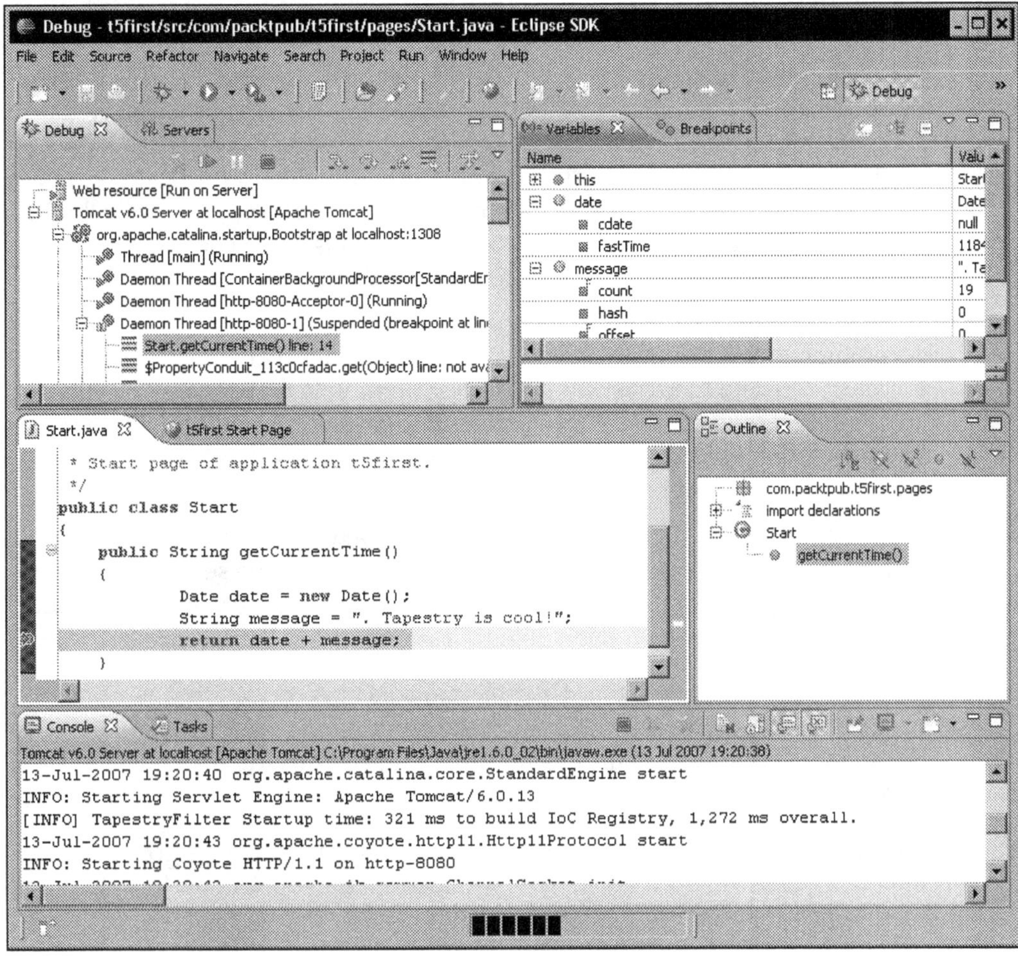

When the debugging is over, press *Ctrl + F2*. You might want to switch back to the Java EE perspective (there is a control for switching perspectives in the top right corner of Eclipse's window).

From here, we can continue developing the application, debugging it when necessary and this is exactly what we are going to do in the chapters that follow.

Summary

- The easiest way to create a foundation for a Tapestry project is to use Maven, a popular project management tool. Maven will create a complete skeleton of the project, with all necessary files and libraries already in place. All we need to do is to download Maven, unpack it and then add its location to the system's PATH variable. We could continue to use Maven to compile, build and deploy an application as we develop it, but it is more convenient and efficient to use an integrated development environment.
- There are two powerful, convenient and completely free integrated development environments available—NetBeans and Eclipse. It is actually a matter of taste which of them to use. My opinion is that NetBeans is better for beginners, as it brings all the necessary ingredients in one convenient package. If you have chosen Eclipse, I advise you to use the Eclipse WTP package, not the bare-bones version.
- In both NetBeans and Eclipse, you can easily make use of the project skeleton created by Maven. You can run the project on the server, updating it when you make some changes, and you can debug the project simply and naturally, as if this were a desktop application.

In the next chapter, we are going to learn the main concepts of Tapestry as a framework. Its ideas are very natural, but, on the other hand they can be quite innovative, and it is important to understand them when working on a Tapestry project.

The discussion that follows isn't going to be a boring theory, as we are going to learn the concepts while playing with a Tapestry application, the foundation for which we have created in this chapter.

3

The Foundations of Tapestry

In this chapter we are going to learn the following concepts:

- A Tapestry application is a set of interactive pages maintained and managed by the framework.
- Each page consists of a page template, which is an XML document, and a page class, which is a POJO (Plain Old Java Object, meaning that it doesn't have to inherit from other classes or implement any interface).
- A Tapestry page can contain extensions and components. We are going to learn almost everything about extensions and introduce a few components, leaving a proper discussion of components for the next two chapters.
- It is important to understand in rough detail the life cycle of a Tapestry page, and how components on a page in a user's web browser are connected to the properties of the page class.
- We can easily navigate from one page to another in a Tapestry application, and there are a few ways how we can do that.
- Tapestry applications can be easily structured according to our needs, and we are going to find out how to keep pages in order by putting them into different subdirectories.
- Any web application needs to remember many things about the current user and his or her choices. We are going to have a look at how an application's state is managed by Tapestry.

Quite a substantial plan for one chapter, but I hope you will enjoy going through it step-by-step. Let's begin.

Tapestry Application is a Set of Interactive Pages

It is natural for a user of a web application to think of it as a set of pages. The user might click on a button, select a value in a drop-down list or do something else, and the page would display different data, or even a completely different page might be shown by the application as a result of user actions.

The design of Tapestry is very close to this natural paradigm, as a Tapestry application actually consists of a number of Tapestry pages.

A Tapestry page is quite a clever entity. It remembers the values entered by the user, and if the user initiates some action, like clicking on a link or clicking on a button, the page will react to that action by running an appropriate fragment of code—an event handler method. It is for us developers to decide what kind of code it will be and how it will use the input provided by the user.

This will sound very familiar to those who have experience of developing desktop applications with some Rapid Application Development environments, such as Borland Delphi or Microsoft Visual Basic. However, web applications are very different from desktop applications, and although working with Tapestry we do not need to deal with complexities that arise from this difference, it is useful to understand how things work, at least in general terms.

Let's say that a Tapestry application is deployed on a web server in the USA, while the user who came to try the application is in Australia. What the user actually sees in his or her web browser is a piece of HTML, perhaps enhanced with images, JavaScript, and styles, but basically this is just a snapshot. It is just one moment in the life of the real Tapestry page, an entity that lives on the server.

When the web server receives a request from a user, it uses an appropriate Tapestry page to generate some output—some HTML page—to be sent to the user. When the user does something with the received HTML page, like putting some data into text boxes or clicking on a button, the information on what was done there is sent back to the Tapestry application. Then, depending on the logic of the application and the contents of user input, this information is passed either to the original Tapestry page, or to some other page to handle the submission and generate an appropriate response.

But what is this mysterious Tapestry page that lives on the server and what does it look like?

Page Template and Page Class

One of the most discussed problems of web development, and perhaps of software development in general, is how to separate presentation (what is being shown to the user) from business logic (what happens behind the scenes). In Tapestry, this separation is achieved cleanly and easily as every Tapestry page has a template and a page class.

A page template is an XML document—something quite similar to a basic XHTML or an HTML file but written to strict XML rules, and with a few elements not available in XHTML. As you already know from the previous chapter, Tapestry page templates have a `.tml` extension (which is for Tapestry Markup Language). A Template must be a well-formed XML document, which means that every element must be either declared as empty or properly closed (say, you can have `<img src=""/>` or `<img src=""></img>`, but not just `<img src="">`), and all attributes' values must be enclosed in quotation marks.

We have already seen a Tapestry page in our first application in the previous chapter and that page was represented by a combination of two files—`Start.tml` and `Start.java`. It is easy to guess that `Start.tml` is the page template. Let's have another look at the contents of this file:

```
<html xmlns:t="http://tapestry.apache.org/schema/tapestry_5_0_0.xsd">
  <head>
    <title>t5first Start Page</title>
  </head>
  <body>
    <h1>Tapestry Start Page</h1>

    <p> This is the start page for this application, a good place
      to start your modifications.
      Just to prove this is live: </p>

    <p> The current date and time is: ${currentTime}. </p>

    <p> [<t:pagelink t:page="Start">refresh</t:pagelink>] </p>
  </body>
</html>
```

You can see that the template is a proper XML document with the `<html>` element as its root (XML declaration is omitted here, and it is not required, as a matter of fact). It also has a namespace declaration:

```
xmlns:t="http://tapestry.apache.org/schema/tapestry_5_0_0.xsd"
```

This declaration basically says that any element or attribute having the `t` prefix belongs to the Tapestry namespace, such as this single component used on the **Start** page:

```
<t:pagelink t:page="Start">refresh</t:pagelink>
```

This is a `PageLink` component. Its purpose is to display a link that leads to a page of the application. In this case, the application has only one page—`Start`, so the component links this page to itself. That is, when the link is clicked on, the same page will be redisplayed (in other words, it will be refreshed).

Tapestry 5 is in many cases case-insensitive. In this case, you are free to write the name of the component and of the page in any case you like, for example, like this:

```
<t:PageLink t:page="start">refresh</t:PageLink>
```

There is also another piece of Tapestry instrumentation in this template, an **expansion** that looks like this:

```
${currentTime}
```

Expansion is a kind of window through which we can see the value of a property in the page class. However, before discussing how expansions work, let's have a look at the page class for the already familiar **Start** page. Its code can be found in `Start.java` file and is shown as follows:

```
package com.packtpub.t5first.pages;
import java.util.Date;
/**
 * Start page of application t5first.
 */
public class Start
{
  public String getCurrentTime()
  {
    Date date = new Date();
    String message = ". Tapestry is cool!";
    return date + message;
  }
}
```

Please note that this class is exactly what is usually termed as POJO (Plain Old Java Object), which means that it is a simple class that doesn't inherit from any framework-specific parent and doesn't implement any framework-specific interfaces. Dealing with POJO has a number of benefits, including easy testing and freedom of class design. We only need to provide some properties to store the page's state and some methods to contain its functionality.

Returning to expansions, they provide a simple way to display the value of some property of the page class on a page. Let's see how this works.

Using Expansions

Let's add the following fragment of code to `Start.java`:

```
private int someValue = 12345;
public int getSomeValue()
{
  return someValue;
}

public void setSomeValue(int value)
{
  this.someValue = value;
}
```

This is how properties are defined in a typical JavaBean class—a private class variable, and public getter and setter methods for it. We could also make this property read-only by omitting the setter method.

Now let's add an expansion to the page template to display this property. Insert the following fragment of code somewhere in `Start.tml`:

```
<p>Here is the value: ${someValue}</p>
```

Run the application and you will see how the page displays the recent addition:

```
Here is the value: 12345
```

What Tapestry does here is that it takes the page template and starts creating an output from it—an HTML page to be sent to a user's browser. When it comes to the `${someValue}` expansion, Tapestry knows that it should find the `getSomeValue` method in the page class and insert whatever that method returns into the output. Tapestry doesn't actually care whether the private field `someValue` exists in the page class. It just needs an appropriate getter method. This is why the `${currentTime}` expansion works fine, although there is no private `currentTime` field. The `getCurrentTime` method provides the value to be displayed. Let's examine this method in its original state, how it looked after being generated by Maven:

```
public Date getCurrentTime()
{
  return new Date();
}
```

The value returned by this method is of the `java.util.Date` type. When displayed as it is, the returned instance is simply converted into a string, and you see that already familiar output. The `Date` class also has a method, `getTime`, that returns the date and time in milliseconds from 12 AM 1st of January 1970. What if we want to display the value returned by this method? In other words, what if we want to display a property of the page class?

Let's modify the page template to look like this:

```
<html xmlns:t="http://tapestry.apache.org/schema/tapestry_5_0_0.xsd">
  <head>
    <title>Tapestry Start Page</title>
  </head>
  <body>
    <h1>Tapestry Start Page</h1>

    <p> The current date and time is: ${currentTime}. </p>

    <p> The same date and time in milliseconds is:
      ${currentTime.time}. </p>

    <p>Here is the value: ${someValue}</p>

    <p>[<t:PageLink t:page="start">refresh</t:PageLink>]</p>
  </body>
</html>
```

The output produced by Tapestry should look like this:

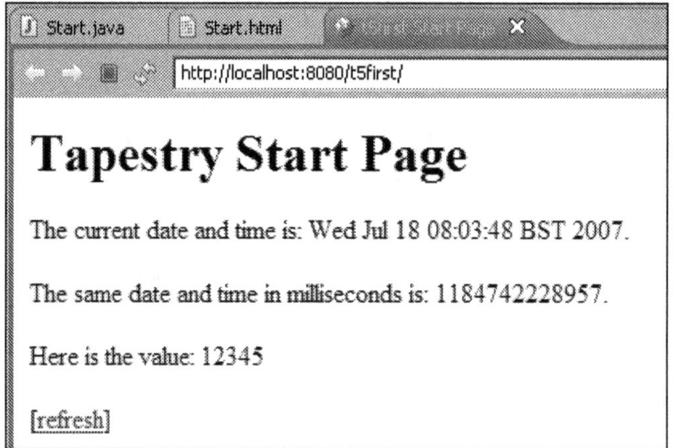

As you can see, using an expansion, we can easily display not only the page property (`currentTime`, as returned by the `getCurrentTime` method of the page class), but also a property of that property (the `time` property as returned by the `getTime` method of the `Date` class).

Here, Tapestry relies on the fact that getter methods are usually named in a standard JavaBean style, by capitalizing the first letter of the property name and appending `get` in front of it. However, there are methods that do not follow this rule. Say, `Date` class also has a method called `hashCode`. What if we want to display the value returned by that method? Let's try and add to the page template the following line of code:

```
And here is the hash code for it: ${currentTime.hashCode}.
```

Run the application, and you will see a glorious **Exception** page provided by Tapestry:

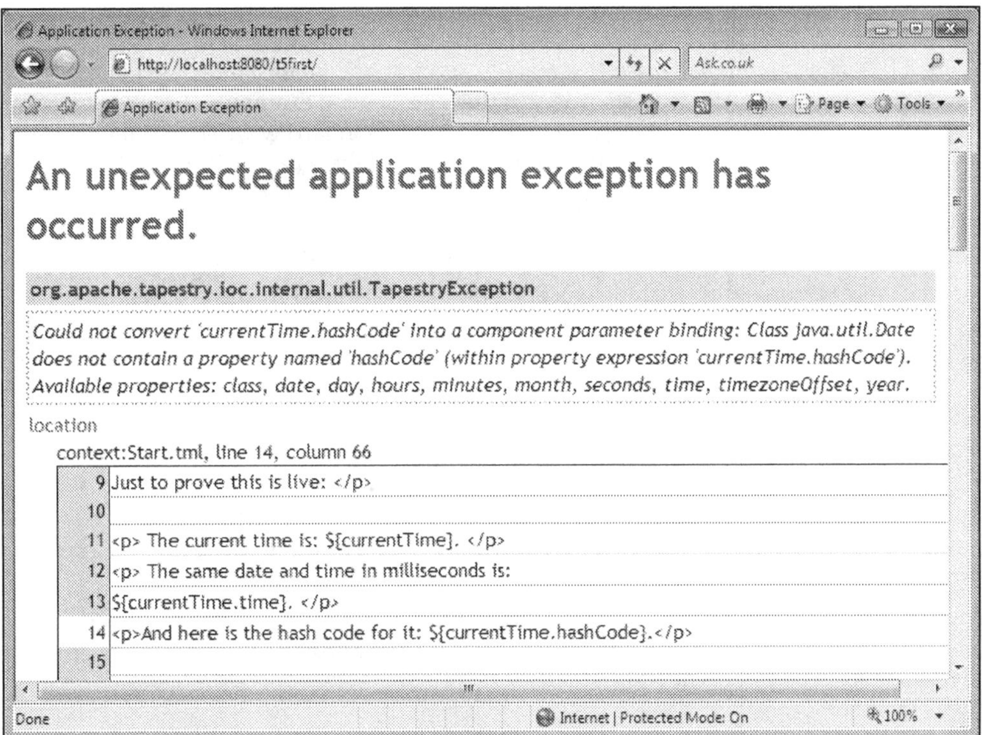

If you were struggling with the obscure error messages of other frameworks, you will greatly appreciate the clarity and precision of the Tapestry **Exception** page which provides you with a wealth of information to help with debugging.

This **Exception** page precisely points to the line of the template that caused the problem—exactly the line that we have just added. It also reports that **Class java.util. Date does not contain a property named 'hashCode'**. This means that Tapestry tried to find a method named `getHashCode`, but couldn't. It also listed all the properties available in the given class, but only those that are named in a standard way, and so `hashCode` is not among them.

How do we display the value of the hash code then? Tapestry expansions do provide a solution for this. If you want to call a method verbatim, let it have brackets in the expansion. Change the recently added line of code in the template to look like this:

```
And here is the hash code for it: ${currentTime.hashCode()}.
```

Seeing the brackets, Tapestry will know that it should not look for a `getHashCode` method, but call the `hashCode` method instead. Run the application, and it should work fine now.

> It is very unlikely that in a real life application you'll be interested in knowing a date's hash code, but there are several examples of popular Java classes with methods named in a non-standard way. To find the size of a Collection implementation, you will call the `size` method on it. Now you know how to do that.

Now you know almost everything about expansions. They can also be used to insert values from property files, but this will be covered in the chapter on internationalization. Next, let's have a look at different ways in which components can be defined on the page.

Using Components

First of all, let's add another page to have more space for experimenting. Right click on the `Start.tml` file in the **Project Explorer** or **Projects view**, depending on which IDE you are using. Click on **Copy,** in the context menu. Then right click on the **WebContent** folder in Eclipse or **Web Pages** folder in NetBeans and then click on **Paste**. Rename the new page to be... well, let it be `Another.tml`. Change the contents of the new page template to look like this:

```
<html xmlns:t="http://tapestry.apache.org/schema/tapestry_5_0_0.xsd">
  <head>
    <title>Another Page</title>
  </head>
  <body>
    <h1>Another Page</h1>
```

```
        <p>
          <t:PageLink t:page="Start">Back to the Start page</t:PageLink>
        </p>
      </body>
    </html>
```

Next, right click on the **com.packtpub.t5first.pages** package and add a new Java class, name it **Another**. Let this class remain empty for the moment. Finally, change the `PageLink` component in the `Start.tml` file to point to the new page:

```
<p>
  <t:PageLink t:page="Another">Go to Another
    page</t:PageLink>
</p>
```

Again, the names for the component and the page are case-insensitive, so you could have them as `<t:pagelink t:page="another">` or `<t:PAGELINK t:page="AnOtHeR">` if you prefer.

Run the application, click on the links, and you should be able to switch between the two pages.

Note that in Tapestry, to navigate between pages you don't need to think in terms of URL, or where the pages are physically located. You just need to tell the framework which page you want to show, by name, and Tapestry figures out everything by itself.

You already have some experience with defining components. Let's add a few others using the same approach. We are going to use a text field to give the user an opportunity to provide some value and a button to submit that value. However, the `TextField` component that we are going to use for the text box is a kind of component that must be surrounded by a `Form` component to work (this is because of the way HTML works: form controls have to be surrounded by the `<form>` element), so we shall provide a `Form` component as well. Add the following fragment to the `Start.tml` template:

```
<html xmlns:t="http://tapestry.apache.org/schema/tapestry_5_0_0.xsd">
  <head>
    <title>Tapestry Start Page</title>
  </head>
  <body>
    <h1>Tapestry Start Page</h1>

    <p> The current date and time is: ${currentTime}. </p>

    <p> The same date and time in milliseconds is:
      ${currentTime.time}. </p>
```

```
        <p> And here is the hash code for it:
          ${currentTime.hashCode()}. </p>

        <p>Here is the value: ${someValue}</p>

        <p>
          <t:PageLink t:page="Another">Go to Another
            page</t:PageLink>
        </p>

        <p>Submit a message:</p>
          <t:form t:id="userInputForm">
          <t:textfield t:value="message"/>
            <input type="submit" value="Submit"/>
          </t:form>
      </body>
    </html>
```

You can see a `Form` component, and there is an ID specified for it. You will see how the ID is used when we come to handling the form submission. Inside the form, there is a Tapestry component `TextField` and an ordinary HTML `<input type="submit"/>` control. The latter will work just fine here when it comes to form submission. There is also a Tapestry control named `Submit`, but we do not have to use it unless there is a good reason for that (see the next chapter for an example).

Please note the `t:value="message"` attribute of the `TextField`. This is where the component is bound to a property of the page class (there is no such property yet, we shall create it in a moment).

When Tapestry renders the page (produces an HTML content to be sent to the user's browser), it asks each component on that page to render itself. The expansions will then insert the values of some properties, the `PageLink` will become a link to another page, and when it comes to the `TextField` component, it will render itself as a text box (more precisely, as an HTML `<input type="text"/>` control). However, should this text box be empty, or should there be some value in it? To find this out, Tapestry will have a look at the `TextField`'s `value` parameter. In our case, its content is "message", which means, the component is bound to the `message` property of the page, and Tapestry will call the `getMessage` method of the page class to find out whether to display something in the text box.

Let's say the user has typed some text into the text box and clicked on the **Submit** button. The contents of the form will be sent back to Tapestry. Tapestry will take the content of the text box and understand that this is the value for the `TextField` component. But where should this value be placed? Since the component is bound to the `message` property of the page class, Tapestry will find the `setMessage` method of the page class and pass to it the submitted value.

Let's now see how this works in practice. Modify the code of the `Start.java` class to look like this:

```
import java.util.Date;
/**
 * Start page of application t5first.
 */
public class Start
{
  private int someValue = 12345;
  private String message="initial value";
  public int getSomeValue()
  {
    return someValue;
  }

  public void setSomeValue(int value)
  {
    this.someValue = value;
  }

  public Date getCurrentTime()
  {
    return new Date();
  }

  public String getMessage()
  {
    return message;
  }

  public void setMessage(String message)
  {
    System.out.println("Setting the message: " + message);
    this.message = message;
  }
}
```

We have provided a private field to store the value submitted by the user. To make things slightly more interesting, we gave this property an initial value, and now we expect that the text box will display this value when the page will render. If we didn't initialize this private field, the text box would remain empty.

We have also provided two public methods, a getter and a setter, to which the `TextField` component will be bound. In the setter method, we are printing out the value to be set to the standard output, to make sure everything works properly.

Do you know that you can have your IDE generating getter and setter methods automatically? Just provide the private field, and then, in NetBeans, select **Refactor | Encapsulate Fields...**, or in Eclipse select **Source | Generate Getters and Setters....** The dialog that opens then should be easy to understand.

Run the application, and you will see that the **Start** page looks like this:

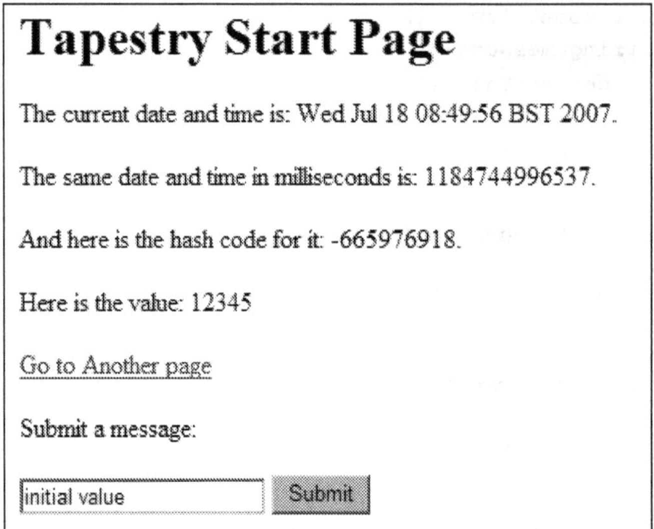

As you see, the initial value is displayed in the text box, exactly as we wanted. Now enter some different value into the text box and click on the **Submit** button.

You will see some output on the console (in Eclipse, it will be in the Console view, in NetBeans—in Bundled Tomcat view), something like this, depending on the message you have entered:

```
Setting the message: hi there!
```

You will notice that the message you have just entered was replaced by the initial value. Why is that? Well, we didn't instruct Tapestry to remember the new value, did we? So it forgot immediately and displayed the initial value again. In fact, we have just witnessed an important Tapestry mechanism at work, but to understand it better, let's consider a more realistic scenario. Usually, if we submit some value we do not want it to be displayed by the same page, but we rather want the application to do something with this value.

For example, we might want the application to pass the entered message to another page.

Passing a Value Between Pages

Let's say we want the **Another** page to display the message we entered at the **Start** page. First of all, we need to provide a property to store the passed value. Modify the `Another` page class (`Another.java` file) to look similar to this:

```
package com.packtpub.t5first.pages;

public class Another
{
  private String passedMessage;
  public String getPassedMessage()
  {
    return passedMessage;
  }

  public void setPassedMessage(String passedMessage)
  {
    this.passedMessage = passedMessage;
  }
}
```

Next, let's use an expansion to display the passed message at the **Another** page. Modify the `Another` page template to look like this:

```
<html xmlns:t="http://tapestry.apache.org/schema/tapestry_5_0_0.xsd">
  <head>
    <title>Another Page</title>
  </head>
  <body>
    <h1>Another Page</h1>

      <p>Received a new message: ${passedMessage}</p>

      <p>
        <t:PageLink t:page="Start">Back to the Start
          page</t:PageLink>
      </p>
  </body>
</html>
```

Now we need to write some code to actually pass the message to the **Another** page. That code should be executed as a result of form submission—in other words, we need to create an event handler for the **submit** event of the `Form` component that we have placed on the page. A `Form` component can generate a few other events too, but this will be explained in a later chapter.

In Tapestry 5 any method can be an event handler, no matter what we name it. To tell Tapestry when to invoke this method, we use the `@OnEvent` annotation, and also provide it with the ID of the component that the event handler should be associated with. For some components like `Form`, we also need to specify which event this method should handle, as the component can produce more than just one event.

Add the following method to the `Start` page class:

```
@OnEvent(value="submit", component="userInputForm")
void onFormSubmit()
{
  System.out.println("Handling form submission!");
}
```

Please note the default (or package) access level used for this method—the method wasn't declared as either private or public. This is a preferred approach for an event handler in Tapestry 5, and it makes a lot of sense. On one hand, this method serves a specific purpose and we do not want to leave it accessible to just everyone by making it public. On the other hand, if we make it accessible for classes in the same package, we shall be able to test this method easily by putting test classes into this package.

There is also an alternative method to define an event handler method without using an annotation. In this case we encode all the relevant information into the method name. The name of an event handler should begin with an `on`, followed by the name of the event, like this:

```
onSubmit() {}
```

Tapestry will automatically invoke this method for every `Submit` event that happens on the page. Say, if you have more than one `Form` component on a page, this method will run every time any of the forms is submitted.

If, however, you want to associate an event handler with a certain component, just add the word `From` to the method name, followed by the component's ID (with first letter capitalized). Here is the annotation-free equivalent of the event handler that was created previously using the `@OnEvent` annotation:

```
void onSubmitFromUserInputForm()
{
  System.out.println("Handling form submission!");
}
```

In fact, using such a naming convention for defining an event handler is the preferred approach for the developers of Tapestry framework. In their opinion, the annotations are for the case when you can't or don't want to use the naming conventions. However, I managed to get used to the annotations, and I like them. So, in the following chapters you will see a combination of both approaches.

Let's run the application. Click on the **Submit** button, and you should see an output in the console confirming that the event handler was invoked on submission:

```
Setting the message: hi there!
Handling form submission!
```

Next, we need to write some code to pass the message to the **Another** page.

First, we need to somehow obtain an instance of the **Another** page. The simplest approach is to inject that page. That is, to simply tell Tapestry that we might need it, like this:

```
@InjectPage
private Another another;
```

Now that we have an instance of the **Another** page, we can pass our message to it easily:

```
another.setPassedMessage(message);
```

Finally, to tell Tapestry that we want it to show the **Another** page as a result of event handling, we need to change the return type of the event handler method to `Object` and return the used instance of the **Another** page from the method. Here is the code for the `Start` page class with all the recent additions.

```
package com.packtpub.t5first.pages;
import java.util.Date;
import org.apache.tapestry.annotations.InjectPage;
import org.apache.tapestry.annotations.OnEvent;
/**
 * Start page of application t5first.
 */
public class Start
{
  private int someValue = 12345;
  private String message="initial value";
  @InjectPage
  private Another another;
  public int getSomeValue()
  {
    return someValue;
  }

  public void setSomeValue(int value)
  {
    this.someValue = value;
  }
```

```
    public Date getCurrentTime()
    {
      return new Date();
    }

    public String getMessage()
    {
      return message;
    }

    public void setMessage(String message)
    {
      System.out.println("Setting the message: " + message);
        this.message = message;
    }

    @OnEvent(value="submit", component="userInputForm")
    Object onFormSubmit()
    {
      System.out.println("Handling form submission!");
      another.setPassedMessage(message);
      return another;
    }
}
```

What Can be Returned From an Event Handler

There are actually a few different options of what you can return from an event handler:

- **Nothing**: This is when the method is void or when it returns a null value. In this case the current page will render the request. That is, it will be redisplayed.
- **String**: Tapestry will expect it to be some application page's logical name, like `another` (the name is case-insensitive). You will find more on logical names later in this chapter.
- **Class**: This should be a page class, like `Another.class`. Returning a class is a preferable approach, as compared to returning a logical name of the page as a string. This is because the logical name can change if application is restructured in the future, while its class will remain the same.

- **Page**: An instance of a page can be returned exactly like we did previously. Tapestry will make sure that page is displayed.
- **Link**: An implementation of a Link interface will be converted into an appropriate URL and the client will be redirected to that URL.
- **Stream**: A stream or more specifically, `StreamResponse` object. This option allows us to send to the user a binary stream—say, a generated PDF or an Excel document.

Any other object returned from an event handler will cause an error.

Run the application, submit some message, and everything will seem to work properly. The messages on the console will be as expected, and the **Another** page will be shown, but it will not display the message that we have just passed to it:

Why is that? To understand what has happened in this case, we need to discuss one subtle but important feature of Tapestry.

Tapestry Pages are Pooled

Tapestry was designed with great scalability in mind. This means that a Tapestry application should be able to easily handle a huge amount of concurrent users, and for this, it should spend minimal efforts to serve every individual request.

Say, a user requests the **Start** page. Should Tapestry create an instance of this page especially for this user and discard it as soon as the user will go to another page? This wouldn't be efficient, as the next moment, twenty other users will come and request an instance of the **Start** page. It would be reasonable not to discard, but to reuse the instance that was just used for the first user.

However, there is a potential problem. The page might have some sensitive data put into it by the first user—say a password, or anything else. To avoid this problem, Tapestry will wipe clean the instance used by the first user before giving it to any other user. It will reset all variables on the page class to their initial values.

In reality, Tapestry maintains a pool of instances for every page, and when a page is requested, it takes an instance from the appropriate pool to serve that request, and then returns the instance to its pool. At the end of the request, Tapestry will wipe clean the variables of the instance of any user-specific data.

This mechanism makes Tapestry very efficient. But we have to remember that even if we think that we are dealing with the same page, in most cases the page will be represented by a different instance (may be even coming from a completely different server, in a clustered environment), and the next instance will have no idea of what we have just told the previous instance. That is, unless we take special care and make sure that the information is passed between instances properly.

What happened when we tried to pass a message to the **Another** page is that we took an instance of it, and put our message into it. Then we told Tapestry to show the **Another** page to this user. What Tapestry 5 does is that it tells the user's browser: "Okay, thank you, I have successfully handled your submission; now go on and ask me to show you Another page". When the browser requests for the **Another** page, it takes a fresh instance of that page from the pool and uses it to produce the output. Unfortunately, that fresh instance will know nothing about the message we wanted to pass.

So how can we make our application work with all this instance pooling and jiggling? Should there be a way to make Tapestry remember the information we have put into the page, no matter which instance of that page is being used?

There are actually two approaches to this:

- We can make a page field persistent. This is a very simple approach, but it has some downsides.
- We can use page activation context. This is a superior approach, but not for every case, and it involves more coding.

Let's try both the approaches and see which one we will prefer for our application.

Making a Page Field Persistent

We can simply tell Tapestry that we want it to remember the value we have set to a page field by using the `@Persist` annotation on that field. Let's try this and add the annotation to the **Another** page class:

```
@Persist
private String passedMessage;
```

If you run the application now, it will work perfectly well, and the **Another** page will successfully display the message we have passed to it. What a simple solution! However, there are two potential problems associated with it. To understand where they come from, let's see how property persistence is achieved in Tapestry.

To store the value we have assigned to a persistent property, Tapestry creates an HttpSession. HttpSession can be understood as a piece of memory on the server associated with a specific user. Web applications have a way of tracking users that came to them, and if they have a session for a particular user, they can store user specific details.

Back to our application, as soon as we have put some value into the persistent message property of the **Another** page, Tapestry will reserve a piece of memory on the server, associate it first with the user, and second, with the **Another** page to which the persistent property belongs. Now every time we request for the **Another** page, Tapestry will notice that the page has a persistent property, and put the value stored for it in the session into that property, no matter what instance of the page is being used. Everything will work automatically, as soon as we have used the correct annotation.

Sounds great, but imagine, there are a few thousand users who are playing with the application simultaneously. For each of them, Tapestry will have to create a session, which might require a substantial amount of memory. Also, it takes some work to store the value into the session and retrieve it from there, even if this happens invisibly.

As a result, having a persistent property makes the application less scalable. This might be not a problem for many applications but would be for busy applications. Let's consider another scenario.

We were so impressed by the message displayed by the **Another** page that we decided to make a bookmark, and returned the next day to contemplate the message again, only to discover that the message is not there anymore. It was stored for that session, and the web application cannot afford to store sessions for all its users eternally. The standard timeout interval is 30 minutes, and if we do not show any activity for longer than this, our session will be invalidated, and any information stored in it will be lost.

Again, this downside is relative. That is, it might not be essential for many pages of our application whether they are bookmarked or not. There is however an approach of passing the value to another page that doesn't involve any session, and it does allow bookmarking. This is covered in the next sub-section.

Using Page Activation Context

Tapestry 5 has a special way to pass a value from one page to another. Let's see how it works. First of all, we need to make the page "activatable", which means that we should add two methods—`onActivate` and `onPassivate` to the page. They will be invoked by Tapestry at the appropriate moments of the HTTP request life cycle. In this case, the **Another** page allows the `@Persist` annotation to be removed and adds the mentioned methods, like the following listing shows:

```
package com.packtpub.t5first.pages;

public class Another
{
  private String passedMessage;
  public String getPassedMessage()
  {
    return passedMessage;
  }

  public void setPassedMessage(String passedMessage)
  {
    this.passedMessage = passedMessage;
  }

  void onActivate(String message)
  {
    System.out.println("Another page is activated! The
      message is: " + message);
    this.passedMessage = message;
  }

  String onPassivate()
  {
    System.out.println("Another page is passivated...");
    return passedMessage;
  }
}
```

Now let's run the application and see what happens. Enter some message into the text box at the **Start** page, and click on the **Submit** button. The **Another** page will appear with the message displayed properly, while in the console we shall see the following output:

```
Setting the message: hi there!
Handling form submission!
Another page is passivated...
Another page is activated! The message is: hi there!
```

Let's see what has happened here. In the code of the **Start** page, we have used an injected instance of the **Another** page to set a message on it. Then we asked Tapestry to show the **Another** page which, as we've seen before, would normally mean wiping out the message (perhaps by sending the instance we have just used back to the pool) and displaying a fresh empty instance of the **Another** page, perhaps just taken from the pool. However, before sending the first instance back to the pool, Tapestry will check whether the **Another** page uses the activation context by implementing the pair of methods, `onActivate` and `onPassivate`. As it does, Tapestry will invoke the `onPassivate` method of that instance, which is like asking "Hey, instance of the **Another** page, is there anything you want me to pass to another instance of your page that will continue your work?".

You can see from the code that the `onPassivate` method will report the contents of the message we have just set, and Tapestry will remember its answer. As soon as it uses another instance of the **Another** page, it will pass the stored message as a parameter to the `onActivate` method of the new instance, and this way we shall be able to see the message properly displayed on the page.

But how will Tapestry remember the message if it does not create a session? Have a look at the URL used to display the **Another** page:

```
http://localhost:8080/t5first/another/hi+there%21
```

The message was recorded into the URL while redirecting the user's browser to the **Another** page, and so Tapestry was able to restore the message without ever creating a session. This also means that the **Another** page can now be bookmarked, and it will show you the message successfully, even if you come to read it after a few months! Now imagine that this page was used to display a product from an online catalog, and you will appreciate the benefits of using the activation context.

This was another way of passing information from one page to another. Now let's return to how we define components on the pages—there are a few different ways to do that too.

Different Ways of Defining Components

So far, we have seen just one approach to defining a component on a page—by using an XML element in the Tapestry namespace, like this:

```
<t:textfield t:value="message"/>
```

However, this simple approach has a downside. If we preview the **Start** page template in a web browser, we'll see something similar to this:

It is not a problem that the values to be inserted into the page are replaced by expansions. This is a static preview, after all. What is worse, some components have simply disappeared. We do not see the link to the **Another** page, and there is no text box.

This means that when we are declaring components as shown above, we are losing the ability to preview the page template in a web browser and to continue editing it using common HTML editors like Dreamweaver.

This might not be a big deal if you are creating both templates and page classes on your own and if the design of the page is not too complicated. However, web applications are often developed by a mixed team where designers work on templates while developers concentrate on page classes. Also, it is often easier to start developing a page from its HTML mock up, discussed and agreed upon with the customer. In these cases, Tapestry's ability to make its instrumentation invisible becomes very important.

Change the `TextField` declaration to look like this:

```
<input type="text" t:type="textfield" t:value="message"/>
```

Here we have hidden both the type of the Tapestry component and its binding inside a standard HTML control. If you run the application now, it should work and look exactly as before, but if you preview the page template in a web browser, you will be able to see a proper text field, not an empty space in place of it.

Try to do a similar cosmetic upgrade for the `PageLink` component:

```
<a href="#" t:type="PageLink" t:page="Another">Go to Another page</a>
```

Now it will look like a link not only on the running page, but on the previewed page template too.

Finally, we can go even further and move most of the components' configuration to the page class. Add the following two private fields with annotations to the `Start` page class:

```
@Component(parameters = {"page=Another"})
private PageLink theLink;

@Component(parameters = {"value=message"})
private TextField theTextBox;
```

Then change the way these two components are placed on the page template:

```
<a href="#" t:id="theLink">Go to Another page</a>
<input type="text" t:id="theTextBox"/>
```

Note that the values used for `t:id` attributes in the page template should be the names of the private properties defined in the page class.

Run the application, and it should work exactly as it did before. As you see, there are three different ways to define a component on a page:

- Explicitly in the template.
- Invisibly in the template.
- In the page class.

With the last option, we achieve the cleanest separation between code and presentation, but, to my taste, those complicated annotations look a bit ugly. On the other hand, having just one attribute, `t:id`, in the page template to represent a potentially complex component is a valuable feature of Tapestry. This can become important in applications with complex design or if you want to make the interaction between designers and developers absolutely minimal.

Right now, while adding new pages, we place templates directly at the root of the web application and page classes under the `pages` sub-package of the application's package, `com.packtpub.t5first`. However, if we wish, we can give our project an additional structure.

Structuring the Application

As the number of pages in our application grows, we might want to structure them in a particular manner. For example, if there is some order handling functionality, we might find it convenient to put all the order-related pages into the `\order` subdirectory. Also, it is often required to limit access to some pages to make them secure, and the standard security solutions often work by limiting access to a certain subdirectory. Let's see how we can create a directory structure in our Tapestry application.

Say we want to have a subdirectory named `\secure`, and put some pages with sensitive content into it.

First of all, create such a subdirectory in the appropriate directory of your IDE (Web Pages or WebContent). Then create a template for a new page, let it be named `Payment.tml`, and put it into the `\secure` subdirectory.

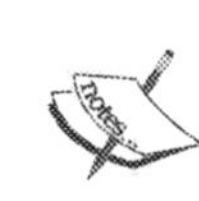

In order not to worry about having the Tapestry namespace right, I find it convenient to copy an existing page template in Project Explorer or Project view, depending on the IDE you are using. Then paste it into a directory where you want to have a new template—say `\secure`, and change its name and contents as you wish.

The contents of the new template can be as simple as this:

```
<html xmlns:t="http://tapestry.apache.org/schema/tapestry_5_0_0.xsd">
  <head>
    <title>Payment Page</title>
  </head>
  <body>
    <h1>Payment Page</h1>

    <p>Some payment functionality goes here.</p>

    <p>
      <t:PageLink t:page="Start">Back to the Start page</t:PageLink>
    </p>
  </body>
</html>
```

Next, right-click on the `com.packtpub.t5first.pages` package and choose to create a new package. Name it `com.packtpub.t5first.pages.secure`. That is, add a sub package with the name of the new subdirectory to the existing package for the application's pages. Create in this new package a Java class named `Payment`—a page class for the new page. Leave this class empty.

Now we need a way to view the `Payment` page. Let's add another `PageLink` component to the **Start** page:

```
<a href="#" t:type="PageLink" t:page="secure/Payment">
  Go to the secure Payment page
</a>
```

As you see, now we have appended the name of the subdirectory to the name of the page. This is what is called the **logical name** of the page in Tapestry—the name of the page itself plus any additional directory structure within the application.

Run the application, and while you are still on the **Start** page, note the URL in the browser's address bar, it should be something like `http://localhost:8080/t5first/`. Now click on the **Go to the secure Payment page** link, and you should see that page. Have a look at its URL—`http://localhost:8080/t5first/secure/payment`. You see that this URL contains the `secure` subdirectory in it. Now we could easily use the Tomcat's built-in security features to authenticate everyone who tries to access the contents of this subdirectory (you will find an explanation of how to do this in any good book on Tomcat).

Now, how about creating a page with the logical name `secure/supersecure/Enigma`? Try it yourself, as an exercise. In fact, you can have the structure of subdirectories as deep as you wish.

Now, let me show one tricky but clever feature of Tapestry 5. Let's create a page named **SecurePage**, and put it into the existing `secure` subdirectory. Do everything like you did with the **Payment** page; only the name of the page will be different.

Finally, use a `PageLink` on the **Start** page to link to the new page. How will you configure it? Perhaps like this:

```
<a href="#" t:type="PageLink" t:page="secure/SecurePage">
  Go to the Secure Page
</a>
```

Now, run the application. What you will see is Tapestry's **Exception** page, as glorious and informative as before:

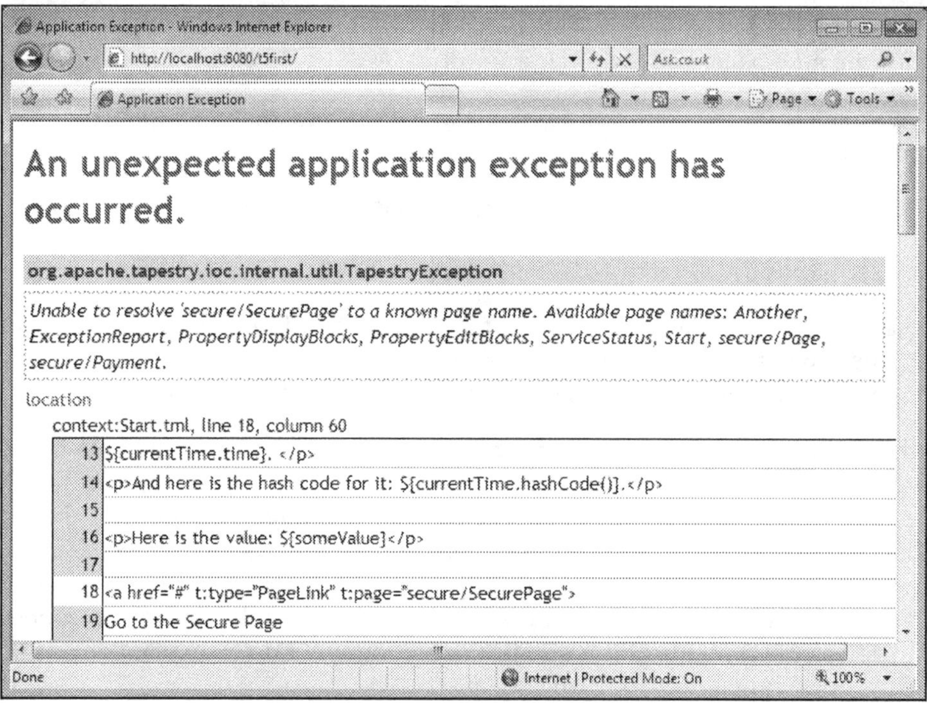

This page is really helpful. It not only it tells us that there is no page named **secure/SecurePage**, but it also provides a list of all the available page names. At the end of this list, we shall find a page named **secure/Page**. You might be surprised to know that this is exactly the page we have just created.

See, Tapestry makes an optimization when it selects a logical name for a page. If the page name contains the name of a folder it is in—like we have a folder named `secure`, and the page name is `SecurePage`, the name of the folder is removed from the page name. This produces a nicer and shorter logical name and URL, while the page files still retain the original name we have given to them.

Do not be surprised when, after creating a page called, `UserRegistration` and placing it into the `\user` subdirectory, you will have to use the logical name `user/registration`, while the page class will still be named `UserRegistration`.

> By the way, do you still remember that Tapestry is case-insensitive when it comes to the names of components and pages? But not the names of classes in Java code!

Since we are already speaking about users, it can be mentioned that quite often we shall want to have some information available for all the pages of our web application, and a typical example of such information is user specific settings, preferences and other details. It would be a burden to pass all this information between pages; we would rather prefer to have it available at any time whenever we need to look up one or another detail. Let's see how we can achieve this in a Tapestry application.

Creating and Using an Application State Object

In Tapestry, an object that is made available for every page of the application is termed Application State Object (ASO). Usually, this is some kind of object we create specially for the purpose of storing some set of data in an organized way. Say, we can have a `User` class for storing information about the application's user. It can be as simple as this:

```
package com.packtpub.t5first.util;
public class User
{
  private String firstName = "John";
  private String lastName = "Smith";
  public String getFirstName()
  {
    return firstName;
  }

  public void setFirstName(String firstName)
  {
    this.firstName = firstName;
  }

  public String getLastName()
  {
    return lastName;
  }

  public void setLastName(String lastName)
  {
    this.lastName = lastName;
  }
}
```

Note that I have placed this class into `com.packtpub.t5first.util` package. Please remember that you should never place anything but page classes into the `pages` sub package (such as `com.packtpub.t5first.pages` in this application).

Go on and create such packages and the class. For simplicity's sake, it contains only first and last names of the user, but we could put as much information as we might find necessary in this class. We have also initialized the properties to some default values.

All we need to make an instance of this class available to the whole application is to create a private field of the type `User` and mark it with the `@ApplicationState` annotation. Add the following snippet to the `Start` page class:

```
@ApplicationState
private User user;

public User getUser()
{
  return user;
}
```

Also, to an Application State Object of the type `User`, we have provided a public getter method so that the page template could access the ASO. Now let's display the user information on the page. Add the following code to the `Start` page template:

```
<p>The user is ${user.firstName} ${user.lastName}</p>
```

Now let's make similar changes to the **Another** page. First of all, the ASO and the getter method for it is:

```
@ApplicationState
private User myUser;

public User getMyUser()
{
  return myUser;
}
```

Hey, but why does the property for the ASO have a different name here? It was just `user`, and now it is `myUser`. Doesn't this mean that the two pages will have different instances of the ASO? No it doesn't. Let's see how all this works.

As soon as a private field of some type (`User` in our case) is marked with the `@ApplicationState` annotation, and if any other private field of the same type is also marked with `@ApplicationState` annotation, it will refer to the same instance of the ASO, no matter how the field is named.

Another important detail to understand is that Tapestry will create an instance of the ASO the first time we request it. This means that whenever we request the ASO, it will always be there, it will never be null.

By default, Application State Objects are stored in session. This means that if the session didn't exist the first time you request an ASO, it will be created. We might need to remember this when creating a highly scalable application.

We shall see how all this works pretty soon. For now, let's display the user information on the **Another** page:

```
<p>The user is ${myUser.firstName} ${myUser.lastName}</p>
```

To complete preparations, we need to provide a way of changing the contents of the ASO. To keep things simple, let's just reuse the existing `TextField`. Currently we are using it to enter an arbitrary message, but let's add some code to accept a new user name entered into it. This additional code will go into the `onFormSubmit` method. Please make the changes shown here:

```
@OnEvent(value="submit", component="userInputForm")
Object onFormSubmit()
{
  System.out.println("Handling form submission!");

  String[] words = message.split(" ");
  if (words.length > 0)
  {
    user.setFirstName(words[0]);
    if (words.length > 1)
    {
      user.setLastName(words[1]);
    }
  }

  another.setPassedMessage(message);
  return another;
}
```

In this code, we are simply splitting the submitted message into words, and then using the first word as the first name and the second word as the last name. We have to check whether there are enough words too.

Run the application, and you will see that the user is **John Smith**. The **Start** page requested the `User` ASO, so it was created by Tapestry and saved into session with default values in it.

Click on the **Go to Another page** link, and you will see that the same **John Smith** is displayed there. Everything as expected. Return to the **Start** page.

Now enter some name into the text box, say, **Jane Johnson**, and click on the **Submit** button. You will see the **Another** page, and the user displayed on it will be **Jane Johnson**! If you remember, to set the new name, we have used the private field named `user` in the **Start** page class, whereas the **Another** page uses its own private field `myUser` to access the ASO. The fact that the **Another** page displays updated information confirms that both private fields are connected to the same instance of the ASO, no matter how they are named, as soon as they have the same type and marked with the `@ApplicationState` annotation.

This convenient feature has one tricky consequence however. Let's say you have created an ASO of type `String` on one of the pages:

```
@ApplicationState
private String someValue;
```

It worked fine for you, but later you decided that you need another ASO for a different piece of information, and it will be a String too:

```
@ApplicationState
private String someCompletelyDifferentValue;
```

However, this will not work in the way that you expected it to. Both Application State Objects will refer to the same string, so as soon as you change the value of one of them, the other one will return the same new value too.

The correct way to use an ASO is to package a number of related pieces of information into a specially created purpose class, like `User` in our example. Of course, if you know that there is already some class you can conveniently reuse, do that. But remember, each ASO must have its own type, or it will be referring to some other already existing ASO.

Was an ASO Already Instantiated?

The final important piece of knowledge about dealing with an ASO is checking whether it exists or not. Consider the following scenario—as soon as the user has successfully logged in, you are storing his or her data in an ASO. On the other pages you are going to check whether the user is logged in and change the displayed information appropriately.

Remember that Tapestry will always give you an ASO as soon as you request for it. So you can request for the `User` ASO, check its contents, and if the contents are default, then the user hasn't logged in yet. All this is fine; but the problem is that you want to make your application highly scalable, which means you do not want to create a session unless it is absolutely necessary. Tapestry will create a session, the first time you request an ASO, even if you just wanted to check whether the values are default.

Fortunately, Tapestry provides a convenient way of checking whether an ASO was ever requested (and so created and stored into session by Tapestry) without initiating its creation.

As soon as you have created an ASO named, say, `user`, you can also create a private boolean field named `userExists`. That is, the name of the ASO field with `Exists` appended to it. As soon as the ASO is requested for somewhere in the application, and so instantiated by Tapestry, this boolean field will be set to `true`, but before that its value will be `false`. Let's use this feature in our application and see how it works.

What if we want to display information about the user on the **Start** page only when the `User` ASO gets instantiated by Tapestry? We can surround the piece of markup that reports about the user by the `If` component, like this:

```
<t:if t:test="userExists">
  <p>The user is ${user.firstName} ${user.lastName}</p>
</t:if>
```

This component simply renders its body (i.e. whatever is surrounded by it) when the condition to which it is bound (`userExists` in this case) evaluates to `true` and or doesn't render anything otherwise.

I hope you do not mind that I am constantly switching between different ways of defining Tapestry components. I do this intentionally, to give you an opportunity to choose which one you prefer.

The final step is to actually create the boolean property named `userExists`. Add the following lines of code to Start page class:

```
private boolean userExists;

public boolean getUserExists()
{
  return userExists;
}
```

This time when you run the application initially, there should be no user information on the **Start** page. However, as soon as you either submit a new name for the user (in which case the `User` ASO will be requested by the **Start** page) or simply click on the **Go to Another page** link (in which case the ASO will be requested by the **Another** page), the ASO will be instantiated. As a result, when you visit the **Start** page next time, you will see the user information displayed there.

Now you know almost everything there is to know about using Application State Objects, and certainly enough to begin using them in your applications. Let's now see what we have learned in this chapter.

Summary

We have covered a lot of ground in this chapter, and as a reward, you should have by now a strong feeling that you know how to work with Tapestry. In particular, you should know how to:

- Create a bare-bones Tapestry project using Maven, and then edit, test and debug it in both NetBeans and Eclipse.
- Add pages to the project, maybe placing them into different subdirectories in order to give your application a logical structure.
- Use expansions to display the values of different properties of the page class (and of properties of those properties too).
- Configure Tapestry components on the page in three different ways—and you are already familiar with a few components: `PageLink`, `TextField`, `Form`, and `If`.
- Navigate between different pages of the application, and how to pass values from page to page if you need to do so.
- Create and use Application State Objects. You even know a couple of tricks that will help you to use ASO more efficiently.

In fact, all you need now to start creating a functionally rich web applications is more knowledge of Tapestry components—and this is exactly what we are going to learn beginning in the next chapter.

In the next chapter, we are going to examine the simplest (and perhaps the most often used) of Tapestry components. You already know some of them, but even so there are additional details which you might find useful.

4
Simple Components

In this chapter, we are going to examine a number of components. I have called them *simple* because they map directly, or almost directly, to HTML controls and elements. Simple components are normally used on every page of a Tapestry web application, and so we should know them quite well.

There are also more complex components in Tapestry. They can save you a lot of work when creating a functionally rich interface. Those components will be discussed in the next chapter.

Instead of giving you a systematic, but dry and boring description of components and their properties, I have decided to take a different approach. We are going to build a web application—more or less close to real life, but somewhat simplified, in order not to overshadow the ideas and principles of Tapestry with details of implementation.

This means that we shall introduce components "in their natural environment", when we need them for the page we are working on—a less systematic, but more practical approach. One of the results is that we shall need to spend some time creating the project, discussing its structure and writing some auxiliary code.

The components we are going to learn in this chapter are:

- `TextField`: You have already met this component in the previous chapter, but I want to show you more of its properties.
- `PasswordField`: This component is similar to TextField, but more convenient for accepting a password from the user.
- `Label`: It is, naturally, used to label other components.
- `PageLink`: This is also familiar to you, but there is more to know about it.
- `ActionLink`: This component looks like an ordinary link, but can have an event handler associated with it.

- `Loop`: This component provides a way to iterate through a number of objects, and perhaps display them as some kind of list.
- `Output`: This component is used to provide a formatted output.
- `Checkbox`: This is very similar to a basic HTML check box, but it is connected to a property of the page class.
- `RadioGroup` and `Radio` components: These work together to provide a control that looks very similar to the familiar set of HTML radio buttons, but, is connected to a property of the page class.
- `If`: This component is already familiar to you, but it has an additional useful feature.
- `Submit`: This component can be used to submit a form, and although it is not required for this purpose, still can be quite useful.
- `Select: This` component provides a way to pick one of several options. It is rendered as an HTML `<select>` control, but being a Tapestry component, has some powerful features too.
- We are also going to use the `Form` component, but only as a required container for the other components. It has some important and powerful features, but they will be fully discussed later, in the chapter on user input validation.

We are going to use these components on the pages of a Tapestry web application named **Celebrity Collector**. We shall only start the project in this chapter, and as we learn more about Tapestry in the following chapters, we shall add more features and functionality to the project.

Celebrity Collector Project

This web application will provide its users an opportunity to maintain a collection of their favorite celebrities. User will be able to display the collection, add more celebrities to it, edit existing information and so on. In order not to distract you to non-Tapestry specific issues, the initial version of **Celebrity Collector** will have no real database. Instead, a simple mock data source will be created to imitate storing and retrieving information. However, if you want to create something closer to real life, Appendix B will explain how to replace this mock data source with a real object database, very lightweight and extremely easy to work with.

First of all, let's create a new Tapestry project following instructions given in Chapter 2. Simply replace the package name in that long Maven command with something like `com.packtpub.celebrities`, and modify the `groupId` and `artifactId` parameters accordingly.

If you have any kind of problem with Maven, or simply want to save time, the code package for this chapter already contains the project tree created by Maven, so you can just copy it and start from there.

From the generated or copied skeleton, create a project in an IDE of your choice, as described in Chapter 2, and then add another two pages—**ShowAll** and **Register** to the already existing **Start** page. You can simply copy and paste the `Start.tml` template twice, renaming it appropriately and removing any page-specific content from the new page templates. Also create two empty, aptly named Java classes for the new pages.

The templates for the new pages can remain as simple as this (replace the title and the text with something reasonable for `ShowAll.tml`):

```
<html xmlns:t="http://tapestry.apache.org/schema/tapestry_5_0_0.xsd">
  <head>
    <title>Celebrity Collector: Registration</title>
  </head>
  <body>
    <h1>Registration</h1>

    <p> Registration form will be created here. </p>
    <a href="#" t:type="PageLink" t:page="Start">
      Back to the Start Page</a>
  </body>
</html>
```

The first iteration of **Celebrity Collector** will be very simple. The **Start** page will contain a login form (for the existing users) and a link to the **Registration** page (for the newcomers). Those who have successfully logged in, and those who have successfully registered will proceed to the **ShowAll** page and see the whole existing collection listed there.

The Auxiliary Classes

Before going into Tapestry-specific work, let's prepare some helper classes. First of all, since we are going to deal with celebrities, it will make sense to create a `Celebrity` class. Create a new package, `com.packtpub.celebrities.model`, and then add to it a new class, naming it `Celebrity`. The contents of this class can be as simple as this:

```
package com.packtpub.celebrities.model;

import java.text.SimpleDateFormat;
import java.util.Date;
```

```
public class Celebrity
{
  private long id;
  private String firstName;
  private String lastName;
  private Date dateOfBirth;
  private Occupation occupation;
  public Celebrity()
  {
  }

  public Celebrity(String firstName, String lastName,
    Date dateOfBirth, Occupation occupation)
  {
    this.firstName = firstName;
    this.lastName = lastName;
    this.dateOfBirth = dateOfBirth;
    this.occupation = occupation;
  }

  public String getFirstName()
  {
    return firstName;
  }

  public void setFirstName(String firstName)
  {
    this.firstName = firstName;
  }

  public String getLastName()
  {
    return lastName;
  }

  public void setLastName(String lastName)
  {
    this.lastName = lastName;
  }

  public Date getDateOfBirth()
  {
    return dateOfBirth;
  }

  public void setDateOfBirth(Date dateOfBirth)
  {
```

```
        this.dateOfBirth = dateOfBirth;
      }

      public Occupation getOccupation()
      {
        return occupation;
      }

      public void setOccupation(Occupation occupation)
      {
        this.occupation = occupation;
      }

      public long getId()
      {
        return id;
      }

      public void setId(long id)
      {
        this.id = id;
      }
    }
```

The `Celebrity` class is very simple. It basically contains five pieces of information—first name, last name, date of birth, occupation and a unique ID. Later we can add more properties if we need them. For an occupation, it will make sense to use an enumeration, perhaps as simple as this:

```
package com.packtpub.celebrities.model;
public enum Occupation
{
  ACTOR, ACTRESS, ARTIST, BUSINESSMAN, COMPOSER,
  MUSICIAN, POLITICIAN, SCIENTIST, SINGER, WRITER
}
```

If required, we can add any other occupation. Admittedly, having `ACTOR` and `ACTRESS` as two different occupations isn't a very good design, but it will work for now. So go on and add such an enumeration to the appropriate package of **Celebrity Collector**.

Next, we need to provide a data source. It would be a good idea to create an interface for this purpose with different methods in it that our application might require. We could then have different implementations of this interface—a mock one, to simplify the initial development, and a real one, for the time when the application will go live. With proper coding, we shall be able to easily substitute one data source for another. Create a new package, `com.packtpub.celebrities.data`, and add to it the following interface:

```
package com.packtpub.celebrities.data;

import com.packtpub.celebrities.model.Celebrity;
import java.util.List;

public interface IDataSource
{
  public List<Celebrity> getAllCelebrities();
  public Celebrity getCelebrityById(long id);
  public void addCelebrity(Celebrity c);
}
```

Following is what a mock implementation, with an odd collection of celebrities, could look like:

```
package com.packtpub.celebrities.data;

import com.packtpub.celebrities.model.Celebrity;
import com.packtpub.celebrities.model.Occupation;
import com.packtpub.celebrities.util.Formats;
import java.util.ArrayList;
import java.util.List;

public class MockDataSource implements IDataSource
{
  private List<Celebrity> celebrities =
    new ArrayList<Celebrity>();
  public MockDataSource()
  {
    addCelebrity(new Celebrity("Britney", "Spearce",
      Formats.parseDate("12/02/1981"),
      Occupation.SINGER));
    addCelebrity(new Celebrity("Bill", "Clinton",
      Formats.parseDate("08/19/1946"),
      Occupation.POLITICIAN));
    addCelebrity(new Celebrity("Placido", "Domingo",
      Formats.parseDate("01/21/1941"),
      Occupation.SINGER));
    addCelebrity(new Celebrity("Albert", "Einstein",
      Formats.parseDate("03/14/1879"),
      Occupation.SCIENTIST));
    addCelebrity(new Celebrity("Ernest", "Hemingway",
      Formats.parseDate("07/21/1899"),
      Occupation.WRITER));
    addCelebrity(new Celebrity("Luciano", "Pavarotti",
      Formats.parseDate("10/12/1935"),
      Occupation.SINGER));
```

```
    addCelebrity(new Celebrity("Ronald", "Reagan",
      Formats.parseDate("02/06/1911"),
      Occupation.POLITICIAN));
    addCelebrity(new Celebrity("Pablo", "Picasso",
      Formats.parseDate("10/25/1881"),
      Occupation.ARTIST));
    addCelebrity(new Celebrity("Blaise", "Pascal",
      Formats.parseDate("06/19/1623"),
      Occupation.SCIENTIST));
    addCelebrity(new Celebrity("Isaac", "Newton",
      Formats.parseDate("01/04/1643"),
      Occupation.SCIENTIST));
    addCelebrity(new Celebrity("Antonio", "Vivaldi",
      Formats.parseDate("03/04/1678"),
      Occupation.COMPOSER));
    addCelebrity(new Celebrity("Niccolo", "Paganini",
      Formats.parseDate("10/27/1782"),
      Occupation.MUSICIAN));
    addCelebrity(new Celebrity("Johannes", "Kepler",
      Formats.parseDate("12/27/1571"),
      Occupation.SCIENTIST));
    addCelebrity(new Celebrity("Franz", "Kafka",
      Formats.parseDate("07/03/1883"),
      Occupation.WRITER));
        addCelebrity(new Celebrity("George", "Gershwin",
        Formats.parseDate("09/26/1898"),
        Occupation.COMPOSER));
  }

  public List<Celebrity> getAllCelebrities()
  {
    return celebrities;
  }

  public Celebrity getCelebrityById(long id)
  {
    for (Celebrity c : celebrities)
    {
      if (c.getId() == id) return c;
    }
    return null;
  }

  public void addCelebrity(Celebrity c)
  {
    long newId = celebrities.size();
    c.setId(newId);
    celebrities.add(c);
  }
}
```

Please add such a class to the `com.packtpub.celebrities.data` package. You can see a utility class—`Formats`, used in it to simplify conversion between dates and strings. Here is the code for it, and it will make sense to put this class into the `com.packtpub.celebrities.util` package:

```
package com.packtpub.celebrities.util;

import java.text.Format;
import java.text.ParseException;
import java.text.SimpleDateFormat;
import java.util.Date;

public class Formats
{
  private static SimpleDateFormat simpleDateFormat =
    new SimpleDateFormat("MM/dd/yyyy");
  public static Date parseDate(String strDate)
  {
    Date date = null;
    try
    {
      date = simpleDateFormat.parse(strDate);
    } catch (ParseException ex)
      {
      throw new RuntimeException(ex);
      }
    return date;
  }

  public static Format getDateFormat()
  {
    return simpleDateFormat;
  }
}
```

The code for the `MockDataSource` is quite simple, at times even primitive. For example, the way that a "unique" ID is generated in the `addCelebrity` method is good only for the case when no celebrities are ever deleted from the collection, but for now, it is good enough.

Another two helper classes that we are going to need for **Celebrity Collector** are `User`, to contain information about the application's users, and `Security` which demonstrates an extremely simplified approach towards user authentication. You will see the code of these classes below, and, of course, all the code from this chapter can be found in the code package provided with the book.

```
package com.packtpub.celebrities.model;

public class User
{
  private String firstName;
  private String lastName;
  public User()
  {
  }

  public User(String firstName, String lastName)
  {
    this.setFirstName(firstName);
    this.setLastName(lastName);
  }

  public String getFirstName()
  {
    return firstName;
  }

  public void setFirstName(String firstName)
  {
    this.firstName = firstName;
  }

  public String getLastName()
  {
    return lastName;
  }

  public void setLastName(String lastName)
  {
    this.lastName = lastName;
  }
}
package com.packtpub.celebrities.util;

import com.packtpub.celebrities.model.User;

public class Security
{
  private static final String USERNAME = "user";
  private static final String PASSWORD = "secret";
  public static User authenticate(String userName,
    String password)
  {
```

```
        if (USERNAME.equals(userName) && PASSWORD.equals(password))
        {
          return new User("John", "Smith");
        }
        return null;
        }
    }
```

You can see that the Security class has a single version for both username and password hard-coded into it. Normally, these two would be retrieved from some kind of storage, and perhaps in an encrypted form. For now, however, the username and password submitted by the user are compared to the fixed values, "user" and "secret". If they are correct, the `authenticate` method returns a `User` object with some default information in it; otherwise, it returns a null. You will see how all this is going to be used in **Celebrity Collector** very soon.

Now that the infrastructure is ready, let's proceed to creating the **Start** page with a few components on it.

TextField, PasswordField and PageLink

The first step is to edit the existing **Start** page. We are going to remove most of its generated content, and instead of it, we are going to create a login form and a link to **Registration** page. What we want to achieve should look similar to this:

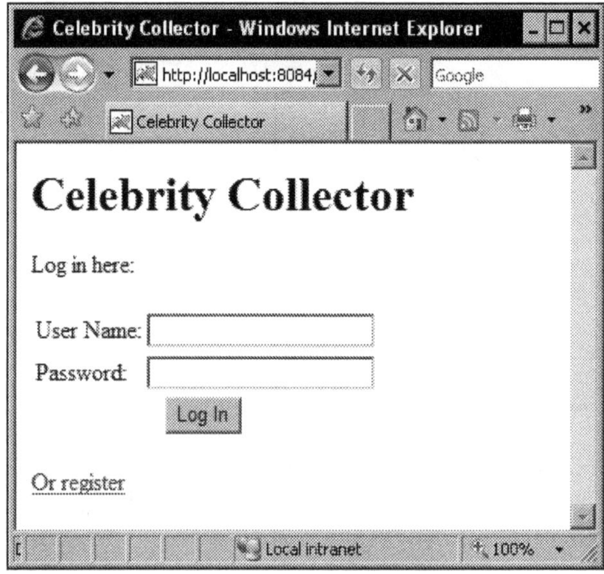

This is a very common solution, you have definitely seen it on many websites that require authentication.

Here is one possible way to create a Tapestry template for such a page:

```
<html xmlns:t="http://tapestry.apache.org/schema/tapestry_5_0_0.xsd">
  <head>
    <title>Celebrity Collector</title>
  </head>
  <body>
    <h1>Celebrity Collector</h1>

    <p> Log in here: </p>

    <t:form t:id="loginForm">
    <table>
      <tr>
        <td>
          <t:label t:for="userName">
          Label for the first text box</t:label>:
        </td>
        <td>
          <input type="text" t:id="userName"
            t:type="TextField" t:value="userName"/>
        </td>
      </tr>
      <tr>
        <td>
          <t:label t:for="password">
          The second label</t:label>:
        </td>
        <td>
          <input type="text" t:id="password"
            t:type="PasswordField" t:value="password"/>
        </td>
      </tr>
      <tr>
        <td colspan="2" align="center">
          <input type="submit" value="Log In"/>
        </td>
      </tr>
    </table>
    </t:form>
    <p>
      <a href="#" t:type="PageLink" t:page="Registration">
        Or register</a>
    </p>
  </body>
</html>
```

Let's see what we have got here. There is a `Form` component that is defined explicitly, as an XML element in a Tapestry namespace. There are four Tapestry components inside this form. Two of them, of the type `Label`, are defined in the same way, explicitly, while two others—`TextField` and `PasswordField`—are hidden inside the `<input type="text">` HTML controls. Why is this mixture of two approaches used when defining Tapestry components?

See, I am trying to follow a certain guideline. Those components that render themselves as HTML controls should preferably be hidden inside such controls. However, those components which are invisible on the page, like `Form`, or render themselves as plain text, like `Label`, are simpler to define in the explicit way.

This is because, in my experience, it makes a lot of sense to start development of a page from its HTML mock-up. If I follow the suggested guideline, then even after inserting Tapestry instrumentation, such a template remains editable by standard HTML tools and can be previewed in a web browser. This keeps developer's efforts when customer's preferences change to a minimum. However, if you prefer a different approach—say, you define all components explicitly, and it works for you, then follow it.

On the other hand, many Tapestry 5 developers prefer to define their components completely in the Java code of the page class (as was demonstrated in the previous chapter), and then only use `t:id` attributes to insert components into the template. Choose which ever approach you prefer.

Let's have a look at this pair of components:

```
<td>
  <t:label t:for="userName">
    Label for the first text box</t:label>:
</td>
<td>
  <input type="text" t:id="userName" t:type="TextField"
    t:value="userName"/>
</td>
```

The second one, `TextField`, is already familiar to us only this time it has a `t:id="userName"` attribute. The first component is new however. We can see that it is of type `Label` and in its `t:for` attribute it references the `t:id` attribute of `TextField`, so this is a label for precisely this text box.

Notice that the `Label` component surrounds some not very meaningful, and probably too lengthy text. I have intentionally used such a weird text for the label so that you could appreciate the miracles that Tapestry does for us. The trick is that when the application runs and the page is rendered, the text surrounded by `Label` component is discarded (it might have been a part of the original mock up, and used for preview purposes only). Instead, a completely different text will be displayed. In our case, it will read "User Name".

How will Tapestry manage to figure out which label to use? In fact, as the `Label` component points to some other component that it labels (in our case `TextField`), it is for that labeled component to define what exactly the label should say.

To define the label of our `TextField`, we could use a special attribute, `t:label`, like this:

```
<input type="text" t:type="TextField" t:id="userName"
  t:label="User Name" t:value="userName"/>
```

However, we have chosen a different approach and provided a `t:id` attribute only, with the value of `userName`. Tapestry can handle this too. If it cannot find a `t:label` attribute, it takes the `t:id` one and then transforms its value by splitting it into words and capitalizes them all. As you see, Tapestry is quite clever.

Next, have a look at the `PasswordField` component. It is defined almost in the same way as `TextField`, and is only displayed differently (it is rendered as a `<input type="password">` HTML control). Any input into this field is masked and not redisplayed when the page is reloaded (when authentication fails, for example). A `PasswordField` also has a `Label` associated with it, and uses the same trick with `t:id` to provide the value for that label.

There is another already familiar component on the **Start** page, `PageLink`. It is disguised as a HTML link and specifies which page should be shown when the link is clicked on:

```
<a href="#" t:type="PageLink" t:page="Registration">
          Or register</a>
```

To complete the page, we need to add the required functionality to the page class— two properties to contain username and password, and an event handler for form submission. Let's implement the following logic in the event handler:

- The previously created `Security` class is used to authenticate the user by checking the submitted information.
- If authentication is successful, the `authenticate` method of Security will return a `User` object. We shall save this `User` as an Application State Object (ASO) and display the **ShowAll** page.

- If validation fails, no `User` is stored as an ASO and the **Registration** page is shown instead. This is for the first iteration of the project only. Later, we are going to redisplay the **Start** page in such a case, with an appropriate message on it.

Here is the complete code for the Start page class:

```
package com.packtpub.celebrities.pages;
import com.packtpub.celebrities.util.Security;
import com.packtpub.celebrities.model.User;
import org.apache.tapestry.annotations.ApplicationState;
import org.apache.tapestry.annotations.OnEvent;
public class Start
{
  private String userName;
  private String password;

  @ApplicationState
  private User user;

  Object onSubmitFromLoginForm()
  {
    Class nextPage = null;
    User authenticatedUser = null;
    authenticatedUser =
      Security.authenticate(userName, password);
    if (authenticatedUser != null)
    {
      user = authenticatedUser;
      nextPage = ShowAll.class;
    }
    else
    {
      nextPage = Registration.class;
    }
    return nextPage;
  }

  public String getUserName()
  {
    return userName;
  }

  public void setUserName(String userName)
  {
    this.userName = userName;
```

```
    }

    public String getPassword()
    {
      return password;
    }

    public void setPassword(String password)
    {
      this.password = password;
    }
  }
```

First of all, please note that the event handler, `onSubmitFromLoginForm` method was named appropriately in order to handle the `submit` event of the `loginForm` component. It returns an object, in this case a class. As the previous chapter explained, this is a preferred, type-safe way of telling Tapestry which page we want it to show next. If validation was successful, the class for the **ShowAll** page will be returned; otherwise the returned class will be for the **Registration** page.

Also, if authentication was successful; that is, the value returned by the `Security.authenticate` method was not null, we assign the returned `User` object to the private class variable named `user`. The latter is marked as an Application State Object, and so Tapestry creates a session and saves the object we have assigned to `user` into it. If, however, authentication fails, no session is created.

At this point, you can run the application and see how it works. If you enter "user" and "secret" for username and password, the **ShowAll** page should be shown, but if either piece of information is wrong, or if you click the **Or register** link, you should see the **Registration** page.

The **Or register** link is implemented as a `PageLink` component and doesn't demonstrate anything new to us. However, if you have a look into the Tapestry 5 documentation for this component (`http://tapestry.apache.org/tapestry5/tapestry-core/component-parameters.html`), you will notice that `PageLink` also has a property named `context`. That property is not required but sometimes can be quite useful.

Do you remember the discussion in Chapter 3 of different ways to pass information when navigating between pages? One of the options was to use the page activation context, and this is exactly the mechanism that can be used by `PageLink` if you provide a value for its *context* property. You will see how to do that later in this chapter.

So far, we have tried to limit access to the **ShowAll** page to only those who were authenticated successfully, but let's see if our solution works properly. Modify the URL in the address bar of your browser to look like this (in your case port number can be different):

```
http://localhost:8084/celebrities/showall
```

Press *Enter*, and the **ShowAll** page will be shown without any authentication. This means that anyone who simply knows the name of the page can easily circumvent our security and view the page, access to which we tried to limit. We need to use a more reliable way to limit access to the page.

Limiting Access to a Page

To efficiently limit access to a page, we can use the `onActivate` method. You should be familiar with this method from Chapter 3 where it was used to pass a value through page activation context. The `onActivate` method is invoked every time the page is loaded, and if there is some value in the activation context, it will be passed as an argument to this method. However, another use for it might be to check whether the user who tries to access the page was successfully authenticated.

If you remember, in the case of a successful authentication, we are storing the `User` object as an ASO. So all we need to do in order to check whether a user was authenticated is to check whether the `User` ASO exists. Add the following code to the `ShowAll` page class:

```
@ApplicationState

private User user;
private boolean userExists;

Object onActivate()
{
  if (!userExists) return Start.class;
  return null;
}
```

Everything is very simple. We are checking the value of the boolean variable associated with the `User` ASO (and automatically set by Tapestry, as you remember). If the ASO was ever created—which means our user was successfully authenticated, the method will return `null`, otherwise it will return the class for the **Start** page.

Here `onActivate()` works similar to an ordinary event handler, with the difference being that it responds not to an event generated by the user but to a page rendering life cycle event. Tapestry will find this method by name, and invoke it at an appropriate time. And since the method is not void, Tapestry will treat the returned value according to the rules for the values returned by an event handler as outlined in the previous chapter.

Those rules say that if the returned value is `null`, Tapestry will display (or redisplay) the same page. In our case, it will proceed by displaying the **ShowAll** page. However, if the method returns something different from `null`, then it should be an indication of the page to be displayed, instead of the current one. Since we are returning the `Start` class, the unauthenticated user will be redirected to the **Start** page.

Try this. Run the application, enter `http://localhost:8084/celebrities/showall` into address bar, and press *Enter*. If you were not authenticated before, or if your session was invalidated, then instead of the **ShowAll** page you will see the **Start** page.

There are two ways of getting your session invalidated—to wait and do nothing for longer than the session timeout period (30 minutes by default), or to close down the browser window and open another one (so that the session cookie will be discarded).

Now we allow access to the **ShowAll** page only to authenticated users, but, at the moment this page displays nothing interesting. We need to add some content to it, and for this we are going to use some new components.

Loop, Output and DirectLink

The following is what we are going to display on **ShowAll** page:

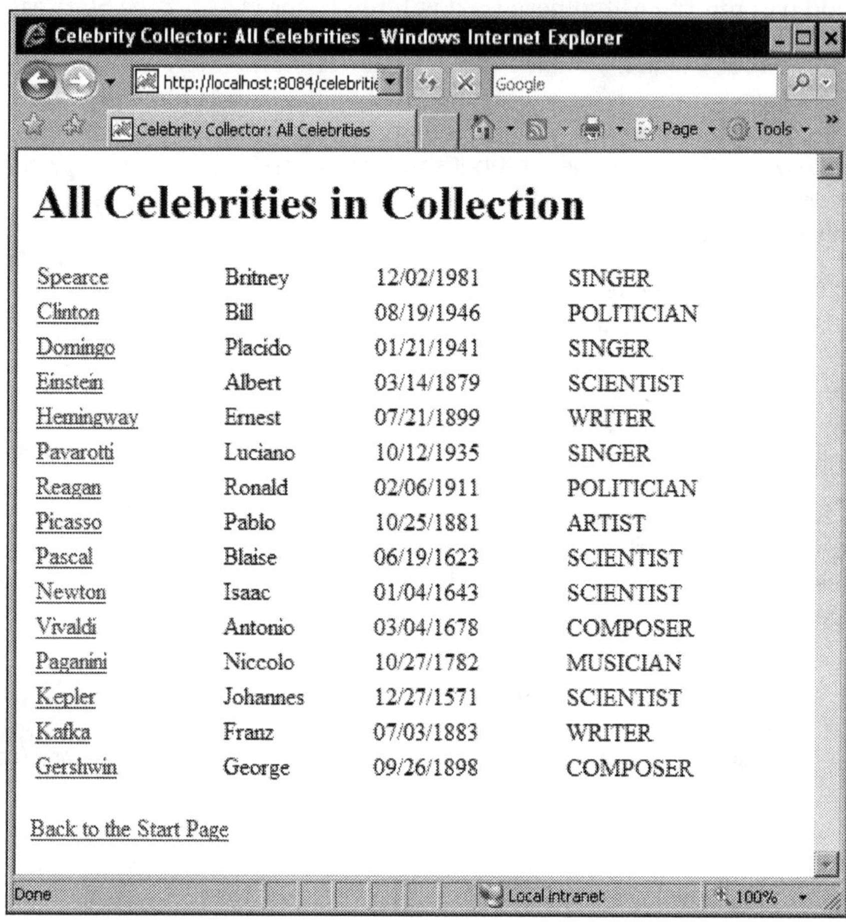

Spearce	Britney	12/02/1981	SINGER
Clinton	Bill	08/19/1946	POLITICIAN
Domingo	Placido	01/21/1941	SINGER
Einstein	Albert	03/14/1879	SCIENTIST
Hemingway	Ernest	07/21/1899	WRITER
Pavarotti	Luciano	10/12/1935	SINGER
Reagan	Ronald	02/06/1911	POLITICIAN
Picasso	Pablo	10/25/1881	ARTIST
Pascal	Blaise	06/19/1623	SCIENTIST
Newton	Isaac	01/04/1643	SCIENTIST
Vivaldi	Antonio	03/04/1678	COMPOSER
Paganini	Niccolo	10/27/1782	MUSICIAN
Kepler	Johannes	12/27/1571	SCIENTIST
Kafka	Franz	07/03/1883	WRITER
Gershwin	George	09/26/1898	COMPOSER

Basically, it lists all celebrities in our collection in a table. The last name serves as a link, and by clicking on it, the user will proceed to a page with all the details about the selected celebrity (we shall add that page to the application a bit later).

Here is the completed template for this page:

```
<html xmlns:t="http://tapestry.apache.org/schema/tapestry_5_0_0.xsd">
    <head>
        <title>Celebrity Collector: All Celebrities</title>
    </head>
    <body>
        <h1>All Celebrities in Collection</h1>
```

```
        <table width="100%">
            <tr t:type="loop" t:source="allCelebrities"
                                            t:value="celebrity">
                <td>
                    <a href="#" t:type="ActionLink"
                          t:context="celebrity.id"
                          t:id="detailsLink">${celebrity.lastName}</a>
                </td>
                <td>${celebrity.firstName}</td>
                <td>
                    <t:output t:format="dateFormat"
                                      t:value="celebrity.dateOfBirth"/>
                </td>
                <td>${celebrity.occupation}</td>
            </tr>
        </table>
            <br/>
        <a href="#" t:type="PageLink" t:page="Start">
                        Back to the Start Page</a>
    </body>
</html>
```

You can see that this template contains an HTML table, and the table contains just one row. This single row has three Tapestry attributes in it, which makes it a disguised Tapestry component. Let's see what sort of information these attributes contain:

```
<tr t:type="loop" t:source="allCelebrities"
  t:value="celebrity">
</tr>
```

The `t:type="loop"` attribute tells us that this is a Tapestry's `Loop` component. It does three things:

1. It accepts a number of objects through its `source` parameter. In our case we used the `t:source="allCelebrities"` attribute, and so Tapestry will be looking for a `getAllCelebrities` method in the page class to provide some number of objects (they can be provided as an `ArrayList`, a `HashSet` or any other Java class that implements an iterable interface).
2. It iterates through the provided collection and displays its body (i.e. whatever is surrounded by the `Loop` component) as many times as there are objects in the collection. When the `Loop` component is embedded into an HTML element, it will display its body surrounded by that element. In our case, we have embedded `Loop` into the `<tr>` element, and as a result, the component will display as many table rows as there are objects in the provided collection.

3. Every time it iterates through an object, `Loop` makes that object available to the page class through the component's `value` parameter. In our case we used the `t:value="celebrity"` attribute which means that Tapestry will be looking for `setCelebrity()` in the page class, and it will pass the current object iterated through by `Loop` as a parameter to that method.

Now let's have a look at what the body of the Loop contains. Basically, there are four table cells (`<td>` elements) with some content in them. In two cases, the content is just an expansion, like this one:

```
<td>${celebrity.firstName}</td>
```

You might remember that in this case Tapestry will look for the `getCelebrity` method in the page class and then try to call the `getFirstName` method on an object returned by `getCelebrity()`.

However, we can also find a new type of component in one of the cells:

```
<t:output t:format="dateFormat" t:value="celebrity.dateOfBirth"/>
```

Instead of this component, we could use an expansion like `${celebrity.dateOfBirth}`, but in this case, the date of birth would be displayed in some default format, which is not appropriate for date of birth; that is, we would have no control over how the date is displayed. The `Output` component provides us exactly that—an opportunity to format the displayed information in any way we want. The information to display is provided through the `value` parameter (`t:value="celebrity.dateOfBirth"` attribute), and the format, through the `format` parameter (`t:format="dateFormat"` attribute). You may have already guessed that the **ShowAll** page class in our application should have the `getDateFormat` method for the latter binding to work.

Finally, there is an `ActionLink` component, disguised as an HTML link, surrounding the last name of each celebrity in the table:

```
<a href="#" t:type="ActionLink" t:context="celebrity.id"
    t:id="detailsLink">
    ${celebrity.lastName}
</a>
```

`ActionLink` is basically a link that is associated with an action, or, in other words, with an event handler. While `PageLinks`'s main aim is to navigate to another page, the `ActionLink`'s purpose is to run some code in an event handler in response to a click on the link. As a result of that code, we can navigate to another page, but not necessarily so.

`ActionLink`'s predecessor in the previous versions of Tapestry, `DirectLink`, was the only natural choice for the pattern where we have a number of entities displayed in a table, and by clicking on a link we want to see the details of one of the items—a kind of master-detail pattern. `ActionLink` should have a `t:id` attribute. This is how we are going to associate an event handler with it. Quite often, it also has a `t:context` attribute, which provides a parameter (or parameters) to the event handler. In our case this parameter is the ID of the celebrity displayed in the given table row. As you will see soon, this ID will allow us to define exactly which celebrity we want to be displayed by the **Details** page.

We already know quite a number of features that have to be present in the `ShowAll` page class, so here is the complete code for this class:

```
package com.packtpub.celebrities.pages;

import com.packtpub.celebrities.data.MockDataSource;
import com.packtpub.celebrities.model.Celebrity;
import com.packtpub.celebrities.util.Formats;
import com.packtpub.celebrities.model.User;
import java.text.Format;
import java.util.List;
import org.apache.tapestry.annotations.ApplicationState;
import org.apache.tapestry.annotations.InjectPage;
import org.apache.tapestry.annotations.OnEvent;

public class ShowAll
{
  @ApplicationState
  private User user;
  private boolean userExists;

  @ApplicationState
  private MockDataSource dataSource;

  @InjectPage
  private Details detailsPage;
  private Celebrity celebrity;
  String onActivate()
  {
    if (!userExists) return "Start";
    return null;
  }
  @OnEvent(component="detailsLink")
  Object onShowDetails(long id)
```

```
    {
      Celebrity celebrity = dataSource.getCelebrityById(id);
      detailsPage.setCelebrity(celebrity);
      return detailsPage;
    }

    public List<Celebrity> getAllCelebrities()
    {
      return dataSource.getAllCelebrities();
    }

    public Celebrity getCelebrity()
    {
      return celebrity;
    }

    public void setCelebrity(Celebrity celebrity)
    {
      this.celebrity = celebrity;
    }

    public Format getDateFormat()
    {
      return Formats.getDateFormat();
    }
  }
```

First of all, notice a private class member named `celebrity` and getter and setter methods associated with it. This is where the exchange of information between the `Loop` component and all those components filling in a row in the table with information happens.

`Loop` receives a list of celebrity objects from the `getAllCelebrities` method. It then displays the rows of the table, and iterates through the received list simultaneously, one by one. It takes the first `Celebrity` object from the list and assigns a reference to this object to the `celebrity` page property. It then displays the first row of the table, and all the expansions and components embedded into that row obtain their details from the first `Celebrity` object in the list. Then the second object is taken, assigned to the `celebrity` property, the second row of the table is displayed, and so on.

You might have noticed that the data source is declared as a `MockDataSource`, that is a concrete implementation rather than a `IDataSource` interface that we have created previously. This is because using an interface for an ASO requires some additional configuration of Tapestry. By the end of this chapter, we shall learn how to do such configuration, but right now, let's just leave everything as it is.

Well, frankly speaking, it is not the best of ideas to provide a data source as an ASO. Application State Object is normally a convenient place to store some information, while it would be better if a data source is maintained as a Tapestry service. However, I find it important to introduce new ideas gradually, step by step. Custom services will appear in the last chapter only. So let the data source be an ASO for now. Not the best design, but it will work.

For this code to work, we need to have a **Details** page in our application. Please add such a page—a template, and an empty page class—in the same way as we did this before with every new page.

When an `ActionLink` component is rendered, it produces an HTML link and whatever we have provided as a context for this component gets recorded into the link. For example, if you hover your mouse over the last name of the fifth celebrity in the list, you should be able to see the following in the status bar of your browser:

```
http://localhost:8084/celebrities/showall.detailslink/4
```

The number `4` at the end of the URL is exactly the value of the ID of the fifth celebrity. When you click on the link, Tapestry will check if there is any method in the page class that is assigned as an event handler for that link, and it will find the following method:

```
@OnEvent(component="detailsLink")
Object onShowDetails(long id)
{
  Celebrity celebrity = dataSource.getCelebrityById(id);
  detailsPage.setCelebrity(celebrity);
  return detailsPage;
}
```

You see that this method accepts a parameter of the type `long`—exactly the type of the `id` property of the `Celebrity` class. So Tapestry will take the ID of the selected celebrity which is embedded into the link, and pass it as a parameter to the event handler. As a result, we shall have an opportunity to retrieve the desired `Celebrity` object from the data source and pass it to the **Details** page.

It is the time to complete the **Details** page properly. Here is what it should look like at run time:

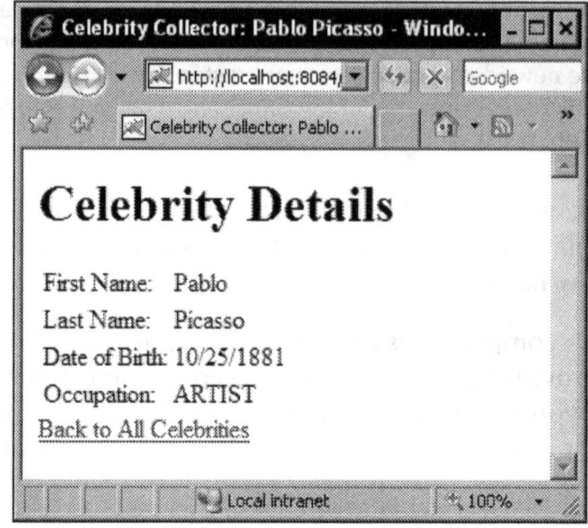

Right now, the occupation of a celebrity is displayed verbatim, as a value of the **Occupation** enumeration. Values of an enumeration are constants, and in Java, constants are named in all capitals by convention. This is why occupations in **Celebrity Collector** are shown in all capitals—a simple, but not a practical solution. One way to overcome this would be to make the **Occupation** enumeration slightly more complex and associate some display label with each of its values. However, we shall see a better solution when we come to internationalization in Chapter 7. For now, let's just leave the occupations in all capitals.

Here is the template for the **Details** page. It contains nothing unknown to you:

```
<html xmlns:t="http://tapestry.apache.org/schema/tapestry_5_0_0.xsd">
    <head>
        <title>Celebrity Collector: ${celebrity.firstName}
          ${celebrity.lastName}</title>
    </head>
    <body>
        <h1>Celebrity Details</h1>
        <table>
            <tr>
                <td>First Name:</td>
                <td>${celebrity.firstName}</td>
            </tr>
            <tr>
```

```
                <td>Last Name:</td>
                <td>${celebrity.lastName}</td>
            </tr>
            <tr>
                <td>Date of Birth:</td>
                <td><t:output t:format="dateFormat"
                                t:value="celebrity.dateOfBirth"/></td>
            </tr>
            <tr>
                <td>Occupation:</td>
                <td>${celebrity.occupation}</td>
            </tr>
        </table>
        <a href="#" t:type="PageLink" t:page="ShowAll">
                        Back to All Celebrities</a>
    </body>
</html>
```

Here is the page class, rather trivial, except perhaps of the persistent property:

```
package com.packtpub.celebrities.pages;

import com.packtpub.celebrities.model.Celebrity;
import org.apache.tapestry.annotations.Persist;
import java.text.Format;

public class Details
{
  @Persist
  private Celebrity celebrity;

  public void setCelebrity(Celebrity c)
  {
    this.celebrity = c;
  }

  public Celebrity getCelebrity()
  {
    return celebrity;
  }

  public Format getDateFormat()
  {
    return Formats.getDateFormat();
  }
}
```

You can run the application now, click on a celebrity's last name and see his or her details displayed on the **Details** page.

Let's suppose that you were so impressed by a celebrity that you decided to bookmark the **Details** page to come and see it later. Let's do this for real, display the details for some celebrity and bookmark the page. Then close the browser window, open another one and try to navigate to the bookmark you have just added. You will get a `NullPointerException`, and the reason for it is that the `celebrity` property of the **Details** page is null. This is because a persistent property like `celebrity` is stored into the session, and by closing the browser window you have invalidated your current session. In other words, you have forced Tapestry to forget which celebrity you were dealing with.

`ActionLink` does record the selected celebrity's ID into the link that it produces, but that ID doesn't go further than the event handler method where it is used to retrieve an appropriate celebrity. That celebrity is assigned to a persistent property of the **Details** page and so, it is destined to be lost when the session is invalidated.

It is not a good idea to have an exception every time a user tries to bookmark a page to see it later. To prevent this, we could use the `onActivate` method to check if the `celebrity` property is `null`, and if it is, to redirect to some other page, but this is not an elegant solution. It is not user friendly either. There is a way to both display the **Details** page, and to make it bookmarkable. Have you already guessed that we can use page activation context?

Another Use of PageLink Component

First of all, replace the `ActionLink` component in the `ShowAll.tml` template with `PageLink`, and specify the page to which this link should lead. You can also remove the `t:id` attribute as it will be not needed anymore. The component definition should look like this:

```
<a href="#" t:type="PageLink" t:page="Details"
                t:context="celebrity.id">
    ${celebrity.lastName}
</a>
```

Remove or comment out the `onShowDetails` event handler method, it is not needed either. Add the `onActivate` method to the `Details` class with the following contents:

```
void onActivate(long id)
{
  celebrity = dataSource.getCelebrityById(id);
}
```

You will also need to provide access to the data source ASO and remove the `@Persistent` attribute from the `celebrity` property:

```
@ApplicationState
private MockDataSource dataSource;
private Celebrity celebrity;
```

Finally, run the application and repeat the experiment. On the **ShowAll** page, click on the last name of some celebrity to see his or her details. Note that this time the ID of the celebrity is present in the URL as displayed in the browser's address bar, like this:

```
http://localhost:8084/celebrities/details/7
```

Create a bookmark and close the browser window. Open another one and navigate to your bookmark. You should successfully see the details for the recently bookmarked celebrity now.

As you can see, in a typical master-detail scenario, the `PageLink` component can do a better job than `ActionLink`. This is not to say however that `PageLink` is always superior. There definitely will be situations where `ActionLink` will be the only reasonable candidate for example, when you want some complex logic to run as a result of a click on a link, and not just pass a piece of information to another page. Anyway, now you know both components and so you can easily choose which one better suits your needs.

We still have the **Registration** page empty, and this is where we are going to meet a significant number of new Tapestry components. Let's fill this page with content.

Radio and RadioGroup

First of all, we need to provide some functionality that is common for registration pages—text boxes for username, password, and re-entered password. They will not give us any additional knowledge right now, but later they will be useful for the user input validation topic.

Then, let's say, we want users to specify their gender. For this, we shall provide a couple of radio buttons, so that the interface looked like this:

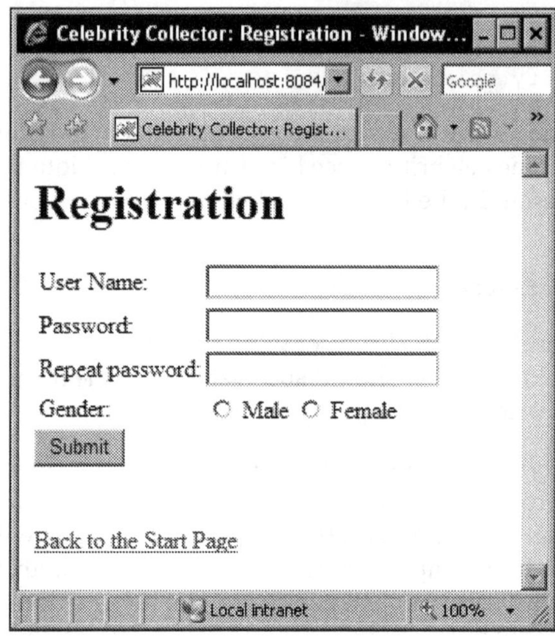

To create such an interface, let's change the `Registration.tml` template to look like this:

```
<html xmlns:t="http://tapestry.apache.org/schema/tapestry_5_0_0.xsd">
  <head>
    <title>Celebrity Collector: Registration</title>
  </head>
  <body>
    <h1>Registration</h1>

      <t:form t:id="registrationForm">
      <table>
        <tr>
          <td><t:label t:for="userName">
                 Label for user name</t:label>:</td>
          <td><input type="text" t:type="textfield"
                 t:id="userName" t:value="userName"/></td>
        </tr>
        <tr>
          <td><t:label t:for="password">
                 Label for password</t:label>:</td>
```

```
            <td><input type="text" t:type="passwordfield"
                            t:id="password" t:value="password"/></td>
          </tr>
          <tr>
            <td><t:label t:for="password2">
                  Label for password 2</t:label>:</td>
            <td><input type="text" t:type="passwordfield"
                  t:id="password2" t:label="Repeat password"
                  t:value="password2"/></td>
           </tr>
           <tr>
             <td>Gender:</td>
             <td>
               <t:radiogroup t:value="gender">
               <input type="radio" t:type="radio"
                   t:value="literal:M"/> Male
               <input type="radio" t:type="radio"
                   t:value="literal:F"/> Female
                   </t:radiogroup>
             </td>
             </tr>
        </table>
        <input type="submit" value="Submit"/>
        </t:form>
      <br/>
      <a href="#" t:type="PageLink" t:page="Start">
         Back to the Start Page</a>
    </body>
  </html>
```

Everything should be familiar to you in this template, except for the following fragment:

```
  <t:radiogroup t:value="gender">
     <input type="radio" t:type="radio" t:value="literal:M"/>
                Male
    <input type="radio" t:type="radio" t:value="literal:F"/>
                Female
  </t:radiogroup>
```

This is how a group of radio buttons is created in Tapestry. Two types of components are used—a `RadioGroup` component that communicates with the page class to define which radio button was selected, and a few `Radio` components that provide options to choose from.

The `value` parameter of the `RadioGroup` component should be connected to a property of the page class. In our case, this property is named `gender`, and we need to ensure that this property exists. We also need to provide a few properties for the username and password components to work properly. All in all, the page class should at this stage look at similar to the following code listing:

```
package com.packtpub.celebrities.pages;

public class Registration
{
  private String userName;
  private String password;
  private String password2;
  private String gender;

  public String getUserName()
  {
    return userName;
  }

  public void setUserName(String userName)
  {
    System.out.println("Setting user name: " + userName);
      this.userName = userName;
  }

  public String getPassword()
  {
    return password;
  }

  public void setPassword(String password)
  {
    System.out.println("Setting password: " + password);
    this.password = password;
  }

  public String getPassword2()
  {
    return password2;
  }

  public void setPassword2(String password2)
  {
    this.password2 = password2;
  }

  public String getGender()
  {
    return gender;
  }
```

```
    public void setGender(String gender)
    {
      System.out.println("Setting gender: " + gender);
      this.gender = gender;
    }
  }
```

The page class is very simple, but note that there are a few basic output statements inserted into the setter methods—they will help us to see what happens when the form is submitted. If you run the application, go to the **Registration** page and submit some information, you will see an output similar to this:

```
Setting user name: john
Setting password: abc123
Setting gender: M
```

We didn't provide any event handler for the form submission yet, and still something is happening in the page class. When we click on the **Submit** button, the values we have entered into the components surrounded by the form are sent to the server. Tapestry extracts these values from the submitted information and assigns them to the appropriate properties of the page class. After all the values are in place, Tapestry checks if there is an event handler for the whole form, and if there is, Tapestry executes it.

Let's provide such an event handler and see if everything works as we expect. Add the following method to the `Registration` page class:

```
void onSubmitFromRegistrationForm()
{
  System.out.println("The form was submitted!");
}
```

This handler does nothing except for giving an output message. Run the application, submit some values at the **Registration** page, click on the **Submit** button, and you should see that the message from the form submission handler appears after the messages from the setter methods—exactly as we expected.

Using Enumerations for Radio Component Values

Right now, when the **Registration** page is rendered, none of the radio buttons are selected. If you want, you can provide a default option by giving the gender property an initial value, like this:

```
private String gender = "F";
```

Now the radio button labeled "Female" will be pre-selected.

The page works properly, but having a gender specified as an arbitrary string isn't a good design. For a set of mutually exclusive options like this, it would be better to have an enumeration. So let's add the following simple enumeration to the `com.packtpub.celebrities.model` package:

```
package com.packtpub.celebrities.model;
public enum Gender
{
  MALE, FEMALE
}
```

We can now modify all the gender-related code to work with the new `Gender` type instead of `String`:

```
private Gender gender;
...
public Gender getGender()
{
  return gender;
}

public void setGender(Gender gender)
{
  this.gender = gender;
}
```

In case you want to provide a default value, you can do it like this:

```
private Gender gender = Gender.FEMALE;
```

We also need to change the template so that each Radio component is associated with an appropriate value. Previously, to provide such a value, we used the `literal` prefix like this:

```
t:value="literal:M"
```

This means, for Tapestry, the value that follows the prefix should be understood literally, in this case, a string. However, the default prefix (the one that is used when no prefix is defined at all) for the `value` property of `Radio` component is `prop`, which means that a property of the page class should be used to obtain the value. Let's change the definition of `Radio` components like this:

```
<input type="radio" t:type="radio" t:value="male"/> Male
<input type="radio" t:type="radio" t:value="female"/> Female
```

Then provide two read-only properties in the page class:

```
public Gender getMale()
{
  return Gender.MALE;
}

public Gender getFemale()
{
  return Gender.FEMALE;
}
```

If you run the application now, it should continue to work as it did before, with the difference that gender is now specified as an enumeration, and both the `RadioGroup` and `Radio` components work with it easily.

I guess you are a little bit puzzled now by all those different prefixes, so let's discuss them properly.

Prefixes: prop and literal

If you look into the Tapestry online documentation at `http://tapestry.apache.org/tapestry5/tapestry-core/component-parameters.html`, you will notice that a component's properties can have either a `prop` or `literal` default prefix. Say, the `label` property of the `TextField` component has the default prefix `literal`, while the `value` property of the same component has the default prefix `prop`. What does this mean?

Say we have provided the following value for the `label` property of some `TextField` component:

```
t:label="User Name"
```

Since the default prefix for this property is `literal`, Tapestry will take whatever we've specified literally, that is, the label for the component will be `User Name`. We could achieve the same result by using the prefix explicitly, but this simply means more typing:

```
t:label="literal:User Name"
```

However, if we wanted the label to be provided by the page class, we would need to explicitly use the `prop` prefix:

```
t:label="prop:theLabel"
```

In this case Tapestry will look for the `getTheLabel` method in the page class and use whatever that method returns as the label.

The reversed version of the same logic works for the `value` property of the `TextField` component. If there is no prefix (like `t:value="userName"`), Tapestry will be looking for an appropriately named property of the page class, as the default prefix is `prop`. However, if for some reason we wanted to treat this value as literal, we would have to use the `literal` prefix explicitly.

The If and Checkbox Components

Let's say during registration we want to give the users an opportunity to subscribe to our newsletter. For this, we are going to add a check box to the registration form, like the one shown here:

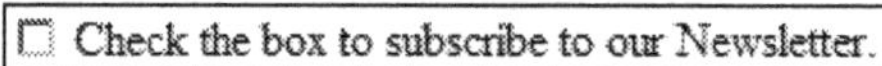

To make the interface slightly more complex, and also to give me an opportunity to show you yet another component, let's say that as soon as the user clicks on the check box, the check box should disappear, and a text box for accepting the user's email should appear instead:

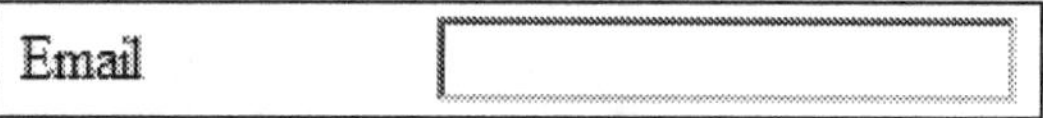

Here is a fragment of the page template that will do the job:

```
<tr>
    <t:if t:test="subscribe">
            <td><t:label t:for="email"/></td>
            <td>
                    <input type="text" t:type="textfield" t:id="email"
                            t:value="email"/>
            </td>
            <t:parameter t:name="else">
                    <td colspan="2">
                    <input type="checkbox" t:type="checkbox"
                                    t:value="subscribe"
                                    onclick="this.form.submit()"/>
            Check the box to subscribe to our Newsletter.
                    </td>
    </t:parameter>
    </t:if>
</tr>
```

Let's see how all this works together. First of all, this is yet another table row (HTML element `<tr>`) to be added to an already existing `Registration` page table, just underneath the row with gender radio buttons. This row contains a Tapestry component of the type `If`, as shown in the following code:

```
<t:if t:test="subscribe">
...
</t:if>
```

The only parameter of this `test` component provides a boolean value. Since the default prefix for this parameter is `prop`, Tapestry will be looking for a `getSubscribe` method in the page class. If this method returns true, the body of the `If` component will be displayed. In our case, the body is represented by two table cells displaying a `TextField` component and a label for it:

```
<td><t:label t:for="email"/></td>
<td>
   <input type="text" t:type="textfield" t:id="email"
         t:value="email"/>
</td>
```

Of course, for this to work, the **Registration** page should have a property named `email`.

The `If` component has another, optional parameter named `else`. This parameter should provide an alternative content to be displayed in case the `test` parameter evaluates to `false`. One possible way to provide the `else` parameter was shown previously, let's have a look at it once again:

```
<t:parameter t:name="else">
   <td colspan="2">
         <input type="checkbox" t:type="checkbox"
               t:value="subscribe"
               onclick="this.form.submit()"/>
   Check the box to subscribe to our Newsletter.
   </td>
</t:parameter>
```

Here we have a `<t:parameter t:name="else"> ... </t:parameter>` element surrounding an alternative markup, namely a Tapestry `Checkbox` component disguised as an ordinary HTML control. Note that the `value` parameter of this control has a value, `subscribe`, which is the same page property as the one that was used for the `test` parameter of the surrounding `If` component.

The `Checkbox` component is also associated with a line of JavaScript that runs when the check box is clicked on. This JavaScript simply submits the surrounding form:

```
onclick="this.form.submit()"
```

Let's see how all this works together. In the very beginning, when the **Registration** page is rendered for the first time, the `subscribe` property will evaluate to `false`, and so the check box that prompts the user to subscribe will be displayed (the alternative content provided as the `else` parameter of the `If` component). If the user decides to subscribe and clicks on the check box, the form gets submitted and the `subscribe` property receives a new value, `true`. We'll want the page to remember this value, so the `subscribe` property should be made persistent.

Since the page class has no event handlers that could potentially redirect the user to another page, the same page will be redisplayed again, but since this time the value of the `subscribe` property will be `true`, the body of the `If` component will be shown, meaning the text box will accept the user's email address.

All we need to do to enable all this logic is to add a `subscribe` persistent property to the `Registration` page class and another property to store the email address, which means adding the following fragment of code:

```
@Persist
private boolean subscribe;
private String email;

public boolean isSubscribe()
{
  return subscribe;
}

public void setSubscribe(boolean subscribe)
{
  System.out.println("Setting subscribe: " + subscribe);
  this.subscribe = subscribe;
}

public String getEmail()
{
  return email;
}

public void setEmail(String email)
{
  this.email = email;
}
```

The output statement in the setter method is, of course, optional. It will simply allow you to see what is happening in the page class.

Run the application, proceed to the **Registration** page, enter some username, password, and then click on the check box, agreeing to subscribe. The text box for email should appear instead of the check box, exactly as we expected, which is good news. But on the other hand, the username and both versions of password disappeared, and gender reverted to the initial value. This shouldn't be a surprise to you if you read the previous chapter attentively—Tapestry doesn't remember anything unless we explicitly ask it to do so. Fortunately, enabling persistence is very easy, we only need to add the `@Persist` annotation to the properties that we want to be remembered:

```
@Persist
private String userName;
@Persist
private String password;
private String password2;
@Persist
private String email;
@Persist
private Gender gender = Gender.FEMALE;
```

There is actually no need to persist the password as it is never redisplayed anyway; however, having the `password` property persistent will become useful a bit later. Now the page should work better, but the problem is that, after we have agreed to subscribe, we have almost no way to see the original check box. This is because the persistent property, `subscribe`, was assigned the value `true`. This value is stored into the session, and we have provided no way to revert it back to `false`. Of course, you can invalidate the session by closing the browser window, but that wouldn't be a natural thing to do.

To solve this problem, let's add another `Checkbox` component next to the `TextField` used for email, like this:

```
<td>
   <input type="text" t:type="textfield" t:id="email"
          t:value="email"/>
   <input type="checkbox" t:type="checkbox"
          t:value="unsubscribe" onclick="this.form.submit()"/>
   I don't want to subscribe
</td>
```

We also need to add another property, `unsubscribe`, to the `Registration` page class:

```
private boolean unsubscribe;
public boolean isUnsubscribe()
{
  return unsubscribe;
```

```
}

public void setUnsubscribe(boolean unsubscribe)
{
  this.unsubscribe = unsubscribe;
}
```

When the user clicks on the new check box, the form will be submitted and the `unsubscribe` property of the page class will become `true`. Now what we want is to set the `subscribe` property to `false` whenever `unsubscribe` is set to `true`. But, where do we implement this logic? The most natural place will be the form submission handler. Modify the `onFormSubmit` method to look like this:

```
void onSubmitFromRegistrationForm()
{
  System.out.println("The form was submitted!");
  if (unsubscribe) subscribe = false;
}
```

Now we can run the application. Go to the **Registration** page, click on the check box to subscribe for the newsletter and then click on the other check box to restore the original interface.

The only problem is that the text box for password doesn't redisplay its value when the page is reloaded, despite the fact that we made password property persistent. This is in the nature of the `PasswordField` component—not to redisplay its value. However, we don't want to annoy our user by the need to re-enter the password every time the page is reloaded. What can we do to avoid this?

One possible solution is to hide the password fields as soon as the password gets submitted. We can use another `If` component for this purpose. Modify the `Registration` page template like this:

```
<t:if t:test="passwordNotSubmitted">
  <tr>
    <td><t:label t:for="password">
       Label for password</t:label>:</td>
    <td><input type="text" t:type="passwordfield"
        t:id="password"
        t:value="password"/></td>
  </tr>
  <tr>
    <td><t:label t:for="password2">
        Label for password 2</t:label>:</td>
    <td><input type="text" t:type="passwordfield"
        t:id="password2"
        t:label="Repeat password" t:value="password2"/></td>
  </tr>
</t:if>
```

From the `test` parameter of this `If` component, you can see that Tapestry will be looking for the `isPasswordNotSubmitted` (or `getPasswordNotSubmitted`) method in the page class. If this method returns `true`, these two table rows with components in them will be displayed, otherwise they will disappear.

Of course, we need to add such a method to the `Registration` page class:

```
public boolean isPasswordNotSubmitted()
{
  return userName == null;
}
```

I am afraid we'll need to close the browser window now to get rid of the session; otherwise the previously stored password will prevent us from testing the new functionality. Run the application, fill in the form, click on the check box, and if you have entered some value for the password, two table rows with password fields in them should disappear.

We now have a rather flexible interface, and we had to write very little code to achieve what we wanted. One of the methods used to enable all this flexibility is the form submission handler. But wait, we didn't create this entire page just to play with it and see how it changes, right? The purpose was to register a new user. We still need to write some code to process the registration, but where do we put this code if the form submission handler was already used for a different purpose?

This is exactly the situation where `Submit` component becomes important.

Submit Component

Right now we are using a basic HTML control to submit the registration form, but it takes very little effort to convert it into a Tapestry `Submit` component. This is how it will look then:

```
<input type="submit" t:type="submit" t:id="submitButton"
                value="Submit"/>
```

We also need to add an event handler for this button to the Registration page class:

```
@OnEvent(component="submitButton")
void onSubmitButton()
{
  System.out.println("Submit button was pressed!");
  // TODO: Some code to actually register the user
}
```

Run the application, enter some values into the registration form and submit it by clicking on the button. You should see an output similar to this:

```
Setting user name: john
Setting password: abc
Setting gender: MALE
Setting subscribe: false
Submit button was pressed!
The form was submitted!
```

The event handler for the submit control runs exactly before the form submission handler, and so all the values submitted by the user are available to it.

Now, to give the logic of the page some completion, we shall perhaps want to imitate user registration—create a new `User` object, fill it with information submitted in the form (although we don't have any details for this at the moment) and store the object into the ASO. We shall also want to display another page, **ShowAll**, at the end. First of all, let's make the `User` ASO available at the **Registration** page:

```
@ApplicationState
private User user;
```

Then we need to create an event handler for the `Submit` component. How do we write it? Based on our previous experience with event handlers, we might write something like this:

```
@OnEvent(component="submitButton")
Object onSubmitButton()
{
  System.out.println("Submit button was pressed!");
  User newUser = new User("John", "Johnson");
  this.user = newUser;
  return ShowAll.class;
}
```

This should be all right, shouldn't it? We are doing what we want to do inside the method, and then returning a class to tell Tapestry which page to display next. This will not work however, at least in the current version of Tapestry. For now, the rule is that the event handler for `Submit` must not return anything. Then how can we navigate to another page?

If you remember, in the output that we received when running the application recently, we could see that a form submission handler was invoked straight after the **Submit** button event handler. It always happens like this, as the `Submit` component is always surrounded by a `Form` component, which gives us an opportunity to solve our problem in the following way:

```
private Class nextPage;
Object onSubmitFromRegistrationForm()
{
  System.out.println("The form was submitted!");
  if (unsubscribe) subscribe = false;
  return nextPage;
}

@OnEvent(component="submitButton")
void onSubmitButton()
{
  System.out.println("Submit button was pressed!");
  User newUser = new User("John", "Johnson");
  this.user = newUser;
  nextPage = ShowAll.class;
}
```

We have modified the form submission handler. It now returns a String, and the value to return is taken from the newly added `nextPage` class variable. We are submitting the form each time a check box is clicked, and each time the form submission handler runs—but that is fine. The value of the `nextPage` variable is `null` (until we specifically assign something to it), so the form submission handler returns `null`, and Tapestry redisplays the same page; that is, everything works as before.

But when the **Submit** button is clicked on, its event handler assigns the class of the **ShowAll** page to the `nextPage` variable. The form submission handler that runs immediately afterwards picks up this value and returns it, and the **ShowAll** page is shown by Tapestry as a result.

As you can see, the use of the `Submit` component gives us significant flexibility while handling form submission—we can have more than one method running in response.

In fact, we can also have more than one `Submit` component in the form.

More Than One Submit Button

Many Web applications give their users an opportunity to quickly "erase" the information they have just entered in case they change their mind. We can also provide a button for this purpose—let it be labeled **Reset**—using a second `Submit` component. Let's position it next to the existing **Submit** button, using the following code:

```
<input type="submit" t:type="submit" t:id="submitButton"
   value="Submit"/>
<input type="submit" t:type="submit" t:id="resetButton"
   value="Reset"/>
```

And of course, we need an event handler for the new component:

```
@OnEvent(component="resetButton")
void onResetButton()
{
  userName = null;
  password = null;
  email = null;
  gender = null;
  subscribe = false;
}
```

We are simply assigning default values to all the persistent properties here. Test the application, and everything should work fine.

This chapter is becoming rather long, but there is only one component left of those we have planned to learn, and this one is very useful.

Select Component

Drop-down lists that allow a user to select one value out of several options are an important part of web interfaces. In Tapestry, we use a `Select` component to display such a drop-down list. Every time we have a fixed set of several options in our code, we need to think of enumeration, and it is natural that the easiest way to use the `Select` component is in combination with an enumeration.

Let's suppose that in the process of registration, we want to ask our users which country they are from. This is how the control we are going to add to the **Registration** page should look:

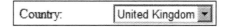

In page template, this addition will look like this:

```
<tr>
    <td>Country:</td>
    <td>
      <select t:type="select" t:model="countries"
              t:value="country">
           <option>Country 1</option>
         <option>Country 2</option>
       </select>
    </td>
</tr>
```

You can see a Tapestry's `Select` component hidden inside of a mocked-up HTML `<select>` control. If you prefer, you can define the same component like this:

```
<t:select t:model="countries" t:value="country"/>
```

This component has two parameters—`model` and `value`. The `value` parameter works in the same way as an similarly named parameter of every other component we've seen before—it connects the component on the page with a property in the page class.

As for the `model` parameter, this parameter provides the option of displaying in the resulting drop-down list. This parameter expects to receive an implementation of the `SelectModel` interface from the page class. There are different ways in which we could provide such an implementation, depending on how much flexibility and power we want. Here we shall consider the simplest approach, and in Chapter 8 we'll experiment with a more powerful one.

First of all, we need to create an enumeration to work with the component. It will be appropriate to name it `Country` and put into the `com.packtpub.celebrities.model` package:

```
package com.packtpub.celebrities.model;
public enum Country
{
  GERMANY, UK, USA
}
```

I have listed only a few countries here, but you can add as many as you wish. Next, let's configure the page class to work with the new component:

```
@Inject
private Messages messages;
public SelectModel getCountries()
{
  return new EnumSelectModel(Country.class, messages);
}

@Persist
private Country country;
public Country getCountry()
{
  return country;
}

public void setCountry(Country country)
{
  this.country = country;
}
```

Interestingly, we are creating an instance of `EnumSelectModel`, one of implementations of the `SelectModel` interface that comes with Tapestry. The constructor of `EnumSelectModel` takes two parameters—the class of an enumeration that should be used as the source of options and some mysterious `Messages` object which we have injected into the page class. What is this Messages object?

Here we are coming very closely to the topic of internationalization and localization that will be thoroughly discussed in Chapter 7. Every Tapestry application can have a number of message catalogs. One of them is the root message catalog that can be used by all the pages and components of the application. It is implemented as an ordinary text file with a `.properties` extension, stored inside of the `WEB-INF` directory. The file should contain key-value pairs for each property separated by the = character, like this:

```
key1=value1
key2=value2
key3=value3
```

When a `Messages` object is injected into a page, this object contains all key-value pairs available for the given page, including those defined in the root message catalog. So what we need to do now is to provide such a root message catalog. Tapestry will use it to define which labels to display for every option in the enumeration. One of the benefits of this is that we can give the properties files to our clients, and they will be able to define how different labels should be displayed without ever touching the source code.

The important thing to remember is that the name of the root message catalog is not arbitrary. It should match the name of the application's Tapestry filter as defined in its deployment descriptor (`web.xml`) file.

Open the deployment descriptor of your application (it can be found directly under `WEB-INF` directory) and view it as an XML code. You should be able to find the following lines in it:

```
<filter>
  <filter-name>app</filter-name>
  <filter-class>org.apache.tapestry.TapestryFilter
  </filter-class>
</filter>
```

From this we can figure out that the name of the Tapestry filter is `app`, and so the name of the root message catalog should be `app.properties`. Please create such a file in the `WEB-INF` directory, and add the following content to it:

```
Country.Germany=Germany
country.UK=United Kingdom
COUNTRY.USA=United States
```

I think the logic in which keys are defined is pretty clear. Note that keys are case-insensitive, and I have intentionally used different case for different options to show this.

Run the application, and you should see a drop-down list that allows you to select a country where the labels are displayed exactly as we've defined them in the message catalog.

We have only one outstanding task for this chapter now, so let's deal with it.

Configuring an Application State Object

Currently, to provide a data source to our pages, we are using an application state object of type `MockDataSource`, like this:

```
@ApplicationState
private MockDataSource dataSource;
```

When we request such an ASO for the first time, Tapestry takes the specified class and creates an instance of it using its no-argument constructor (naturally, such a constructor should exist). It then stores this instance into the session and gives us a reference to it.

All this works okay, but imagine that one day we have created a real data source, and so now we want to have the data source ASO like this:

```
@ApplicationState
private RealDataSource dataSource;
```

We would have to find all the references to this ASO and change them then. Not impossible, but this isn't a good design. To avoid this, we create the `IDataSource` interface, and our `MockDataSource` implements it. Ideally, we would wish the ASO to be defined in a generic way, like this:

```
@ApplicationState
private IDataSource dataSource;
```

This way, we could have any implementation of `IDataSource` working as an ASO—they will all look exactly the same for the pages. But how to tell Tapestry which class to instantiate when we define an ASO as an interface? This is exactly what we are going to find out now.

We shall see some lengthy names of Tapestry-specific classes, but don't be afraid. The logic of what we are going to do is quite simple.

From the very beginning, we had a package named `com.packtpub.celebrities.services` in our application, and a single class, `AppModule` in it, generated for us by Maven. Now we are going to make use of this class. Skim through its source code, just to appreciate that this is the place where we can interact with the inner working of Tapestry—configure, extend existing services or maybe even create some custom services.

We are going to influence the way in which Tapestry manages application state objects. All we need to do for this is to add one more method, `contributeApplicationStateManager` to `AppModule`, thus contributing our own way to manage an ASO. Here is how this method should look:

```
public void contributeApplicationStateManager(
  MappedConfiguration<Class, ApplicationStateContribution>configuratio)
{
   ApplicationStateCreator<IDataSource> creator =
       new ApplicationStateCreator<IDataSource>()
    {
    public IDataSource create()
    {
      return new MockDataSource();
    }
  };

  configuration.add(IDataSource.class,
     new ApplicationStateContribution("session", creator));
}
```

First of all, we create an implementation of the `ApplicationStateCreator` interface (which is a part of Tapestry), associated with type, `IDataSource`:

```
ApplicationStateCreator<IDataSource> creator = ...
```

To do this, we are employing a convenient feature of the Java language named "anonymous inner class". We are creating an instance of a class that implements `ApplicationStateCreator`, and in this case the interface is associated with the `IDataSource` type—the type we are going to use for our ASO. We don't even care to name the class which is used to create the instance, so it remains anonymous:

```
... = new ApplicationStateCreator<IDataSource>()
{
  ...
}
```

The `ApplicationStateCreator` interface has only one method, `create()`. This method should return an instance of the type with which the interface is associated, and this is exactly where we define which class should be instantiated for the ASO. You can also do some custom configuration in this method if you need like, obtain some resources, pass them as parameters to the class constructor, and so on. In our case this method is very simple:

```
public IDataSource create()
{
  return new MockDataSource();
}
```

If you later create another implementation for the data source, you will have to change one single line to make the new data source available throughout the application:

```
return new RealDataSource();
```

Finally, we add the new creator to the application's configuration and, once again, associate it with the type of ASO that the creator should be used for.

Now, find all the references to the `MockDataSource` ASO (there should be two of them, at the **ShowAll** and **Details** pages) and replace the `MockDataSource` type with `IDataSource`. That's it. Now, as soon as you request for the ASO, Tapestry will check its configuration to see whether there is a creator for the requested `IDataSource` type. We have just provided one, and so it will be used to do the job (and generate an instance of `MockDataSource` behind the scenes). I hope this isn't difficult to understand.

Summary

We have learned a lot in this chapter:

- We are now closely familiar with a number of Tapestry components— `TextField`, `PasswordField`, `Label`, `PageLink`, `ActionLink`, `Loop`, `If`, `Output`, `RadioGroup` and `Radio`, `Checkbox`, `Submit` and `Select`. This knowledge is not just theoretical as we used all these components in a web application and saw how they work.
- We now have a good understanding of how form submission works. We have plenty of flexibility in defining which code and when it should run in the process of submission.
- We have explored how to implement a master-detail-like pattern in two different ways—with `ActionLink` and `PageLink` components.

- We have created a good foundation for the future **Celebrity Collector** web application. It already has four pages and some auxiliary code too. We shall continue to develop this application in the coming chapters.
- We have learned to influence the inner working of Tapestry, by providing a custom creator for an application state object.

In the next chapter, we are going to use some really powerful Tapestry components. They bring with them complete sophisticated pieces of interface which require very little configuration, so we can get a lot of functionality with minimal effort. As before, we shall learn new components not just theoretically but by using them in our **Celebrity Collector** web application.

5
Advanced Components

We are already familiar with a significant number of Tapestry components, and using them, we can build sophisticated and functionally rich interfaces. It so happens however, that many web applications have certain patterns repeating on their pages. For example, they have tables that display different data or they have forms that accept user input and then put the submitted details into some kind of Java Bean object.

Wouldn't it be convenient to have such repeating patterns already implemented as components, ready to be dropped onto a page? It certainly would, and the current version of Tapestry 5 already comes with a few components of this kind. They are great effort savers for us, and in this chapter we are going to introduce them and use them in our **Celebrity Collector** application.

Following are some of the components, we'll examine:

- The `Grid` component allows us to display different data in a fairly sophisticated table. We are going to use it to display our collection of celebrities.
- The `BeanEditForm` component greatly simplifies creating forms for accepting user input. We shall use it for adding a new celebrity to our collection.
- The `DateField` component provides an easy and attractive way to enter or edit the date.
- The `FCKEditor` component is a rich text editor, and it is as easy to incorporate into a Tapestry 5 web application, just as a basic `TextField` is. This is a third party component, and the main point here is to show that using a library of custom components in a Tapestry 5 application requires no extra effort. It is likely that a similar core component will appear in a future version of the framework.

Grid Component

Previously, we were able to display our collection of celebrities with the help of the `Loop` component. It wasn't difficult, and in many cases, that will be exactly the solution you need for the task at hand. But, as the number of displayed items grow (our collection grows) different problems may arise.

We might not want to display the whole collection on one page, so we'll need some kind of a pagination mechanism and some controls to enable navigation from page to page. Also, it would be convenient to be able to sort celebrities by first name, last name, occupation, and so on. All this can be achieved by adding more controls and more code to finally achieve the result that we want, but a table with pagination and sorted columns is a very common part of a user interface, and recreating it each time wouldn't be efficient.

Thankfully, the `Grid` component brings with it plenty of ready to use functionality, and it is very easy to deal with. Open the `ShowAll.tml` template in an IDE of your choice and remove the `Loop` component and all its content, together with the surrounding table:

```
<table width="100%">
  <tr t:type="loop" t:source="allCelebrities"
      t:value="celebrity">
    <td>
      <a href="#" t:type="PageLink" t:page="Details"
        t:context="celebrity.id">
        ${celebrity.lastName}
      </a>
    </td>
    <td>${celebrity.firstName}</td>
    <td>
      <t:output t:format="dateFormat"
        t:value="celebrity.dateOfBirth"/>
    </td>
    <td>${celebrity.occupation}</td>
  </tr>
</table>
```

In place of this code, add the following line:

```
<t:grid t:source="allCelebrities"/>
```

Run the application, log in to be able to view the collection, and you should see the following result:

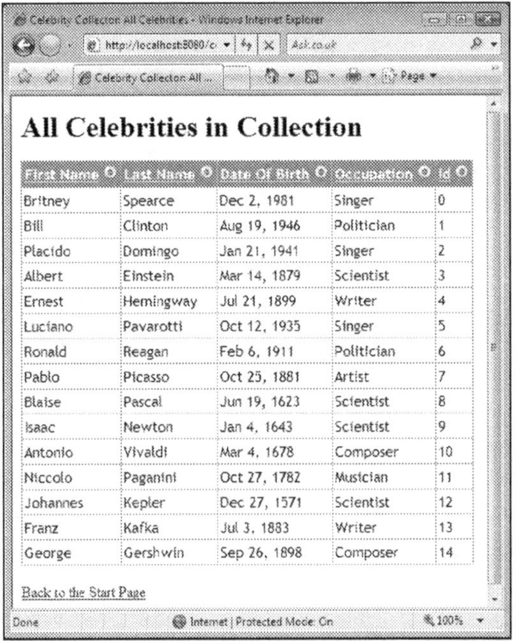
All Celebrities in Collection

First Name	Last Name	Date Of Birth	Occupation	Id
Britney	Spearce	Dec 2, 1981	Singer	0
Bill	Clinton	Aug 19, 1946	Politician	1
Placido	Domingo	Jan 21, 1941	Singer	2
Albert	Einstein	Mar 14, 1879	Scientist	3
Ernest	Hemingway	Jul 21, 1899	Writer	4
Luciano	Pavarotti	Oct 12, 1935	Singer	5
Ronald	Reagan	Feb 6, 1911	Politician	6
Pablo	Picasso	Oct 25, 1881	Artist	7
Blaise	Pascal	Jun 19, 1623	Scientist	8
Isaac	Newton	Jan 4, 1643	Scientist	9
Antonio	Vivaldi	Mar 4, 1678	Composer	10
Niccolo	Paganini	Oct 27, 1782	Musician	11
Johannes	Kepler	Dec 27, 1571	Scientist	12
Franz	Kafka	Jul 3, 1883	Writer	13
George	Gershwin	Sep 26, 1898	Composer	14

Back to the Start Page

Quite an impressive result for a single short line of code, isn't it? Not only are our celebrities now displayed in a neatly formatted table, but also, we can sort the collection by clicking on the columns' headers. Also note that occupation now has only the first character capitalized—much better than the fully capitalized version we had before.

Here, we see the results of some clever guesses on Tapestry's side. The only required parameter of the `Grid` component is `source`, the same as the required parameter of the `Loop` component. Through this parameter, `Grid` receives a number of objects of the same class. It takes the first object of this collection and finds out its properties. It tries to create a column for each property, transforming the property's name for the column's header (for example, `lastName` property name gives **Last Name** column header) and makes some additional sensible adjustments like changing the case of the `occupation` property values in our example.

All this is quite impressive, but the table, as it is displayed now, has a number of deficiencies:

- All celebrities are displayed on one page, while we wanted to see how pagination works. This is because the default number of records per page for `Grid` component is 25—more than we have in our collection at the moment.

- The last name of the celebrities does not provide a link to the **Details** page anymore.
- It doesn't make sense to show the **Id** column.
- The order of the columns is wrong. It would be more sensible to have the **Last Name** in the first column, then **First Name**, and finally the **Date of Birth**.

By default, to define the display of the order of columns in the table, Tapestry will use the order in which getter methods are defined in the displayed class. In the `Celebrity` class, the `getFirstName` method is the first of the getters and so the **First Name** column will go first, and so on.

There are also some other issues we might want to take care of, but let's first deal with these four.

Tweaking the Grid

First of all let's change the number of records per page. Just add the following parameter to the component's declaration:

```
<t:grid t:source="allCelebrities" rowsPerPage="5"/>
```

Run the application, and here is what you should see:

You can now easily page through the records using the attractive pager control that appeared at the bottom of the table. If you would rather have the pager at the top, add another parameter to the `Grid` declaration:

```
<t:grid t:source="allCelebrities" rowsPerPage="5"
  pagerPosition="top"/>
```

You can even have two pagers, at the top and at the bottom, by specifying `pagerPosition="both"`, or no pagers at all (`pagerPosition="none"`). In the latter case however, you will have to provide some custom way of paging through records.

The next enhancement will be a link surrounding the celebrity's last name and linking to the **Details** page. We'll be adding an `ActionLink` and will need to know which `Celebrity` to link to, so we have the `Grid` store using the `row` parameter. This is how the `Grid` declaration will look:

```
<t:grid t:source="allCelebrities" rowsPerPage="5"
  row="celebrity"/>
```

As for the page class, we already have the `celebrity` property in it. It should have been left from our experiments with the `Loop` component. It will also be used in exactly the same way as with `Loop`, while iterating through the objects provided by its `source` parameter, `Grid` will assign the object that is used to display the current row to the `celebrity` property.

The next thing to do is to tell Tapestry that when it comes to the contents of the **Last Name** column, we do not want `Grid` to display it in a default way. Instead, we shall provide our own way of displaying the cells of the table that contain the last name. Here is how we do this:

```
<t:grid t:source="allCelebrities" rowsPerPage="5"
  row="celebrity">
  <t:parameter name="lastNameCell">
    <t:pagelink t:page="details" t:context="celebrity.id">
      ${celebrity.lastName}
    </t:pagelink>
  </t:parameter>
</t:grid>
```

Here, the `Grid` component contains a special Tapestry element `<t:parameter>`, similar to the one that we used in the previous chapter, inside the `If` component. As before, it serves to provide an alternative content to display, in this case, the content which will fill in the cells of the **Last Name** column. How does Tapestry know this? By the name of the element, `lastNameCell`. The first part of this name, `lastName`, is the name of one of the properties of the displayed objects. The last part, `Cell`, tells Tapestry that it is about the content of the table cells displaying the specified property.

Finally, inside `<t:parameter>`, you can see an expansion displaying the name of the current celebrity and surrounding it with the `PageLink` component that has for its context the **ID** of the current celebrity.

Run the application, and you should see that we have achieved what we wanted:

Click on the last name of a celebrity, and you should see the **Details** page with the appropriate details on it.

All that is left now is to remove the unwanted **Id** column and to change the order of the remaining columns. For this, we'll use two properties of the `Grid`—`remove` and `reorder`. Modify the component's definition in the page template to look like this:

```
<t:grid t:source="celebritySource" rowsPerPage="5"
  row="celebrity"
  remove="id"
  reorder="lastName,firstName,occupation,dateOfBirth">
  <t:parameter name="lastNameCell">
  <t:pagelink t:page="details" t:context="celebrity.id">
    ${celebrity.lastName}
  </t:pagelink>
  </t:parameter>
</t:grid>
```

Please note that re-ordering doesn't delete columns. If you omit some columns while specifying their order, they will simply end up last in the table.

Now, if you run the application, you should see that the table with a collection of celebrities is displayed exactly as we wanted:

Changing the Column Titles

Column titles are currently generated by Tapestry automatically. What if we want to have different titles? Say we want to have the title, **Birth Date**, instead of **Date Of Birth**.

The easiest and the most efficient way to do this is to use the message catalog, the same one that we used while working with the `Select` component in the previous chapter. Add the following line to the `app.properties` file:

```
dateOfBirth-label=Birth Date
```

Run the application, and you will see that the column title has changed appropriately. This way, appending `-label` to the name of the property displayed by the column, you can create the key for a message catalog entry, and thus change the title of any column.

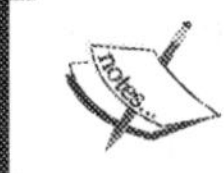

> Right now, we are using the root message catalog, which is common for all the pages of the application. Later, in Chapter 7, you will see how to create a message catalog for every page.

Now you should be able to adjust the `Grid` component to most of the possible requirements and to display with its help many different kinds of objects. However, one scenario can still raise a problem.

Add an output statement to the `getAllCelebrities` method in the `ShowAll` page class, like this:

```
public List<Celebrity> getAllCelebrities()
{
  System.out.println("Getting all celebrities...");
  return dataSource.getAllCelebrities();
}
```

The purpose of this is simply to be aware when the method is called. Run the application, log in, and as soon as the table with celebrities is shown, you will see the output, as follows:

```
Getting all celebrities...
```

The `Grid` component has the `allCelebrities` property defined as its source, so it invokes the `getAllCelebrities` method to obtain the content to display. Note however that `Grid`, after invoking this method, receives a list containing all 15 celebrities in collection, but displays only the first five.

Click on the pager to view the second page—the same output will appear again. `Grid` requested for the whole collection again, and this time displayed only the second portion of five celebrities from it. Whenever we view another page, the whole collection is requested from the data source, but only one page of data is displayed. This is not too efficient but works for our purpose.

Imagine, however, that our collection contains as many as 10,000 celebrities, and it's stored in a remote database. Requesting for the whole collection would put a lot of strain on our resources, especially if we are going to have 2,000 pages.

We need to have the ability to request the celebrities, page-by-page—only the first five for the first page, only the second five for the second page and so on. This ability is supported by Tapestry. All we need to do is to provide an implementation of the `GridDataSource` interface.

Here is a somewhat simplified example of such an implementation.

Using GridDataSource

First of all, let's modify the `IDataSource` interface, adding to it a method for returning a selected range of celebrities:

```
public interface IDataSource
{
  List<Celebrity> getAllCelebrities();
  Celebrity getCelebrityById(long id);
  void addCelebrity(Celebrity c);
  List<Celebrity> getRange(int indexFrom, int indexTo);
}
```

Next, we need to implement this method in the available implementation of this interface. Add the following method to the `MockDataSource` class:

```
public List<Celebrity> getRange(int indexFrom, int indexTo)
{
  List<Celebrity> result = new ArrayList<Celebrity>();

  for (int i = indexFrom; i <= indexTo; i++)
  {
    result.add(celebrities.get(i));
  }
  return result;
}
```

The code is quite simple, we are returning a subset of the existing collection starting from one index value and ending with the other. In a real-life implementation, we would probably check whether `indexTo` is bigger than `indexFrom`, but here, let's keep things simple.

Here is one possible implementation of `GridDataSource`. There are plenty of output statements in it that do not do anything very useful, but they will allow us to witness the inner life of `Grid` and `GridDataSet` in tandem. Have a look at the code, and then we'll walk through it step-by-step:

```
package com.packtpub.celebrities.util;

import com.packtpub.celebrities.data.IDataSource;
import com.packtpub.celebrities.model.Celebrity;
import java.util.List;
import org.apache.tapestry.beaneditor.PropertyModel;
import org.apache.tapestry.grid.GridDataSource;

public class CelebritySource implements GridDataSource
{
```

```
    private IDataSource dataSource;
    private List<Celebrity> selection;
    private int indexFrom;

    public CelebritySource(IDataSource ds)
    {
      this.dataSource = ds;
    }

    public int getAvailableRows()
    {
      return dataSource.getAllCelebrities().size();
    }

    public void prepare(int indexFrom, int indexTo,
                        PropertyModel propertyModel, boolean ascending)
    {
      System.out.println("Preparing selection.");
      System.out.println("Index from " + indexFrom + " to " + indexTo);
      String propertyName = propertyModel == null?
      null : propertyModel.getPropertyName();
      System.out.println("Property name is: " + propertyName);
      System.out.println("Sorting order ascending: " + ascending);
      selection = dataSource.getRange(indexFrom, indexTo);
      this.indexFrom = indexFrom;
    }

    public Object getRowValue(int i)
    {
      System.out.println("Getting value for row " + i);
      return selection.get(i - this.indexFrom);
    }

    public Class getRowType()
    {
      return Celebrity.class;
    }
  }
```

First of all, when creating an instance of `CelebritySource`, we are passing an implementation of `IDataSource` that will imitate an actual data source to its constructor. In real life this could be some Data Access Object.

The `GridDataSource` interface that we implemented contains four methods: `getAvailableRows()`, `prepare()`, `getRowValue()`, and `getRowType()`. The simplest of them is `getRowType()`. It simply reports which type of objects are served by this implementation of `GridDataSource`.

The getAvailableRows method returns the total number of entities available in the data source (this is needed to know the number of pages and to construct the pager properly). In our case, we are simply returning the size of a collection. In real life, this method could contain a request to the database that would return the total available number of records in a search result, without actually returning all those records.

If you insert an output statement into this method, you will notice that it is invoked by Grid several times, even while a single page of the table is displayed. You will not want to call the database that many times, so you will need to include some logic to cache the result returned by this method, and update it only when necessary. But, again, we are looking at the principles here, so let's keep everything simple.

The prepare method does the main job of requesting the database and obtaining a subset of entities from it to be displayed by the current page of the table. The subset is limited by the first two parameters—indexFrom and indexTo, which are the indexes of the first and the last entities to be returned. They might be used in a SELECT statement which would command the database to select all the entities and then limit the selection in one way or another, depending on the SQL dialect.

The third parameter of this method, propertyModel, is used to define the column by which the result should be sorted. Again, we could use this parameter in a SELECT statement, but here we are simply outputting the name of the property to see what the Grid has passed to the method.

Finally, the ascending parameter could be used to define the order in which the results should be sorted when speaking to the database, but we are just outputting its value.

The last of the four methods, getRowValue(), returns the entity requested by Grid using its index as a parameter. You will see how all this works soon.

To make use of the created CelebritySource, add the following method to the ShowAll page class:

```
public GridDataSource getCelebritySource()
{
  return new CelebritySource(dataSource);
}
```

Then change the source parameter of the Grid component in ShowAll.tml template:

```
<t:grid t:source="celebritySource" rowsPerPage="5"
  row="celebrity" t:model="model">
```

Run the application. Log in to view the **ShowAll** page, and as soon as the table with celebrities is displayed, you should see the following output:

```
Preparing selection.
Index from 0 to 4
Property name is: null
Sorting order ascending: true
Getting value for row 0
Getting value for row 1
Getting value for row 2
Getting value for row 3
Getting value for row 4
```

From this you can see that to display the first page of results, the `Grid` component invoked the methods of the `GridDataSource` implementation provided by its source parameter in a certain succession. The output shows that the `prepare` method was invoked with the `indexFrom` parameter set to 0, and the `indexTo` parameter set to 4. These are indexes of the first five celebrities in collection. The `propertyModel` parameter was `null`, so no specific sorting was requested. Finally, the `getRowValue` method was invoked five times to obtain an object to be displayed by each of the five rows in the table.

Click on the pager to view the second page of results and the result will be similar, only the indices will be different:

```
Preparing selection.
Index from 5 to 9
Property name is: null
Sorting order ascending: true
Getting value for row 5
Getting value for row 6
Getting value for row 7
Getting value for row 8
Getting value for row 9
```

Click on the header of one of the columns, and you will see the change in the property name passed to the `prepare` method:

```
Property name is: lastName
Sorting order ascending: true
```

Now the data source will be requested to sort the result by last name. Of course, no sorting will take place in our simplified example as we are simply outputting the name of the property and not using it in an actual request to a database.

Click on the same column once again, and this time you will see that the order of sorting is changed:

```
Property name is: lastName
Sorting order ascending: false
```

You can see from this example that Tapestry allows us to define precisely how a database (or other data source) should be called, and we can request data, page-by-page by creating an implementation of `GridDataSource` interface. The `Grid` component will then invoke the methods of this interface and display the information returned by them appropriately.

Next, we are going to see another advanced component, `BeanEditForm`. It is somewhat similar to `Grid` in that it also can make use of `BeanModel`, and its configuration is pretty similar too.

BeanEditForm Component

Our current collection of celebrities is tiny, and it would be a good idea to provide in the application functionality for adding new celebrities. Let's begin by adding a template and a page class for a new page named **AddCelebrity**. Add to the page class a single persistent property named `celebrity`, so that its code looks like this:

```
package com.packtpub.celebrities.pages;

import com.packtpub.celebrities.model.Celebrity;
import org.apache.tapestry.annotations.Persist;

public class AddCelebrity
{
  @Persist
  private Celebrity celebrity;
  public Celebrity getCelebrity()
  {
    return celebrity;
  }

  public void setCelebrity(Celebrity celebrity)
  {
    this.celebrity = celebrity;
  }
}
```

In the page template, declare one single component of type `BeanEditForm` and let its `id` be the same as the name of the property of the page class, in our case, `celebrity`:

```
<html xmlns:t="http://tapestry.apache.org/schema/tapestry_5_0_0.xsd">
  <head>
    <title>Celebrity Collector: Adding New
      Celebrity</title>
  </head>
  <body>
    <h1>Adding New Celebrity</h1>
    <t:beaneditform t:id="celebrity"/>
  </body>
</html>
```

We also need to somehow connect the new page to the rest of the application. For instance, we could add this new `PageLink` component somewhere at the bottom of the `ShowAll` page:

```
<a href="#" t:type="PageLink" t:page="AddCelebrity">Add new
  Celebrity
</a><br/>
<a href="#" t:type="PageLink" t:page="Start">
  Back to the Start Page
</a>
```

Finally, to make things more interesting, add another couple of properties to the `Celebrity` class (don't forget to generate getters and setters for them):

```
private String biography;
private boolean birthDateVerified;
```

Say we could store a brief biography in the first property, and the second could be set to true whenever we verify in some way that the birth date is correct.

Run the application, log in, and at the **ShowAll** page, click on the link leading to the new **AddCelebrity** page. You will see the `BeanEditForm` in all its glory:

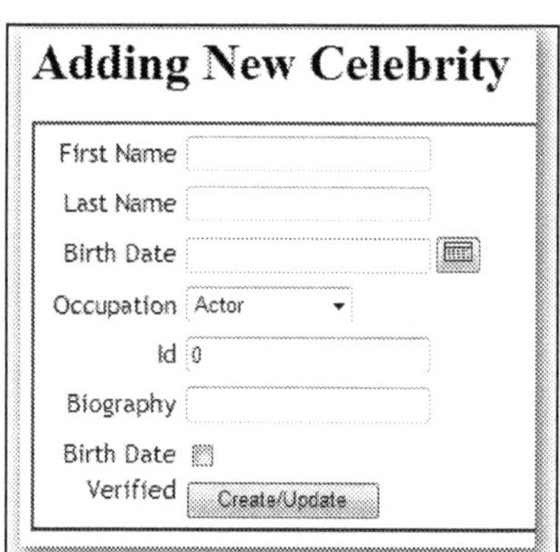

Isn't it amazing how much can be done for us by Tapestry when we just drop one component onto the page, with virtually no configuration? Let's see how all this magic works:

- Since we didn't specify any *object* parameter for `BeanEditForm`, Tapestry decided that the name of the property should be the same as the `id` of the `BeanEditForm` component.
- We didn't initialize the `celebrity` property, so its value is null, and still everything works fine since `BeanEditForm` can create an instance of the edited property as required. One consequence of this is that the type of property should be a concrete class, not an interface.
- `BeanEditForm` took all the properties of the edited class and created a field in the form for each of them.
- For each property that it can edit, `BeanEditForm` automatically selects a certain control. For a string or a numeric property it displays a text box, for an enumeration—a drop-down list, for a boolean property—a checkbox, for a date—a `DateField` component (which will be described soon). However, we can easily override the default choice if needed.
- `BeanEditForm` generates a label for each property based on the property name in the same way as the Grid component did. And in the same way we can override the default label by providing an alternative for it in the application's message catalog, with a key like the `propertyName` label.
- If the object edited by `BeanEditForm`, as provided by the page class, contains some values in it, those values will be displayed in appropriate fields of the form. As soon as you click on the **Create/Update** button, the values in the form fields will be put into the appropriate properties of the edited object.

This list of features already looks quite impressive for a default configuration, but there are more miracles to see. Purely for the purpose of demonstration, enter some non-numeric value, like **abc**, into the **Id** field and click on the **Create/Update** button. You will see something similar to this:

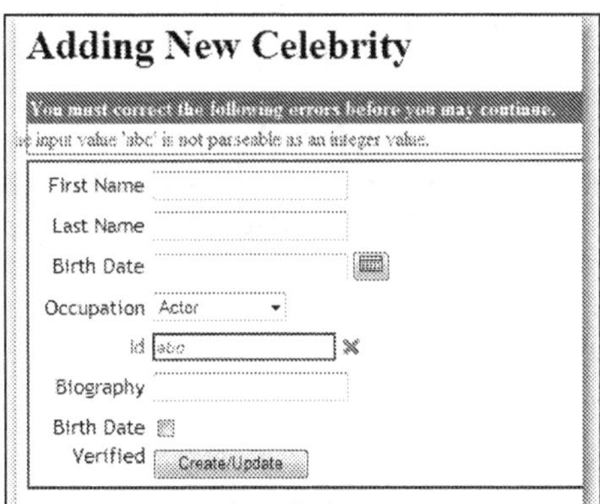

Which means that in addition to everything else, `BeanEditForm` comes with a pre-configured system of user input validation, and applies reasonable restrictions to its fields, like it prevents entering a non-integer value for an integer property.

User input validation is the topic for the next chapter, but you can already see that without any efforts from our side, the validation system of Tapestry 5 does quite a lot—it changes the style of the field in error, its label and adds an error marker, and also displays an appropriate error message at the top of the form. In Chapter 7 you will see that it can even display error messages in many different languages! Well, the error message is somewhat misplaced at the moment, but we'll deal with this problem later.

Do you still remember that to obtain all this wealth of functionality, all we had to do is to insert a short line of markup into the page template? Here it is again:

```
<t:beaneditform t:id="celebrity"/>
```

Tweaking BeanEditForm

There are a few parameters that we could use to tweak the component. First of all, you will probably want the submit button to display a different label, not the default **Create/Update**. Nothing could be easier:

```
<t:beaneditform t:id="celebrity" t:submitLabel="Save"/>
```

You can also explicitly specify the object that `BeanEditForm` should work with, and use an arbitrary id:

```
<t:beaneditform t:id="celebrityEditor" t:object="celebrity"
  t:submitLabel="Save"/>
```

Although `BeanEditForm` made a lot of clever guesses, in many cases we shall want to somehow influence the way it works. As with the `Grid` component in the previous section, we'll want to remove the `Id` field and change the order of fields in the form, so that the **Birth Date Verified** check box is underneath the **Birth Date** control.

By the way, did you notice that the label for this control is **Birth Date**, not **Date Of Birth**, as would be automatically generated by Tapestry? This is because of the entry that we've added to the `app.properties` file. That file is used by the whole application, and every label associated with the `dateOfBirth` ID will automatically receive the value from the message catalog.

The way we tidy up the `BeanEditForm` is very similar to what we did with the `Grid` component:

```
<t:beaneditform t:id="celebrity" t:submitLabel="Save"
  remove="id"
  reorder="firstName,lastName,dateOfBirth,birthDateVerified,
  occupation,biography"/>
```

The other change we might want to make is to change the control that is used for **Biography**. Even though the biography will be brief, a text box is not convenient for entering a long string. There is a much more convenient control for this purpose in HTML, `<textarea>`. In Tapestry, such control can be displayed by the `TextArea` component. Here is what we should do to override the default choice for editing the biography property of the displayed object:

```
<t:beaneditform t:id="celebrity" t:submitLabel="Save"
  remove="id"
  reorder="firstName,lastName,dateOfBirth,birthDateVerified,
    occupation,biography">
  <t:parameter name="biography">
    <t:label for="biography"/>
    <t:textarea t:id="biography"
      t:value="celebrity.biography"/>
  </t:parameter>
</t:beaneditform>
```

In a way similar to what we did with the `Grid` component to override the default rendering of a certain column, we are using a `<t:parameter>` element. Here it repeats the name of the property for which we want to provide an alternative editor. Inside this element we are using a `TextArea` component, in the same way as we used `TextField` in the previous chapter.

If you run the application now, the form should look like this:

This is already better. If you think that you'd prefer to have more space for a biography, try this:

```
<t:textarea t:id="biography" t:value="celebrity.biography"
  cols="30" rows="5"/>
```

As `cols` and `rows` attributes do not belong to parameters of Tapestry's `TextArea` component, they will be simply passed to the resulting `<textarea>` HTML control. Run the application and see how the form looks now.

At this point, let's distract ourselves to explore the new component that magically appeared in `BeanEditForm`, it deserves it.

DateField Component

This is a new addition that appeared only in the latest 5.0.6 version of Tapestry. Now we can use this beautiful, JavaScript-powered control without seeing even a single line of JavaScript.

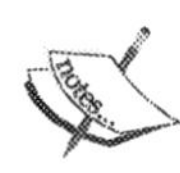

`DateField` is based on an open source DHTML/JavaScript calendar that can be found at `http://www.dynarch.com/projects/calendar/`.

Let's add one more piece of information to those that we already collect from the users at the **Registration** page—**Date Of Birth**. Add this table row to the template, perhaps straight under the controls used for gender selection:

```
<tr>
  <td>Gender:</td>
  <td>
    <t:radiogroup t:value="gender">
      <input type="radio" t:type="radio" t:value="male"/>
          Male
      <input type="radio" t:type="radio" t:value="female"/>
          Female
    </t:radiogroup>
  </td>
</tr>
<tr>
  <td>Birth Date:</td>
  <td>
    <input type="text" t:type="datefield"
        t:value="dateOfBirth"/>
  </td>
</tr>
```

We'll also need a property to store the selected date in the `Registration` page class:

```
@Persist
private Date dateOfBirth;

public Date getDateOfBirth()
{
  return dateOfBirth;
}

public void setDateOfBirth(Date dateOfBirth)
{
  this.dateOfBirth = dateOfBirth;
}
```

Run the application, go to the **Registration** page, and you will see the new control on it:

Click on the small icon to the right, and in the beautiful calendar that opens you will be able to choose a date:

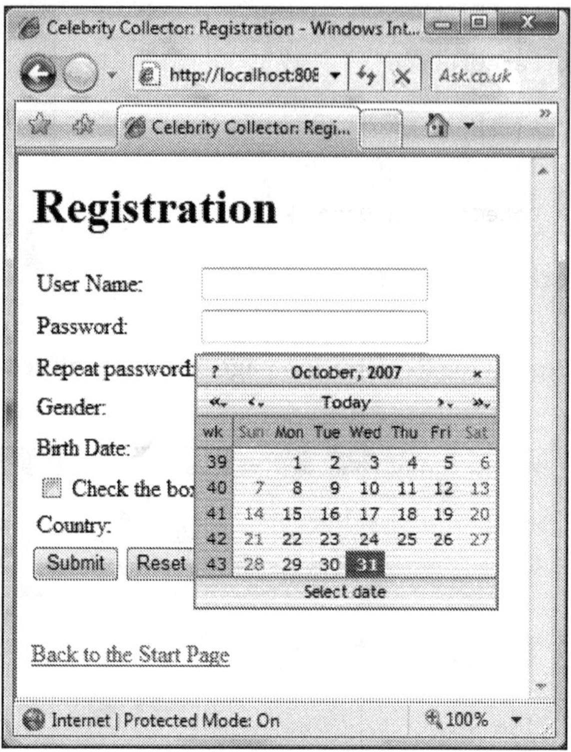

However, by default the selected date will be displayed in the American format, like **10/31/07** for the 31st of October. What if you would rather prefer to see it in the European format, **31/10/07**? We can use the format property of the `DateField` component to display the date how we like:

```
<input type="text" t:type="datefield" t:value="dateOfBirth"
  t:format="%d/%m/%y"/>
```

You can also construct a completely different date format. For example, `%b %e, %Y` will produce the result Oct 31, 2007. For the complete list of formatting characters check `http://www.dynarch.com/demos/jscalendar/doc/html/reference.html#node_sec_5.3.1`, but the following are a few that might be most useful:

Formatting character	Its meaning
%a	Abbreviated weekday name
%A	Full weekday name
%b	Abbreviated month name
%B	Full month name
%d	The day of the month (00...31)
%e	The day of the month (0...31)
%m	Month (01...12)
%y	Year without the century (07)
%Y	Year including the century (2007)

We can use the `DateField` component everywhere we need to edit a property of the `java.util.Date` type. Whenever the `BeanEditForm` components finds a property of this type in the edited `JavaBean`, it selects `DateField` to edit that property automatically.

Changing the Styles of Grid and BeanEditForm

Everything works fine but looks less than perfect. For example, the labels of `BeanEditForm` are cramped on the left side of the form so that lines like **Birth Date Verified** have to split into two lines, and it misplaces the other labels as a result. Also, the background color and the font used by default for `Grid` and `BeanEditForm` might not fit the design of your application. Fortunately, the appearance of these components is defined by CSS styles, and so we can easily influence how they look by changing the styles.

Tapestry provides a default stylesheet, named appropriately `default.css`, and this is exactly where the styling of its components is defined. Tapestry adds the default stylesheet in such a way that it will always be the first for every page, and so any stylesheet that we provide can override whatever is defined in `default.css`. To make the desired changes, we need to provide a stylesheet of our own and in it declare the same styles as in `default.css`—with the same names, but with different content.

As the first step, we might want to look into the `default.css` file. It can be found in the Tapestry source code package that can be downloaded from `http://tapestry.apache.org/download.html`. The name of the package will be similar to `tapestry-src 5.0.6 binary (zip)`. The `default.css` file can be found inside the package, in the `tapestry-core\src\main\resources\org\apache\tapestry` subdirectory.

This file contains a significant number of styles, but those related to `BeanEditForm` have `t-beaneditor` in their name, and those related to `Grid` contain `t-data-grid`. Let's say we want to change the background of `BeanEditForm` to white, the surrounding border to green and give more space to the labels. Admittedly, I am not an expert in CSS, but it is not actually difficult to figure out what exactly should be changed. These are the two style definitions we shall want to tweak:

```
DIV.t-beaneditor
{
  display: block;
  background: #ffc;
  border: 2px solid silver;
  padding: 2px;
  font-family: "Trebuchet MS", Arial, sans-serif;
}

DIV.t-beaneditor LABEL
{
  width: 10%;
  display: block;
  float: left;
  text-align: right;
  clear: left;
  padding-right: 3px;
}
```

The first of them defines the appearance of the form in general, the second—the appearance of the labels used for the fields in the form. It is easy to guess that the first definition will allow us to change, most significantly, the background, the border and the font of the form, while the second allows us to change the space given to the labels (currently only 10% of the width of the page).

But where do we put our own style definitions? It will be convenient to have a directory for all the assets of our web application, let's name it appropriately, `styles`. It should be created at the root of the web application, on the same level where page templates are placed.

To create it in NetBeans, right click on the **Web Pages** folder inside the project structure. Select **New | File/Folder...**, then **Other** in **Categories** and **Folder** in **File Types**. Click on **Next**, give the new folder a name, and then click on **Finish**. Now right click on the new **styles** folder and again select **New | File Folder...**. Choose **Other** for **Categories**, **Empty File** for **File Types**, click on **Next** and name the new file something like **styles.css**.

In Eclipse, the sequence of actions will be similar, but the new **styles** folder should be added to the **WebContent** folder in the project structure.

Now we can put the aforementioned style definitions into `styles.css`, and change them as required. Let's try something like this:

```
DIV.t-beaneditor
{
  display: block;
  background: white;
  border: 2px solid green;
  padding: 2px;
  font-family: "Trebuchet MS", Arial, sans-serif;
}
DIV.t-beaneditor LABEL
{
  width: 150px;
  display: block;
  float: left;
  text-align: right;
  clear: left;
  padding-right: 3px;
}
```

In fact, it should be enough to leave only the highlighted lines here as the other details were already specified in the default style sheet.

We can also influence the positioning of the **Save** button:

```
input.t-beaneditor-submit
{
  position: relative;
  left: 150px;
}
```

However, to see the changes, we need to make the new stylesheet available to the web page. Tapestry can inject an asset, be it a stylesheet or an image, into the page class when we ask it to do that, so let's add to the `AddCelebrity` page class to the following lines of code:

```
@Inject
@Path("context:styles/styles.css")
private Asset styles;

public Asset getStyles()
{
  return styles;
}
```

Finally, provide in the page template a link to the stylesheet:

```
<head>
  <title>Celebrity Collector: Adding New Celebrity</title>
  <link rel="stylesheet" href="${styles}" type="text/css"/>
</head>
```

If you run the application now, you will notice a significant difference in the form's appearance:

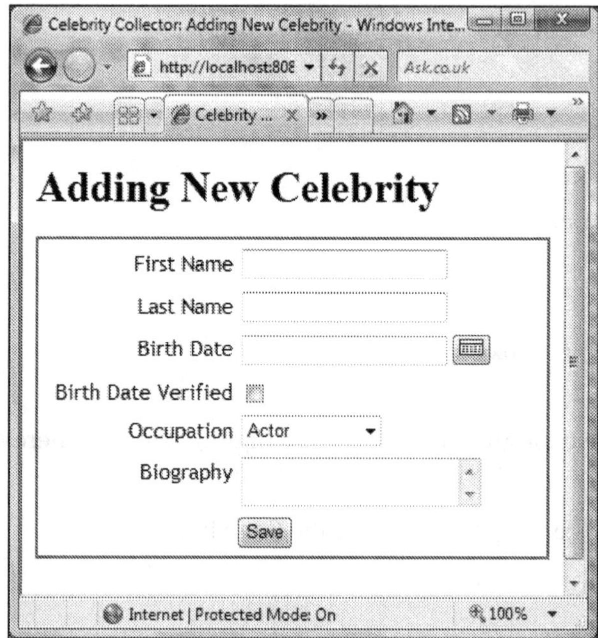

You can continue experimenting from here with styles on your own, using the `default.css` file and the source code of the rendered page (where you can see which styles are used for what) as your starting point.

But let me show you one more very useful component.

FCKEditor Component

Quite often, we might want to give the users of our application an opportunity not only to enter a message, but also to format it similarly to how they would do this in a familiar word processor. There are JavaScript-enabled rich text editors available for this purpose, the most famous of them is perhaps `FCKEditor` (`http://www.fckeditor.net/`), but integrating such an editor into a web application might require additional knowledge and effort.

Thankfully, there is a custom Tapestry 5 component developed by Ted Steen and Olof Naessen that wraps `FCKEditor`. As a result, we can use this excellent rich text editor in the same way like any other Tapestry component. The component can be downloaded from `http://code.google.com/p/tapestry5-fckeditor/` as a JAR file (make sure you pick the version, 1.0.2 or later). The name of the file will be similar to `tapestry5-fckeditor-1.0.2.jar`. Please put it into the `WEB-INF/lib` subfolder of our web application. In Eclipse, you might want to press *F5* to make sure that the IDE has noticed the addition.

Let's use the `FCKEditor` component to enter a celebrity's biography at the **AddCelebrity** page. All we need to do is to change the type of component used to edit the `biography` property in the page template:

```
<t:parameter name="biography">
  <t:label for="biography"/>
  <t:fckeditor.editor t:id="biography"
    t:value="celebrity.biography"/>
</t:parameter>
```

The result of this change might look a bit overwhelming:

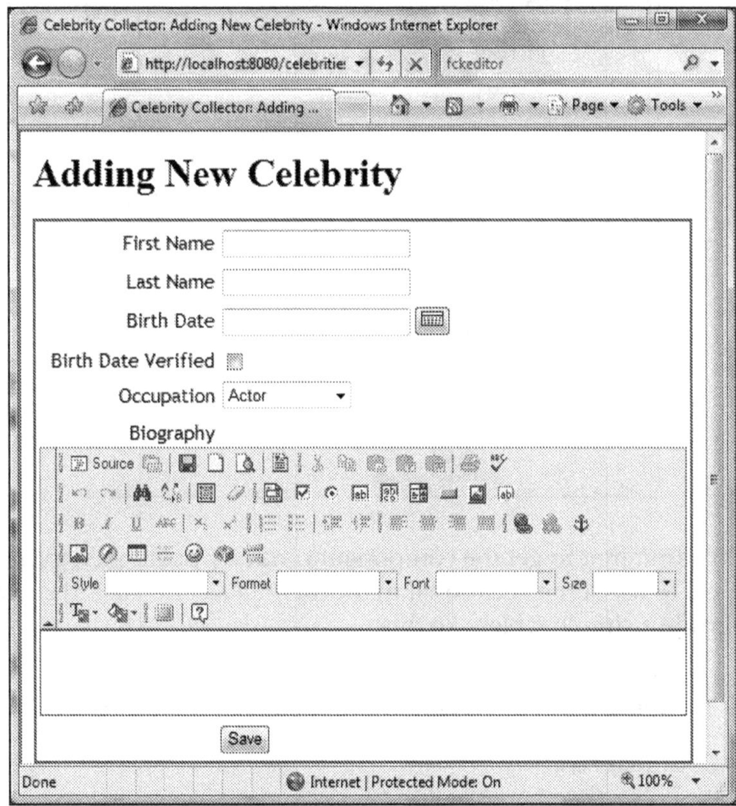

By default, the component is huge as it displays all the goodies made available by the original `FCKEditor`. In many cases you will not need all that, and there is an easy way to both change the number of displayed toolbars and change the size of the component.

There are three toolbar sets available—Default, Simple and Medium, and we can choose using the `toolbarSet` parameter. There are also `width` and `height` parameters that allow us to specify the size of the component. Here is one possible combination of settings:

```
<t:fckeditor.editor t:id="biography"
  t:value="celebrity.biography"
  t:toolbarSet="Simple" t:width="300" t:height="150"/>
```

And here is how the resulting component looks:

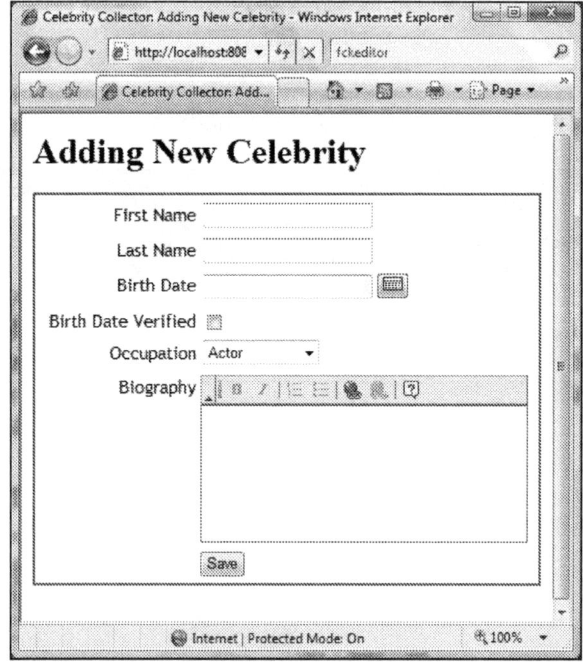

Well, I have to admit that to get the component properly positioned in Internet Explorer 7, I had to use some additional markup, to place the `FCKEditor` component and its label inside a simple table, like this:

```
<t:parameter name="biography">
  <table cellpadding="0" cellspacing="0">
    <tr>
      <td valign="top">
        <t:label for="biography"/>
```

```
        </td>
        <td>
          <t:fckeditor.editor t:id="biography"
            t:value="celebrity.biography"
            t:toolbarSet="Medium" t:width="350"
            t:height="200"/>
        </td>
      </tr>
    </table>
  </t:parameter>
```

My favorite toolbar set is the medium one. This is how it looks:

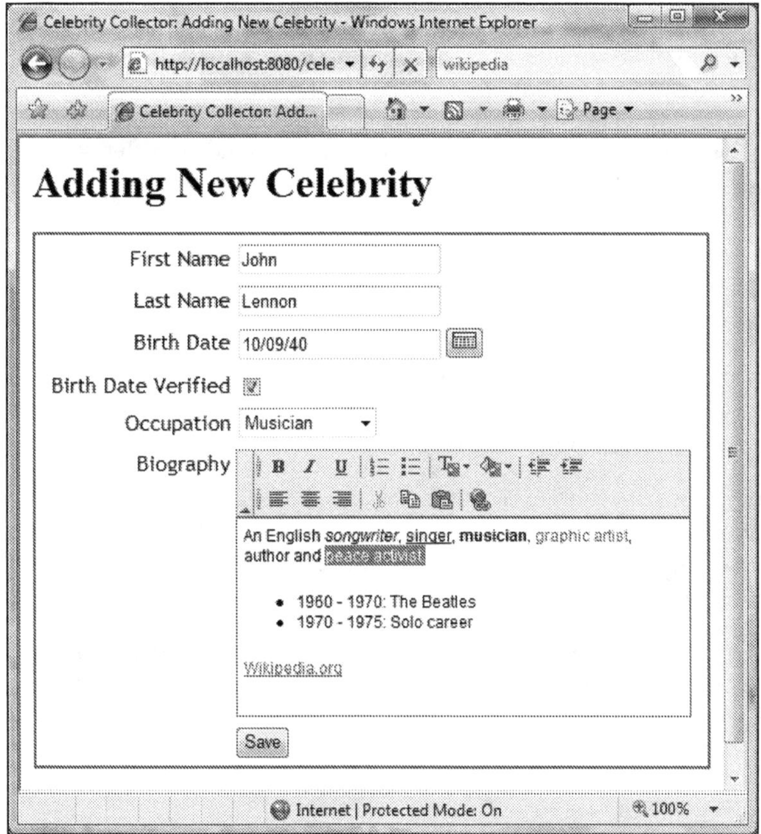

After the text of the biography is entered, formatted and submitted, what gets sent to the server (and is stored in a property of the page class) is a piece of HTML with all the markup that is needed to reproduce the formatting. We can later display the biography on the details page, but right now we need to make sure that the new information (and a new `Celebrity` object containing it) is stored properly in the data source.

All we need to do for this is to add the following fragment of code to the **AddCelebrity** page:

```
@ApplicationState

private IDataSource dataSource;
Object onSubmitFromCelebrity()
{
  dataSource.addCelebrity(celebrity);
  return ShowAll.class;
}
```

We are handling form submission here, so our event handler handles the `submit` event and is named appropriately, according to convention. Looks all right, doesn't it? This will work for now, but in the next chapter, we'll find out that in such a situation we should handle the "success" event. So the method should be better named `onSuccessFromCelebrity`.

We have added an event handler and a reference to the data source ASO. When the form with the new celebrity is submitted, we store the resulting `Celebrity` object using the data source existing for this purpose and display the **ShowAll** page.

However, at the moment the table that displays our collection has two extra columns, for `biography`, and `birthDateVerified` properties. We do not want to see them, so let's modify the **ShowAll** page template:

```
<t:grid t:source="celebritySource" rowsPerPage="5"
  row="celebrity"
  remove="id, biography, birthDateVerified"
  reorder="lastName,firstName,occupation,dateOfBirth">
```

Finally, to get the biography displayed at the **Details** page, let's make the necessary preparations. All we need to do is to add the following piece of markup to the page template:

```
<tr>
  <td>Occupation:</td>
  <td>${celebrity.occupation}</td>
</tr>
<tr>
  <td valign="top">Biography:</td>
  <td>
    <t:outputraw t:value="celebrity.biography"/>
  </td>
</tr>
```

Now add a new celebrity and a brief biography for him or her as I did above for John Lennon. Format the biography using different styles and colors to your heart's content and then click on the **Save** button. You will see the **ShowAll** page and the newly added celebrity will be somewhere at the end of collection, perhaps on page four.

Find the new celebrity and click on the last name to see the details. Depending on how you formatted the biography, you should see something similar to this:

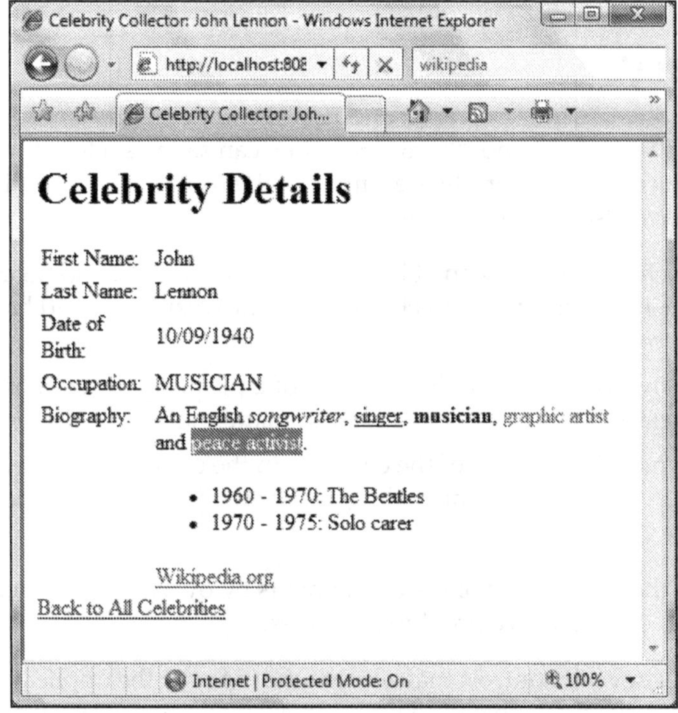

As you can see, all the formatting is displayed properly, and this is the reason why we used a new component, OutputRaw in the last example. In fact, this component is quite similar to an ordinary Output component, or even to a basic extension—it simply outputs whatever is given to it as a value. The difference is that both regular output and extension encode the content that they insert into the page while OutputRaw just inserts into the resulting HTML its value, no matter what it contains.

For instance, if the value provided by the component's binding is <b>bold text</b>, then regular output will encode angle brackets and produce the following result: <b>bold text</b>. As a result, instead of formatted text, the page will display the tags verbatim: <b> bold text</b>. The OutputRaw however will insert into the page what was given to it, and as a result, we'll see bold text.

Security Note: Please use the `OutputRaw` component with caution. If you will use it to freely display any content entered by a random user, someone might enter a hostile script and achieve sinister results that you cannot even imagine.

All right, we had enough of work and study in this chapter. Now we can relax and review what was done.

Summary

We have learned to use four powerful and useful components—`Grid`, `BeanEditForm`, `DateField` and `FCKEditor`. They can save us a lot of work since with minimal configuration, they produce a rather sophisticated, functionally rich piece of interface. We have also found out that:

- We can change the way an object is displayed by `Grid` and `BeanEditForm` components, in terms of which properties are displayed and how they are ordered.
- We can override the default rendering of a property by `Grid` or the default editor selected for it by `BeanEditForm`, using the `<t:parameter>` element.
- We can modify the titles of the columns in the `Grid` or the labels of the fields in the `BeanEditForm` by providing appropriate messages in the application's message catalog.

We can change the appearance of the components by overriding the default CSS styles in the stylesheet that we provide ourselves.

We already have several controls that accept user input in the application, but nowhere have we checked what kind of input is submitted so far. This is acceptable at the initial stage of development, when we are the only users of the application, and we know for sure which kind of information should be entered in each field.

However, every real life application must validate user input, and if there are errors, it should inform the user about them in a friendly and clear way. The next chapter will discuss the powerful validation system of Tapestry 5.

6
User Input Validation

One of the benefits of having a web application is that it can be very easily accessed by everyone around the world. One of the downsides of this is that when so many people use your application, they are going to have errors in their input. Some people are not attentive, others are tired and, finally, everyone in this world has his or her individual style of thinking, so something that seems obvious to the developers of the application might puzzle someone else.

A well-designed web application should immediately be able to define that the input is wrong and stop—otherwise all kinds of errors can happen inside of the application. If this application is user-friendly, it should:

- Clearly and unambiguously inform the user that some part of the input is erroneous, and should be corrected.
- Identify the field that is erroneous and mark it in some way.
- If possible, display the erroneous value, and maybe even explain why exactly it is wrong.

Let's see how Tapestry 5, being a highly efficient and user-friendly framework, handles these issues.

Adding Validation to Components

Have a look at the **Start** page of the running **Celebrity Collector**. There is a login form that expects the user to enter some values into its two fields. But, what if the user didn't enter anything and still clicked on the **Log In** button? Currently, the application will decide that the credentials are wrong and the user will be redirected to the **Registration** page, and receive an invitation to register. This logic does make some sense; but, it isn't the best line of action, as the button might have been pressed by mistake.

These two fields, **User Name** and **Password**, are actually mandatory, and if no value was entered into them, then it should be considered an error. All we need to do for this is to add a `required` validator to every field, as seen in the following code:

```
<tr>
  <td>
    <t:label t:for="userName">
      Label for the first text box</t:label>:
  </td>
  <td>
    <input type="text" t:id="userName" t:type="TextField"
      t:label="User Name" t:validate="required"/>
  </td>
</tr>
<tr>
  <td>
    <t:label t:for="password">
      The second label</t:label>:
  </td>
  <td>
    <input type="text" t:id="password" t:label="Password"
      t:type="PasswordField" t:validate="required"/>
  </td>
</tr>
```

Just one additional attribute for each component, and let's see how this works now. Run the application, leave both fields empty and click on the **Log In** button. Here is what you should see:

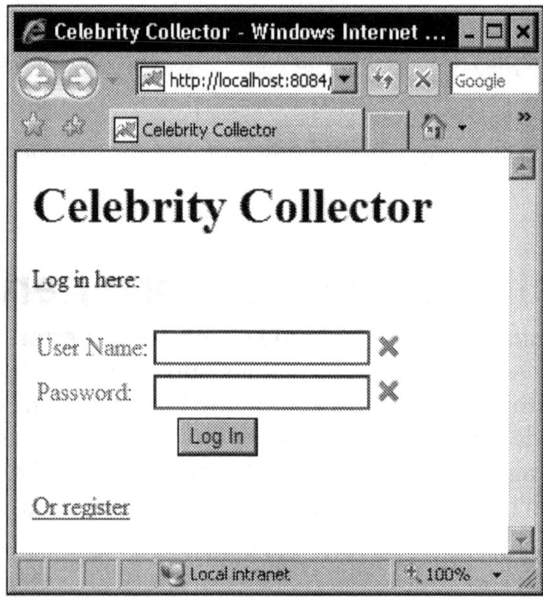

Both fields, including their labels, are clearly marked now as an error. We even have some kind of graphical marker for the problematic fields. However, one thing is missing—a clear explanation of what exactly went wrong. To display such a message, one more component needs to be added to the page. Modify the page template, as done here:

```
<t:form t:id="loginForm">
  <t:errors/>
  <table>
```

The `Errors` component is very simple, but one important thing to remember is that it should be placed inside of the `Form` component, which in turn, surrounds the validated components. Let's run the application again and try to submit an empty form. Now the result should look like this:

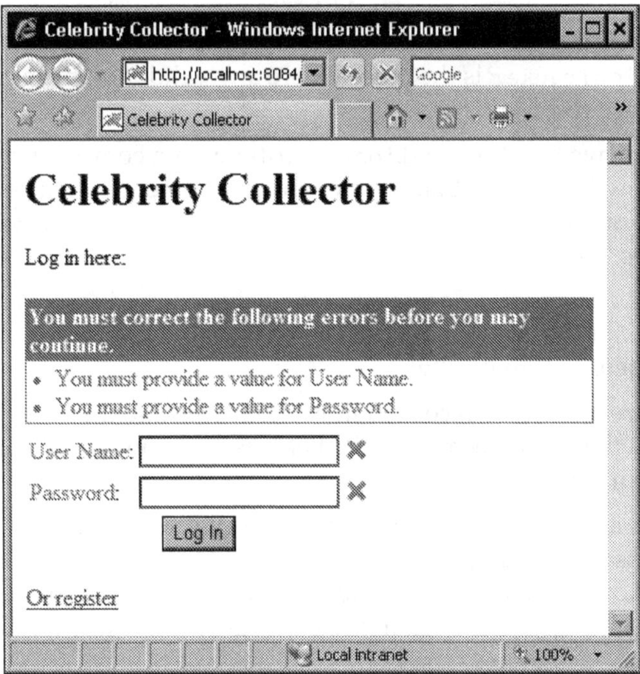

This kind of feedback doesn't leave any space for doubt, does it? Of course if you wish, you can override the default styles, by following the instructions given in the previous chapter for styling `BeanEditForm`.

> If you see that the error messages are strongly misplaced to the left, it means that an error in the `default.css` file that comes with Tapestry distribution still hasn't been fixed. To override the faulty style, define it in our application's `styles.css` file like this:
>
> ```
> DIV.t-error LI
> {
>   margin-left: 20px;
> }
> ```
>
> Do not forget to make the stylesheet available to the page, as described in the previous chapter.

I hope you will agree that the efforts we had to make to get user input validated are close to zero. But let's see what Tapestry has done in response to them:

- Every form component has a `ValidationTracker` object associated with it. It is provided automatically, we do not need to care about it. Basically, `ValidationTracker` is the place where any validation problems, if they happen, are recorded.
- As soon as we use the `t:validate` attribute for a component in the form, Tapestry will assign to that component one or more validators, the number and type of them will depend on the value of the `t:validate` attribute (more about this later).
- As soon as a validator decides that the value entered associated with the component is not valid, it records an error in the `ValidationTracker`. Again, this happens automatically.
- If there are any errors recorded in `ValidationTracker`, Tapestry will redisplay the form, decorating the fields with erroneous input and their labels appropriately.
- If there is an `Errors` component in the form, it will automatically display error messages for all the errors in `ValidationTracker`. The error messages for standard validators are provided by Tapestry while the name of the component to be mentioned in the message is taken from its label.

A lot of very useful functionality comes with the framework and works for us "out of the box", without any configuration or set-up!

Tapestry comes with a set of validators that should be sufficient for most needs. Let's have a more detailed look at how to use them.

Validators

The following validators come with the current distribution of Tapestry 5:

- `Required` – checks if the value of the validated component is not null or an empty string.
- `MinLength` – checks if the string (the value of the validated component) is not shorter than the specified length. You will see how to pass the length parameter to this validator shortly.
- `MaxLength` – same as above, but checks if the string is not too long.
- `Min` – ensures that the numeric value of the validated component is not less than the specified value, passed to the validator as a parameter.
- `Max` – as above, but ensures that the value does not exceed the specified limit.
- `Regexp` – checks if the string value fits the specified pattern.

We can use several validators for one component. Let's see how all this works together.

First of all, let's add another component to the **Registration** page template:

```
<tr>
  <td><t:label t:for="age"/>:</td>
  <td><input type="text" t:type="textfield" t:id="age"/></td>
</tr>
```

Also, add the corresponding property to the `Registration` page class, `age`, of type double. It could be an `int` indeed, but I want to show that the `Min` and `Max` validators can work with fractional numbers too. Besides, someone might decide to enter their age as **23.4567**. This will be weird, but not against the laws.

Finally, add an `Errors` component to the form at the **Registration** page, so that we can see error messages:

```
<t:form t:id="registrationForm">
  <t:errors/>
  <table>
```

Now we can test all the available validators on one page. Let's specify the validation rules first:

1. Both **User Name** and **Password** are required. Also, they should not be shorter than three characters and not longer than eight characters.
2. **Age** is required, and it should not be less than five (change this number if you've got a prodigy in your family) and not more than 120 (as that would probably be a mistake).
3. **Email** address is not required, but if entered, should match a common pattern.

Here are the changes to the **Registration** page template that will implement the specified validation rules:

```
<td>
  <input type="text" t:type="textfield" t:id="userName"
    t:validate="required,minlength=3,maxlength=8"/>
</td>
...
<td>
  <input type="text" t:type="passwordfield" t:id="password"
    t:validate="required,minlength=3,maxlength=8"/>
</td>
...
<td>
  <input type="text" t:type="textfield" t:id="age"
    t:validate="required,min=5,max=120"/>
</td>
...
<input type="text" t:type="textfield" t:id="email"
  t:validate="regexp"/>
```

As you see, it is very easy to pass a parameter to a validator, like `min=5` or `maxlength=8`. But, where do we specify a pattern for the `Regexp` validator? The answer is, in the message catalog. Let's add the following line to the `app.properties` file:

```
email-regexp=^([a-zA-Z0-9_.-])+@(([a-zA-Z0-9-])+.)
  +([a-zA-Z0-9]{2,4})+$
```

This will serve as a regular expression for all `Regexp` validators applied to components with ID `email` throughout the application. In the next chapter you will see how to create page-specific message catalogs.

Run the application, go to the **Registration** page and, try to submit the empty form. Here is what you should see:

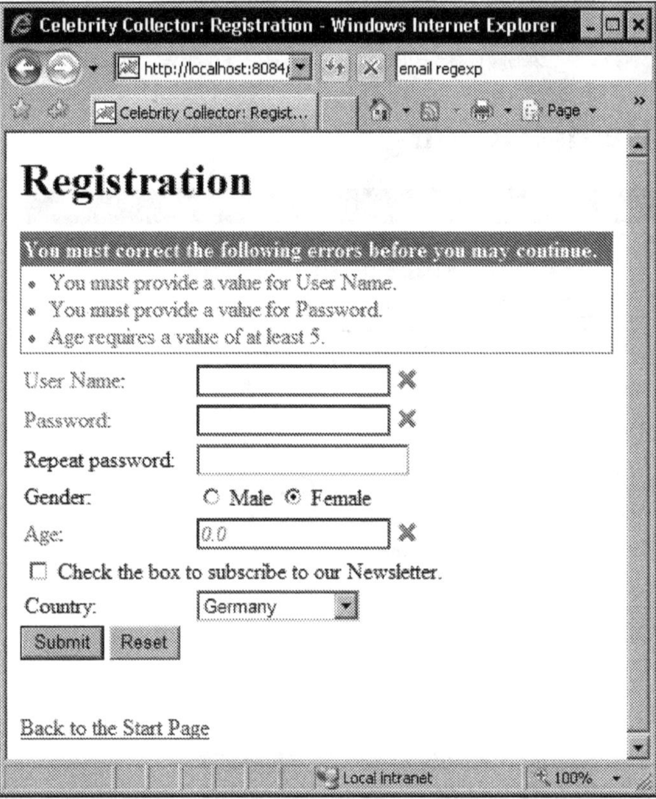

Looks all right, but the message for the age could be more sensible, something like **You are too young! You should be at least 5 years old.**. We'll deal with this later. However for now, enter a very long username, only two characters for password and an age that is more than the upper limit, and see how the messages will change:

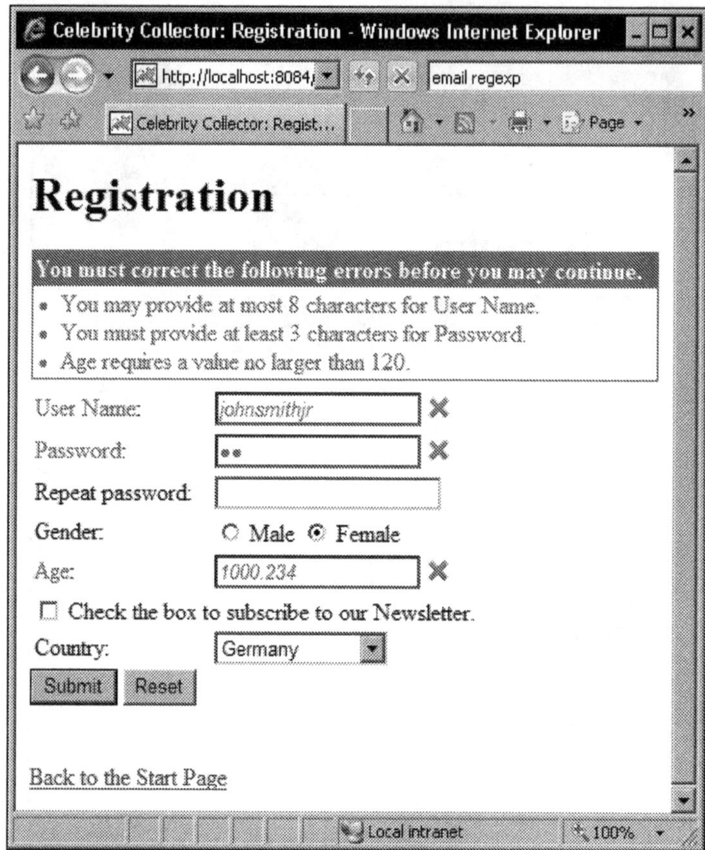

Again, looks good, except for the message about age. Next, enter some valid values for **User Name**, **Password** and **Age**. Then click on the check box to subscribe to the newsletter. In the text box for email, enter some invalid value and click on **Submit**. Here is the result:

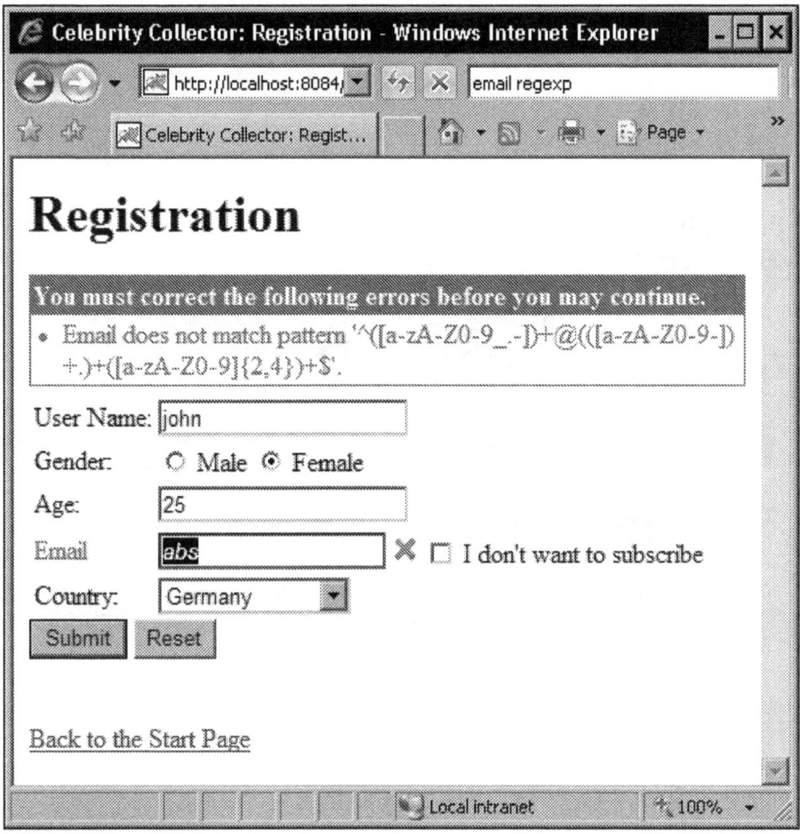

Yes! The validation worked properly, but the error message is absolutely unacceptable. Let's deal with this, but first make sure that any valid email address will pass the validation.

Providing Custom Error Messages

We can provide custom messages for validators in the application's (or page's) message catalog. For such messages we use keys that are made of the validated component's ID, the name of validator and the "message" postfix. Here is an example of what we could add to the `app.properties` file to change error messages for the `Min` and `Max` validators of the `Age` component as well as the message used for the email validation:

```
email-regexp-message=Email address is not valid.
age-min-message=You are too young! You should be at least 5 years
  old.
age-max-message=People do not live that long!
```

Still better, instead of hard-coding the required minimal age into the message, we could insert into the message the parameter that was passed to the `Min` validator (following the rules for `java.text.Format`), like this:

```
age-min-message=You are too young! You should be at least %s years
  old.
```

If you run the application now and submit an invalid value for age, the error message will be much better:

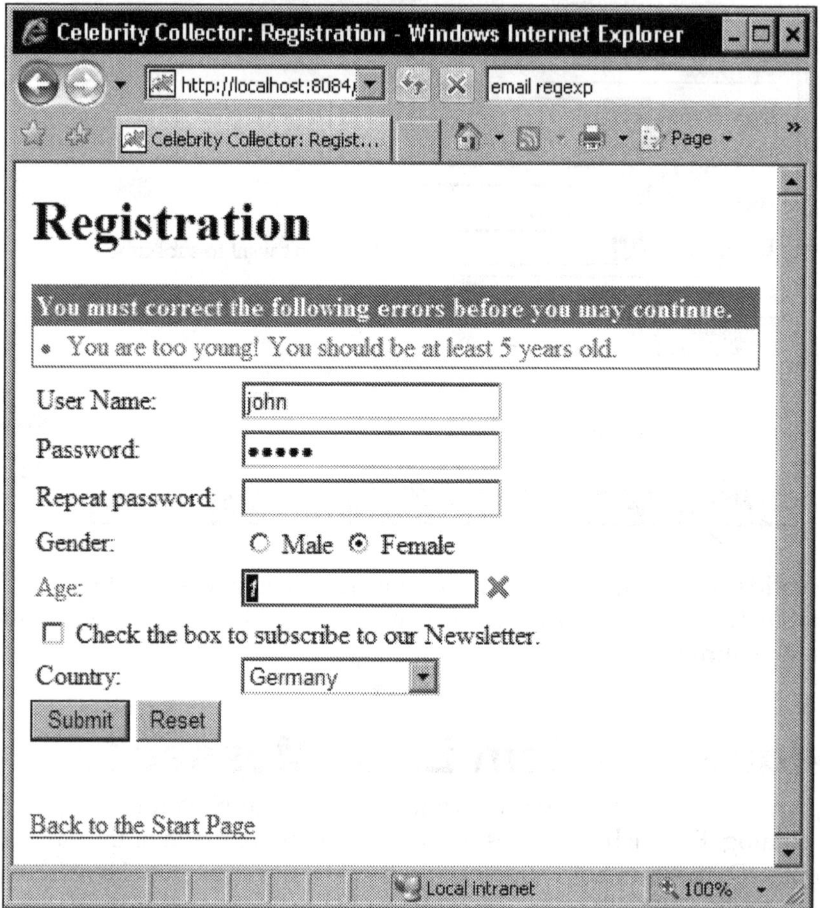

You might want to make sure that the other error messages have changed too.

We can now successfully validate values entered into separate fields, but what if the validity of the input depends on how two or more different values relate to each other? For example, at the **Registration** page we want two versions of password to be the same, and if they are not, this should be considered as an invalid input and reported appropriately. Before dealing with this problem however, we need to look more thoroughly at different events generated by the `Form` component.

Handling Validation-Related Form Events

Previously, while writing a Form submission handler, we used either an annotation like this:

```
@OnEvent(value="submit", component="registrationForm")
```

or an appropriately named method like `onSubmitFromRegistrationForm()`.

As you already know, this means that the event handler method should be invoked in response to the submit event generated by the component with a specified ID. The `Form` component generates a few other events too. There are three events related to validation—`validate`, `success`, and `failure`. Let's implement event handler methods for all these events.

This is where following the naming convention for event handlers, as opposed to using the `@OnEvent` annotation, will save us some effort. If Tapestry will find a method named `onSuccess()` in the page class, it will understand that this is the event handler for any `success` event that happens on the page. Let's modify the existing handler for the `submit` event and add handlers for the other events mentioned above. Here is how these methods should look in the `Registration` class:

```
String onSubmit()
{
  System.out.println("The form was submitted!");
  if (unsubscribe) subscribe = false;
  return nextPage;
}

void onValidate()
{
  System.out.println("In onValidate.");
}

void onSuccess()
{
  System.out.println("In onSuccess.");
}

void onFailure()
{
  System.out.println("In onFailure.");
}
```

As usual, we have inserted some output statements to have a glimpse into the inner life of Tapestry.

If you run the application now, enter some invalid values and then click on the newsletter checkbox (use the **Reset** button to return the form to its initial state when needed) you should see the following output:

```
In onValidate.
In onFailure.
The form was submitted!
```

From this we can see that the `validate` event was fired first, then `failure`, and finally `submit`.

If however, we provide correct input, the output will be different:

```
Setting user name: John
Setting password: Smith
In onValidate.
Submit button was pressed!
In onSuccess.
The form was submitted!
```

Here is how all this works.

In the very beginning, as soon as we click on the **Submit** button, the `Form` component performs an automatic single field validation of the values using the validators we have specified. You might have noticed that if you click on the **Submit** button in an empty form no event handlers are invoked at all. This is because the initial stage of validation happens on the client side, without submitting the form to the server. However, for client side validation to work, the components used on the page should provide some appropriate JavaScript (those components that come with Tapestry do provide such JavaScript), and of course JavaScript should be enabled in the user's browser.

If this first stage of validation was successful, the `Form` component sends the values provided by the user to the server, so they can be set to the appropriate properties of the page class. This is why we saw the following lines of output:

```
Setting user name: John
Setting password: Smith
```

If however the first stage revealed a problem, the values submitted by the user are not set to the properties of the page class, and none of the event handlers get invoked.

On the next step, the `Form` component fires the `validate` event, and Tapestry invokes our `onValidate` method. This is where we should put any custom validation logic, additional to that performed automatically by the form on single fields. If our additional logic defines a problem, we can record a validation error with a message of our choice. This is what we'll be doing in the next section.

After the `onValidate` method does its job, Tapestry checks if there are any errors recorded in `ValidationTracker`—either automatically or by ourselves. If there are, then the `failure` event is generated and the `onFailure` method is invoked, otherwise the `success` event is fired and the `onSuccess` method runs. Finally, the `submit` event is generated, and so the `onSubmit` method runs no matter what.

From this logic, we can make an inference that the proper place for any code that should run only in case of successful validation is the `onSuccess` method, and so we need to change the code of the `Registration` class like this:

```
void onSubmit()
{
  System.out.println("The form was submitted!");
}

String onSuccess()
{
  System.out.println("In onSuccess.");
  if (unsubscribe) subscribe = false;
  return nextPage;
}
```

Another conclusion is that if we want to perform any additional validation, this should be done in the `onValidate` method.

Cross-Form Validation

We do need to perform custom validation in a couple of places. First of all, at the **Registration** page we should check whether the two versions of password are identical, and if not, we should report a problem.

To begin with, we need to have a reference to the `Form` component to record any eventual error in the page class code, and it is very easy to get:

```
@Component
  private Form registrationForm;
```

Here the name of the private class member is the same as the ID of the `Form` component, so we do not need to clarify exactly which form we mean here.

We can record an error in the form in two ways—specifying the component which is in error and without mentioning any components. In the first case, the specified component will be marked as an error. Let's say that if passwords do not match, we want to mark the `password` component as an error. For this, we need to have a reference to this component in the page code:

```
@Component(id="password")
  private PasswordField passwordField;
```

Here we couldn't give the reference the same name as the ID of the component, since there is already a class member named `password`. So we used a different name for the reference (`passwordField`) and specified exactly which component we meant in the `id` parameter passed to the `@Component` annotation.

Also, we'll want to provide an error message to be automatically displayed by the `Errors` component. The proper place for such a message is the application's (or page's) message catalog, so let's add some error message to the `app.properties` file:

```
passwords-dont-match=Two versions of password do not match.
```

And then we need to provide a reference to this catalog in the page class:

```
@Inject
  private Messages messages;
```

Finally, we can write the contents for the `onValidate` method:

```
void onValidate()
{
  System.out.println("In onValidate.");
  if (!password.equals(password2))
  {
    password = null;
    registrationForm.recordError(passwordField,
      messages.get("passwords-dont-match"));
  }
}
```

We are setting the password property to `null` if passwords do not match so that previously implemented logic (that hides password fields after password was submitted) worked properly. Then we are recording an error into the form, specifying the component in error and providing an error message. If some errors were recorded into the form, Tapestry will always redisplay the same page, so we don't need to bother about any navigation issues. Now, if you run the application and enter two different values for password you should see something like this:

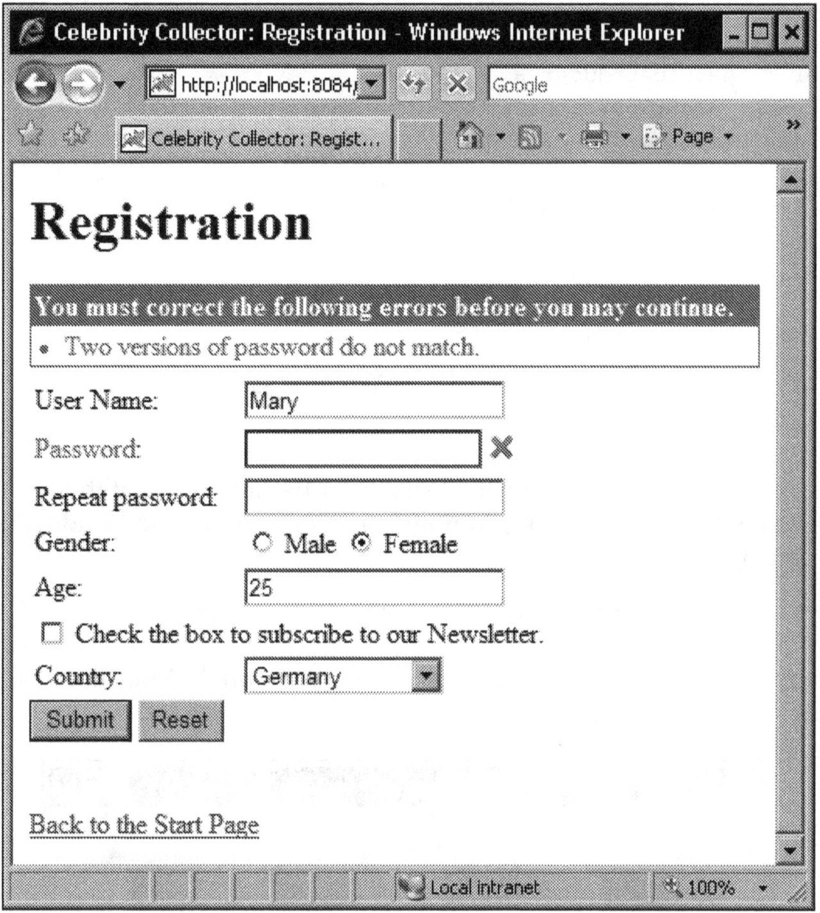

The second place in the application where the `onValidate` method becomes useful is the **Start** page. If you remember, in the case of failed authentication we are simply redirecting the user to the **Registration** page. It would be much better to just display an error message in this case. As we are not going to associate this error with any component, here is the addition to the **Start** page class that will do the job:

```
@Component
private Form loginForm;

@Inject
private Messages messages;

Object onSuccess()
{
  return ShowAll.class;
}
```

```
void onValidate()
{
  User authenticatedUser =
           Security.authenticate(userName, password);
  if (authenticatedUser != null)
  {
    user = authenticatedUser;
  }
  else
  {
    loginForm.recordError(
      messages.get("authentication-failed"));
  }
}
```

Of course, you will need to remove the listener for the submit event that was used on this page before. Also, some appropriate error message should be added to the message catalog:

```
authentication-failed=We couldn't authenticate you.
  Try again or register.
```

Run the application and try to log in using wrong credentials. You should see something similar to this:

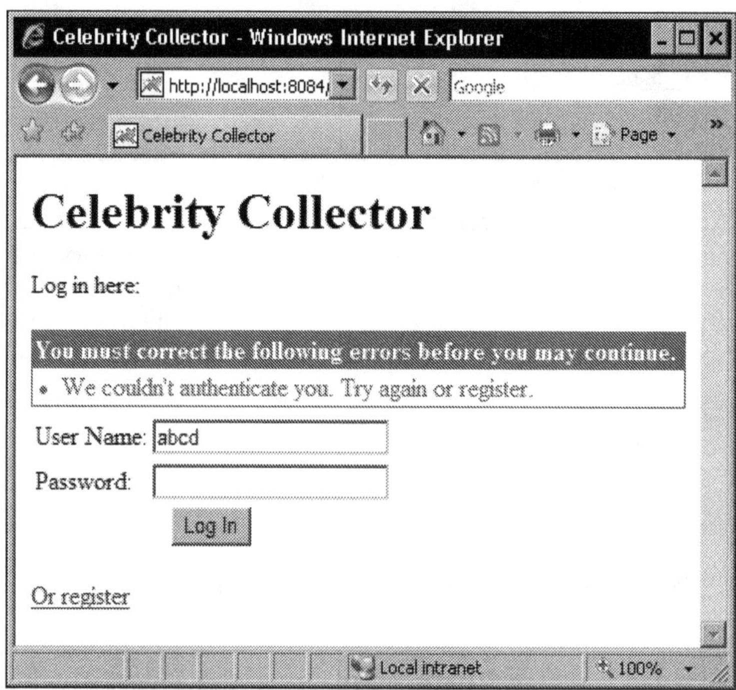

So far, we've successfully managed different cases of validation by dealing directly with components in the form, or by recording errors directly to the `Form` component; but, how about validation in `BeanEditForm`? This sophisticated component does so much for us automatically that it doesn't make sense to use many of the skills we've just learned.

BeanEditForm Validation

Let's say that when we are adding a new celebrity to our collection the first name should be mandatory. This can be easily achieved by adding a `@Validate` annotation to either getter or setter method of the `Celebrity` class, like this:

```
@Validate("required")
public String getFirstName()
{
  return firstName;
}
```

If you try to add a celebrity without specifying a first name, you will see an appropriate error message, as the `Errors` component is already incorporated into the `BeanEditForm`.

You can also specify a custom error message if you do not like the default one. Try something like this:

```
firstName-required-message=You cannot have a celebrity without a name!
```

And of course you combine different validators like we did before.

Summary

Here is what we have learned in this chapter:

- Tapestry 5 comes with a powerful framework for user input validation. To use it, we have to do very little, while Tapestry does a lot for us—applies validators, decorates fields in error, and displays error messages.
- We can provide custom error messages and `Regexp` patterns using message catalogs. Although this wasn't explained in the chapter, you can also change the styles used to display errors by overriding them in your stylesheet.
- Tapestry 5 comes with five validators that will cover most needs. You can combine several of them to achieve the desired result.

- You can provide custom validation, for example cross-form validation, in the `validate` event handler.
- To validate the fields of `BeanEditForm`, the `@Validate` annotation should be used on either the getter or setter method of the validated property in the edited class.

You have already seen that it is possible to have both application-wide and page-specific message catalogs, and the next chapter will explain how exactly this can be done. But the main topic of the next chapter is how to display Tapestry application in different languages, and this is another area where, with minimal effort, we can achieve some very impressive results.

7

Internationalization and Localization

Internationalization (commonly abbreviated as *i18n*—first "i", then 18 other characters, then "n") and localization (*l10n*) are two inseparable parts of the same process—the process of making an application able to display itself in different locales. A **locale** is a set of language and country-specific attributes that most obviously include the language spoken in that part of the world, but also other details like number or currency format specific to a certain culture.

Internationalization means, making the application technically able to display itself in different languages. While localization provides locale-specific resources, but since these two processes are so inter-dependent, let's just refer to them both as **internationalization** in the remaining part of this chapter. Here we are going to learn:

- What Tapestry can do for us in terms of internationalization.
- What does it take to internationalize labels, messages and other string resources.
- How to create a page-specific message catalog, plus to the root one.
- How an image can be changed according to the current locale.
- What else can we do to make our multi-lingual web application.

Internationalization on the Java Platform

The Java platform has substantial support for internationalization. The foundation of this support is formed by two classes—`Locale` and `ResourceBundle`. The first of these classes, `java.util.Locale`, basically defines a language, but also can be narrowed down to a country (to distinguish, say, between British English, and American English) or even to a variant of the language (Chinese traditional versus Chinese simplified, as an example).

The `Locale` class has many useful constants that allow us to obtain a properly configured instance of it, like `Locale.ENGLISH` or `Locale.GERMAN`. We can also use a constructor of this class, which gives us more flexibility. For example, we can create `new Locale("en", "UK")` for British English, or new `Locale("de", "CH")` for Swiss German. You can find more information on the subject in Java API at `http://java.sun.com` website.

The second class, `ResouceBundle`, represents resources that are specific to a given Locale. However, we don't need to know anything about this class as it is managed by Tapestry behind the scenes. All we need to do as Tapestry developers is to create a proper Locale and to provide resources for it.

Internationalization in Tapestry

Multi-lingual support works in Tapestry as follows:

If several locales are supported by a Tapestry web application and some user visits the application for the first time, Tapestry checks for the preferred language of the user's browser (you can set the preferred language in Internet Explorer by going to **Tools** | **Internet Options** | **General** | **Appearance** | **Languages**, in Firefox, by going to **Preferences** | **Advanced** | **General** | **Languages**). If the web application supports the preferred language, Tapestry displays it in that language; otherwise the application is displayed in the default language.

While doing this, Tapestry applies some reasonable logic. Say, if the preferred language as set in the browser is either English (United Kingdom) or English (United States) and the supported locales are defined as "en" and "de", Tapestry will display the web application in the "en" locale.

If, while working with the application, the user switches the locale (you will see soon how this can be done), Tapestry will remember the choice by setting a special cookie into the user's browser. The Next time the same user visits the application, Tapestry will check to see if such a locale-remembering cookie exists, and if it does, the application will be displayed in the locale specified by the cookie, even if the browser's preferred language is different.

The First thing we need to do to enable multi-lingual support in a Tapestry application is to edit the `contributeApplicationDefaults` method of the `AppModule` class that was automatically generated for us by Maven in the very beginning. If we decided to support two languages, English and German, the method should look like this:

```
public static void contributeApplicationDefaults(
                    MappedConfiguration<String, String> configuration)
{
  configuration.add("tapestry.supported-locales", "en,de");
}
```

Next step is perhaps the most important part of internationalization—providing the appropriate message catalogs for the supported locales. In the previous chapters, we have already created the application-wide message catalog, `app.properties` file. Now it is the time to learn more about message catalogs.

Creating and Using Message Catalogs

Just to remind you—a application-wide, or root, message catalog should be placed into the `WEB-INF` directory. Its extension should be `properties`, and its name should be the same as the name of Tapestry filter defined in the deployment descriptor `web.xml`—hence `app.properties` in our case. Here is the content of this file accumulated throughout the previous chapters:

```
Country.GERMANY=Germany
country.uk=United Kingdom
COUNTRY.USA=United States
dateOfBirth-label=Birth Date
email-regexp=^([a-zA-Z0-9_.-])+@(([a-zA-Z0-9-])+.)+
([a-zA-Z0-9]{2,4})+$
email-regexp-message=Email address is not valid.
age-min-message=You are too young! You should be at least %s years
old.
age-max-message=People do not live that long!
passwords-dont-match=Two versions of password do not match.
authentication-failed=We couldn't authenticate you. Try again or
register.
firstName-required-message=You cannot have a celebrity without a
name!
```

If we look through the entries, we shall realize that some of them might be needed by several pages of our growing application, while others are very much page-specific. For example, the message with the key `authentication-failed` is certainly needed only for that single page where we are checking user's credentials.

The application will work fine if we continue to keep all the messages in the root catalogue, but if we do so, and as the number of pages in the application increases, this catalog can quickly become unmanageable. This is why Tapestry provides an opportunity to have page-specific message catalogs that contain messages for only one page. We can also have component-specific method catalogs, as you will see in the next chapter.

Right now, let's create a message catalog for the **Start** page. The trick is that in the current version of Tapestry, message catalogs for pages should be placed under the same structure of subdirectories under which page classes exist in their packages. Say, if the fully qualified name of the **Start** page is `com.packtpub.celebrities.pages.Start`, and so the page class can be found under the corresponding structure of subdirectories (`com\packtpub\celebrities\pages`). Its message catalog, to be successfully found by Tapestry, should be placed under the same structure of subdirectories.

The easiest way to achieve this is to create a `Start.properties` file and place it straight inside the `com.packtpub.celebrities.pages` package in your IDE—the same package that contains the source code of the `Start` page class.

In NetBeans, right-click on the mentioned package and select **New | File/Folder...** In the dialog that opens, select **Other** for **Categories** and **Empty File** for **File Types**. Click on **Next** and name the new file, `Start.properties`. Then click on **Finish**. The new file will appear next to the source code files.

In Eclipse you can achieve the same result by right-clicking on the source package and then selecting **New | Other...**, and then, under the **General** category, **File**.

Now we can move the `authentication-failed` message from the root message catalogue to the `Start.properties` file. Also, as a part of the process of page internationalization, we need to "externalize" all the strings used on that page—titles, labels, links text and so on—everything that should be later displayed in different languages.

You can create any reasonable key for the messages that you create. For example, this is what the contents of the `Start.properties` file could look like after the externalization is completed:

```
authentication-failed=We couldn't authenticate you. Try again or
register.
login-here=Log in here
```

```
user-name=User Name
password=Password
or-register=Or register
log-in=Log In
```

The page title and header—**Celebrity Collector**, also needs to be externalized, but it will most likely be needed by the other pages too, so let's add the following message to the root message catalog, `app.properties` file:

```
celebrity-collector=Celebrity Collector
```

We also need to do something with the page template so that it can retrieve the appropriate strings from message catalogs. There are actually a few slightly different ways to retrieve a message, let's try them all.

The first option is to use an expansion with the `message:` prefix in it. Here is how the upper portion of the page template will look after applying such expansion:

```
<html xmlns:t="http://tapestry.apache.org/schema/tapestry_5_0_0.xsd">
  <head>
    <title>${message:celebrity-collector}</title>
    <link rel="stylesheet" href="${styles}" type="text/css"/>
  </head>
  <body>
    <h1>${message:celebrity-collector}</h1>
    <p> ${message:login-here}: </p>
```

When Tapestry sees an ordinary expansion like `${styles}` in the listing above, it will go to the page class and try to retrieve an appropriate value from there. However, when it sees the `message:` prefix inside the expansion, it will understand that what follows after the prefix is the key into the message catalogs that are available to the page. Both page-specific and root catalogs are made available to it, but the page-specific one is checked first. If there are two messages with the same key in different catalogs, the most specific one will be used. For example, the message in the page-specific catalogue will override the one in the root catalog.

In the example above, the `login-here` message will be easily found in the page's catalog, but for the `celebrity-collector` message Tapestry will have to look into the root one. All this works automatically though.

The other way we can obtain a message in the page template is by using `message:` prefix inside an attribute value. The following fragment of the **Start** page template demonstrates this approach:

```
<tr>
  <td>
    <t:label t:for="userName">
      Label for the first text box</t:label>:
  </td>
  <td>
    <input type="text" t:id="userName" t:type="TextField"
      t:label="message:user-name" t:validate="required"/>
  </td>
</tr>
<tr>
  <td>
    <t:label t:for="password">The second label</t:label>:
  </td>
  <td>
    <input type="text" t:id="password"
      t:label="message:password" t:type="PasswordField"
      t:validate="required"/>
  </td>
</tr>
```

You already know two prefixes—`literal:` which tells Tapestry that whatever follows should be taken literally, and `prop:` which tells Tapestry that the value should be provided by a property of the page class. So here is the third one, `message:` which tells Tapestry that the value should be obtained from the message catalog using the provided key.

Another variety of this approach is to use an expansion inside of an attribute value, as the following fragment demonstrates:

```
<tr>
  <td colspan="2" align="center">
    <input type="submit" value="${message:log-in}"/>
  </td>
</tr>
```

We can also obtain a message in the code of the page class, not only in the template. To quickly demonstrate this opportunity, we shall do something not very logical. We shall obtain a text for the "Or register" link from a property of the page class. This is for demonstration purposes only; normally we would use a `${message:key}` expansion here. However, this approach may become very useful if you format the message in the code, perhaps inserting some parameters into it (for instance, using the `format` method of the `MessageFormat` class) and then make it available to the page template. Here is how our example will look in the template:

```
<a href="#" t:type="PageLink"
  t:page="Registration">${orRegisterLabel}</a>
```

And here is the method that returns a text for this link:

```
@Inject

private Messages messages;
public String getOrRegisterLabel()
{
  return messages.get("or-register");
}
```

Through the `Messages` object, Tapestry gives our code access to message catalogs—both page-specific and root ones.

Providing a German Message Catalog

What we have done so far is an example of internationalization—we made the page able to display itself in different languages by moving all of its textual messages and labels into message catalogs. Now we need to localize the page into the German locale by providing a German message catalogs.

Whenever Tapestry retrieves some file for the needs of the application—a page template, an image, a message catalog or almost anything else—it tries to do that in a proper locale. For this, it tries to find a file with an appropriate, locale-specific suffix appended to the file name. If the current locale of the application is German, and Tapestry wants to find a message catalog for the **Start** page, it will be looking for a file named `Start_de.properties`. If the current locale is English, Tapestry will be looking for the `Start_en.properties` file. If it finds such a file, it uses it, if not, it uses the default file, without any suffixes, which is called `Start.properties`.

So what we need to do now is to create another file, this time named `Start_de.properties`, in the same way as we created `Start.properties`, and fill it with messages translated into German. I do not know German, but at this stage of development perfect translation is not required. What is actually required is a set of strings that will look like German, or at least will be clearly distinguishable from English messages and labels.

In practice, I use an online tool, like Babel Fish Translation (`http://babelfish.altavista.com/`) or Google Language Tools (`http://www.google.com/language_tools`). Here is what I was able to produce:

```
authentication-failed=Wir könnten nicht dich beglaubigen. Versuchen
noch einmal oder Register.
login-here=LOGON hier
user-name=Benutzer-Name
password=Kennwort
or-register=Oder Register
log-in=LOGON
```

This is probably a very rough approximation of a proper German text, but it will do for now. At a later stage, when preparing the close to completion application for deployment, we shall send all the message catalogs to real translators, and they will do everything properly.

Okay, we have German messages ready, but to see them displayed by the application, we need to learn how to switch the application's locale first.

Switching Locale

Basically, to switch the locale of our web application, all we need to do is to tell Tapestry which locale we want to see as current. Tapestry has a special service named `PersistentLocale`. To get access to this service we simply inject it into the page. This is how it looks:

```
@Inject
private PersistentLocale persistentLocale;
```

And then we use the service's `set` method to set the new locale, like this:

```
persistentLocale.set(Locale.GERMAN);
```

It's that simple! However, to make this functionality work, we need to run the above line of code in some event handler. For simplicity, let's use the `ActionLink` component at this stage.

We could use two links, one of them saying **Switch to German**, another **Switch to English**, but, it will be slightly closer to a real life functionality if we use just one link, **Switch Locale**, and it will do the job whatever the current locale is. Here is how such a link could look in the page template:

```
<p align="right">
  <t:actionlink t:id="switchlocale">
    Switch Locale
  </t:actionlink>
</p>
```

Before writing an event handler for this link, let's inject into the page yet another resource—the current application's locale:

```
@Inject
private Locale currentLocale;
```

And here is the event handler:

```
@OnEvent(component="switchlocale")
void changeLocale()
{
  if (currentLocale.equals(Locale.GERMAN))
  {
    persistentLocale.set(Locale.ENGLISH);
  }
  else
  {
    persistentLocale.set(Locale.GERMAN);
  }
}
```

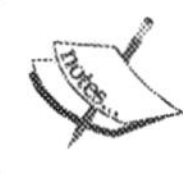

Please note that to compare locale objects, you will need to use the `equals` method. Something like `currentLocale == Locale.GERMAN` will not work for you.

Now, running the application, you should see the already familiar page, plus the new link on it:

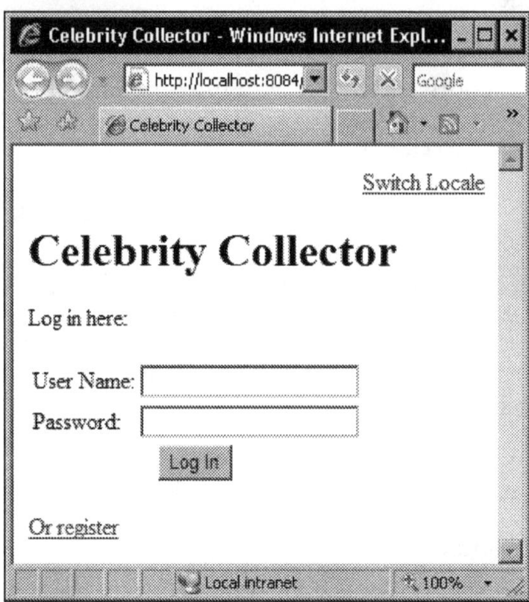

Click on the **Switch Locale** link, and the language of the application will change:

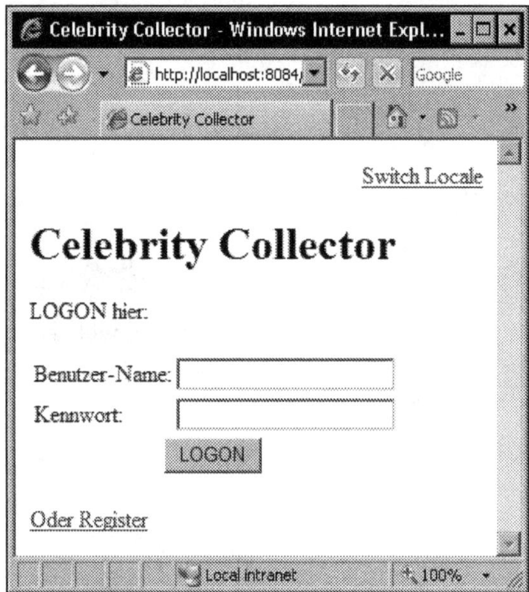

We have just internationalized our first Tapestry page! And it was easy, wasn't it? What happened here is that when the locale of the application was switched to German, Tapestry looked for a German message catalog for the page, and found the `Start_de.properties` file. So it took the labels from it, except for the one, with `celebrity-collector` key. It kept looking for a German root message catalog that would look like `app_de.properties`, but couldn't find any. So it took the default root catalog, `app.properties`, and retrieved the value for the `celebrity-collector` key from there.

Everything works now, but there is still a space for an enhancement. Wouldn't it be better if the text of the link for switching the locale was more informative? Imagine that a German-speaking user came to the application and cannot understand anything because it is displayed in English. He or she will probably look around in search for some hint, and if they see a link saying **Deutsch**, they will certainly click on it. So let's change the text of the link so that it says **Deutsch** when the current locale of the application is English, and **English** when the current locale of the application is German.

Here is how the link will look now in the page template:

```
<p align="right">
  <t:actionlink t:id="switchlocale">
    ${localeLabel}
  </t:actionlink>
</p>
```

And here is the code that will make it work:

```
@Persist
private String localeLabel;

public String getLocaleLabel()
{
  if (localeLabel == null)
  {
    if (currentLocale.equals(Locale.GERMAN))
    {
      localeLabel =
        new Locale("en").getDisplayName(Locale.ENGLISH);
    }
    else
    {
      localeLabel =
        new Locale("de").getDisplayName(Locale.GERMAN);
    }
  }
```

```
    return localeLabel;
  }
  @OnEvent(component="switchlocale")
  void changeLocale()
  {
    localeLabel = currentLocale.getDisplayName(currentLocale);
    if (currentLocale.equals(Locale.GERMAN))
    {
      persistentLocale.set(Locale.ENGLISH);
    }
    else
    {
      persistentLocale.set(Locale.GERMAN);
    }
  }
```

Run the application, and it should work and look quite well now. But wouldn't it look even better if, we also displayed an image of the flag appropriate for the alternative locale? Say, when the link says **Deutsch**, we could display the German flag. Let's try this.

Internationalization of Images

First of all, let us simply display an image of German flag next to the link. Find an appropriate image (or simply take the one named `flag.gif` from the source code package for this chapter) and put it into the `assets` folder, where we already have our `styles.css` file. Place a regular `<img>` tag somewhere in the page template, but the source for it will be provided by an expansion, like this:

```
<p align="right">
  <img src="${flag}"/>
  <t:actionlink t:id="switchlocale">
    ${localeLabel}
  </t:actionlink>
</p>
```

Now we need to add some code to the page class in order to make the `flag.gif` image available to the page template. Here is the code that will do the job:

```
@Inject
@Path("context:/assets/flag.gif")
private Asset flag;

public Asset getFlag()
{
  return flag;
}
```

This way you can obtain any kind of asset in your code—image, stylesheet, text or XML file—anything at all, as long as it is located in an appropriate directory of your application. When it comes to an image however, there is a simpler way to do that. You will not need to add any code to the page class at all if you write the image tag like this:

```
<img src="${asset:context:/assets/flag.gif}"/>
```

Run the application, and you should see the flag displayed like this:

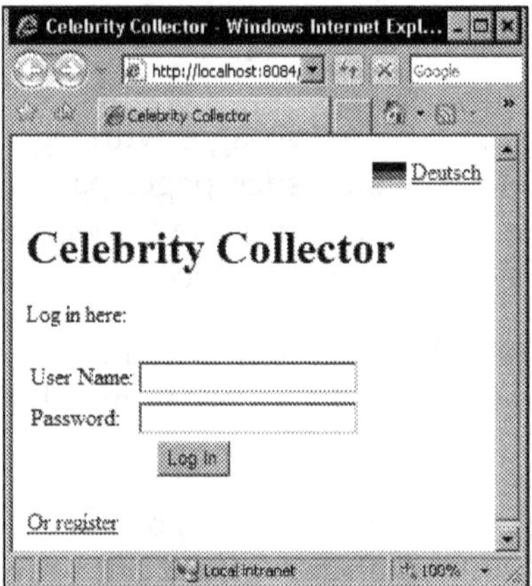

This however, is not enough, as changing locale doesn't change a flag. When the current locale is German, we want an English flag to be displayed in assistance to those users who might want to switch the language back to English. To enable this, all you have to do is to place an appropriate flag image into the `assets` directory and name it `flag_de.gif` (again, you will find such an image in the source code for the chapter). Do this, and whenever you will have current locale set to German, the English flag will be displayed on the page:

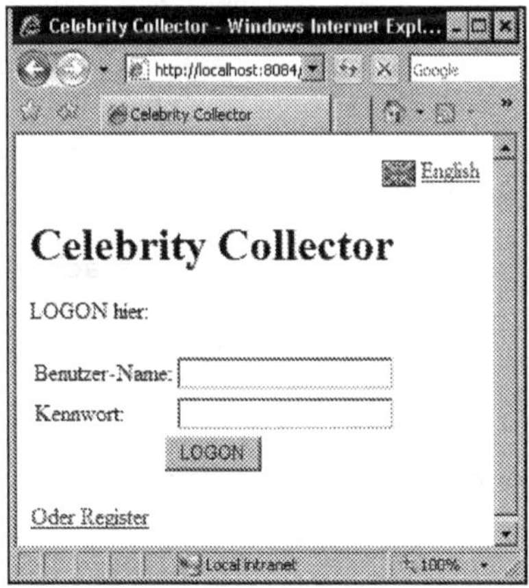

As you see, most of what we have to do to internationalize a web application is to provide the appropriate resources in different languages, and then to write a tiny bit of code to make those resources available to the application, and to be able to change the current locale. All the low-level work of obtaining and using the correct resources is done for us by Tapestry.

Sometimes, we don't need to write any code at all, as the next section shows.

Using Localized Templates

Many applications have pages with significant textual content and very few components on them, if any. These can be pages with legal information, terms and conditions and so on. Internationalizing such pages paragraph by paragraph, placing all text into message catalogs, doesn't sound like a good idea. Fortunately, Tapestry has an alternative solution for this purpose—localized templates.

Let's add yet another page to the application, and this one will be extremely simple. First add a new empty class to the package containing all the other page classes and name it `Terms`.

Next, add to the application two new templates, one of them named `Terms.tml`, another one `Terms_de.tml`. In real life we would put some lengthy English text into the `Terms.tml` file while its German translation would go into the `Terms_de.tml`. However to save space, we'll make the content of these files very simple, just enough to see that they are different. This is what `Terms.tml` might look like:

```
<html xmlns:t="http://tapestry.apache.org/schema/tapestry_5_0_0.xsd">
  <head>
    <title>Terms and Conditions</title>
  </head>
  <body>
    <p>Miscellaneous terms and conditions can be found
      here.</p>
  </body>
</html>
```

And here is the possible content for `Terms_de.tml`:

```
<html xmlns:t="http://tapestry.apache.org/schema/tapestry_5_0_0.xsd">
  <head>
    <title>Terms and Conditions in German</title>
  </head>
  <body>
    <p>Same terms and conditions but in German.</p>
  </body>
</html>
```

Finally, we need to add to one of the existing pages a link that will allow us to see the **Terms** page. We could place this link somewhere at the bottom of the **Start** page:

```
<p>
  <t:pagelink t:page="terms">Terms and Conditions</t:pagelink>
</p>
```

If you now run the application and click on the new link, if the current locale is English you should see the text that you've put into the `Terms.tml` template. However, if the current locale is German, you will see the text from the `Terms_de.tml` template. This is because, while loading the template for a page, Tapestry always tries to add the template that fits the current locale (and has an appropriate file name suffix). If there is no such localized template, it uses the default one, without any suffix.

Other Examples of Internationalization

If you remember, there is a drop-down list with country names on the **Registration** page. How could we display the names of the countries in German? Nothing can be easier. Currently, the English labels for this drop-down list are defined in the root message catalog like this:

```
Country.GERMANY=Germany
country.uk=United Kingdom
COUNTRY.USA=United States
```

We can create a separate message catalog for the **Registration** page if we wish so and move these entries there, or leave everything as it is in case the same messages might be needed for some other page. To provide the countries labels in German, all we need is to create an appropriate German message catalog, with German values for the labels.

Let's create a new file, `app_de.properties` in WEB-INF directory. We could translate all the contents of the `app.properties` file, put the translations into the new message catalog and then internationalize all the labels of the **Registration** page. However, you already know how to do that, so let's leave that work as an exercise for you. For now, let's just provide German labels for the Country enumeration, like this:

```
country.germany=Deutschland
country.uk=Grossbritannien
country.usa=Staaten von Amerika
```

Run the application and at the **Start** page change the locale to German and then proceed to the **Registration** page. You should see that now all the countries' names are displayed in German:

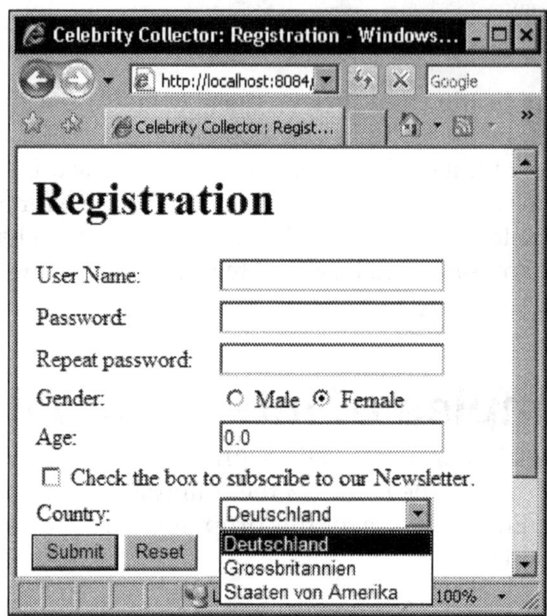

Similarly, we can easily internationalize the names of the columns of the `Grid` component. Let's do one more exercise. Create two files, `ShowAll.properties` and `ShowAll_de.properties` in the `com.packtpub.celebrities.pages package`, as explained above. Move the `dateOfBirth-label` message from `app.properties` to `ShowAll.properties`, then put the following content into the `ShowAll_de.properties` file (or make a legible translation if you know the language):

```
dateOfBirth-label=Geburt Datum
lastName-label=Letzter Name
firstName-label=Vorname
occupation-label=Besetzung
```

Run the application, set the current locale to German and log in to see the collection. Note the column titles of the table are in German now:

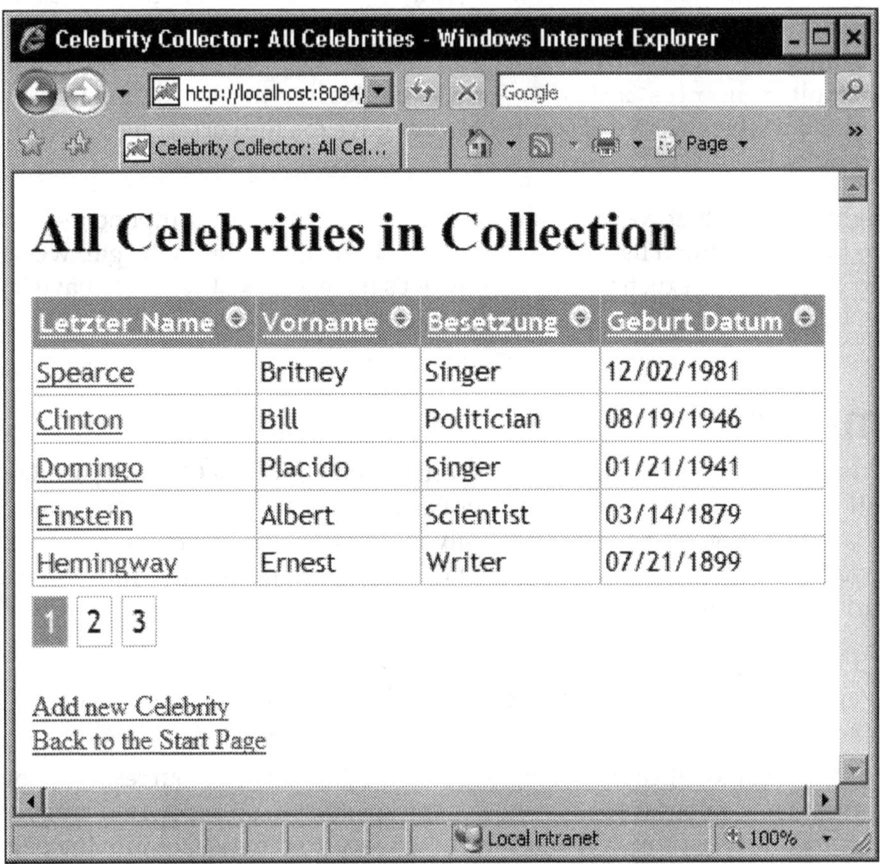

Guess what you need to do to internationalize the labels of the fields of `BeanEditForm`? Exactly the same—just provide an appropriate message catalog and put messages into it with keys like `firstName-label`. The same holds true for error messages and any other contents of message catalogs, of course, only the keys will be different (like `age-min-message`, for example).

In fact, as soon as you realize that for any resource requested by the application, Tapestry tries to find its localized version, you will see many different opportunities. For example, in my first Tapestry project I wanted to create a drop-down list, like above, but containing all (well, most) countries of the world. That application was bi-lingual, English and German, so the application was required to display the countries' names in one of these languages depending on the current locale.

At that time enumerations didn't exist in the Java language, and anyway, it would be hardly reasonable to create an enumeration with so many options in it. I had the lists of countries in XML files and I was going to use the JDOM library for easy XML manipulation. All I needed was to get a proper XML file for the current locale. So I simply named the list in German as `countries_de.xml` and left the list in English as the default, `countries.xml`. Then I put both files into the assets directory and retrieved them when needed. Tapestry always gave me the correct file depending on the current locale.

You might say here that we don't know enough about `Select` components yet in order to fill a drop-down list with an arbitrary content, but this is the gap we are going to close in the next chapter. For now, let's have a look at what we have learned so far.

Summary

In this chapter we have internationalized only one page of the **Celebrity Collector** application and only one enumeration, but as soon as you know the basics, you should be able to continue work, and easily internationalize the remaining pages. What you have discovered about support of internationalization in Tapestry can be summarized as follows:

- First of all, we need to tell Tapestry which language this web application is going to support by providing a list of locales in the `contributeApplicationDefaults` method of the `AppModule` class.
- To internationalize labels, messages and other string resources, we provide message catalogs (root as well as page-specific) in all supported languages, name the files properly, and then insert localized messages into the page templates using one of the few available approaches.
- To display an internationalized image, we provide as many images as there are supported locales, name them appropriately and then make them available for the page as assets (there are two ways we can do that).
- If a page contains a lot of text, it can be more efficient to use localized templates for it, rather than to localize it paragraph-by-paragraph.
- To internationalize enumerations, the `Grid` and `BeanEditForm` components used in the application, we simply provide appropriate messages in the message catalogs.

Did you notice one annoying thing about our web application? As soon as we want to make the `styles.css` stylesheet available for a page, we need to do the same steps again and again—insert a link into the page template, make the stylesheet available to the page class as an asset and add a getter method to the page. Could we somehow avoid copying and pasting the same code into different pages?

It would also be nice to have a link for switching locale on every page, but in that case we would need to write even more code again and again, on every page.

As soon as we notice that some content or functionality is reproduced in the application more than just once, we should think of creating a custom component. This is exactly what we are going to learn in the next chapter—how to create interesting, powerful, non-trivial components that can be used and reused throughout the application, or even in many different applications.

8 Creating Custom Components

There are a few different reasons why one might want to create a custom component. Quite often there are pieces of interface or functionality that are replicated on different pages, so we have to write the same code again and again until we package the repeating pattern into a custom component.

Also, every framework is necessarily limited in terms of the number of components that come pre-packaged with it. Now and again we shall find that the component we need wasn't created by anyone. Or maybe the existing component just doesn't fit our needs, or the requirements of our clients. A developer friendly framework should provide an opportunity to easily extend it by being able to creating custom components. Tapestry does just this.

In particular, we are going to learn:

- What it takes to create a Tapestry 5 component.
- How to create a `Border` component that will contain all the elements common for all the pages and that will provide an easy way to ensure a common layout.
- How to unleash the power of the `Select` component by creating a custom model.
- How to create an alternative component for date input that consists of three `Select` components.
- How to create a universal locale switcher that will automatically adapt to those locales that are supported by the application.
- How to create a custom Tapestry service if the existing services do not provide the functionality we need.
- How to package custom components into a library and make them available for everyone.

How to Create a Tapestry 5 Component

In fact, components in Tapestry 5 are very similar to pages. They can have a template that looks pretty similar to a Tapestry page. The component's Java class is a POJO, just like a page class. In this class, we can inject different resources and services, create event handlers and so on—anything we would normally do in a page class.

The difference between a page and a component is that components often have parameters—pieces of information passed to them to influence their appearance and functionality. Also, page classes are always created in the `pages` sub-package of the application's package structure. Whereas component classes always go into the `components` sub-package, and their templates should be placed into this sub-package as well (or, more precisely, the templates should be placed under the same structure of subdirectories as component classes).

There can also be components without templates. If they need to display themselves in some way, they generate any mark up in their Java code. We are not going to create such components, but if you want to see an example, please refer to the Tapestry 5 User Guide (`http://tapestry.apache.org/tapestry5/tapestry-core/guide/component-classes.html`).

In many cases, creating a custom component will be very similar to creating a custom page, and this will especially be true for the component created in the next section.

Creating the Border Component

In any real life web application, there is always some content that is repeated on many pages. Such content can include—logo, navigation menu, copyright message, standard links to legal information, contact page and so on. Also, there is almost always a link to a stylesheet in the page code, and if the application is internationalized, it might make sense to have a locale switcher on every page too.

It would be convenient to create all this content just once, and then reuse it on as many pages as we wish, and in this section we are going to build a component that will encapsulate all the common page elements.

Let's start by creating a template and a Java class. The steps required for creating them are the same as when creating a template and a class for a new page, with the only difference being that these should be created in the `com.packtpub.celebrity.components` package. Please create such a package and then add to it an empty Java class named `Border`. Also, add an empty file named `Border.tml` to the new package, in the same way as we add message catalogs to source code packages.

Here is possible content for the first version of the component template, `Border.tml` file:

```
<html xmlns:t="http://tapestry.apache.org/schema/tapestry_5_0_0.xsd">
  <head>
    <title>Celebrity Collector</title>
    <link rel="stylesheet"
      href="${asset:context:/assets/styles.css}"
      type="text/css"/>
  </head>
  <body>
    <p align="right">
      <img src="${asset:context:/assets/flag.gif}"
        align="middle"/>
      <t:actionlink t:id="switchlocale">
        ${localeLabel}
      </t:actionlink>
    </p>
    <t:body/>
  </body>
</html>
```

Basically, we have put here content that is common for every page, and only one element, `<t:body/>`, is something new for us. This is just a special Tapestry element; its only purpose is to be replaced by any page content that is surrounded by the `Border` component. You will see how this works soon.

We managed to configure the link to the stylesheet completely in the template, so no code in the component class will be needed. However, to enable locale switching, we are going to need some code; but we can simply copy it from the `Start` page class. The completed `Border` class should look like this:

```
package com.packtpub.celebrities.components;

import java.util.Locale;
import org.apache.tapestry.annotations.Inject;
import org.apache.tapestry.annotations.OnEvent;
import org.apache.tapestry.annotations.Persist;
import org.apache.tapestry.services.PersistentLocale;

public class Border
{
  @Inject
  private PersistentLocale persistentLocale;

  @Inject
  private Locale currentLocale;

  @Persist
  private String localeLabel;
  public String getLocaleLabel()
```

```
    {
      if (localeLabel == null)
      {
        if (currentLocale.equals(Locale.GERMAN))
        {
          localeLabel =
            new Locale("en").getDisplayName(Locale.ENGLISH);
        } else {
          localeLabel =
            new Locale("de").getDisplayName(Locale.GERMAN);
        }
      }
      return localeLabel;
    }

    @OnEvent(component="switchlocale")
    void changeLocale()
    {
      localeLabel = currentLocale.getDisplayName(currentLocale);
      if (currentLocale.equals(Locale.GERMAN))
      {
        persistentLocale.set(Locale.ENGLISH);
      }
      else
      {
        persistentLocale.set(Locale.GERMAN);
      }
    }
  }
```

Also, to see immediately that the stylesheet is available to the page, we can add a couple of simple style definitions to the `styles.css` file, but this is certainly optional:

```
body, table, input, select
{
    font-family: Verdana, Arial, Helvetica, sans-serif;
    font-size: 10pt;
}

h1
{
    font-family: Arial, Helvetica, sans-serif;
    font-size: 20pt;
    font-weight: bold;
    color: #204060;
}
```

Next, we need to change all the page templates, removing all the common content from them and surrounding the remaining content with the `Border` component. The following example shows the changed version of the **AddCelebrity** page. Please transform all the other pages in a similar way:

```
<t:border xmlns:t="http://tapestry.apache.org/schema/tapestry_5_0_
0.xsd">
  <h1>Adding New Celebrity</h1>
  <t:beaneditform t:id="celebrityEditor"
      t:object="celebrity"
      t:submitLabel="Save" t:model="model">
    <t:parameter name="biography">
      <t:label for="biography"/>
      <t:textarea t:id="biography"
        t:value="celebrity.biography" cols="30" rows="5"/>
    </t:parameter>
  </t:beaneditform>
</t:border>
```

We had to declare Tapestry name space inside of the opening tag of the border component; otherwise it would not be clear to any XML parser what exactly the `t:` prefix means.

You can now see that the opening and closing tags of the `Border` component are surrounding the content of the page. This content will replace the `<t:body/>` element that we placed inside of the `Border` template when the page is rendered.

The final step is to remove any code that is related to common functionality from page classes, anything that serves for providing the stylesheet or switching the locale. We also need to remove the locale switcher from the **Start** page.

After all this is done, run the application, and you should immediately see that all its pages have a certain new style and a locale switcher at the top of them. Here is how the **ShowAll** page should look now:

This is already closer to a real life application, but all those "quick and dirty" links that connect pages to each other are not a proper means for navigation. We need a navigation menu.

Adding a Navigation Menu

Let me admit from the very beginning that I am not going to show a production quality menu. That would require a serious use of styles, and I don't want to create such a distraction for you. We are going to use a simple table for layout, and a set of links. This will provide a decent foundation, and you can add any kind of styling to it when you have time.

All work will concentrate on the `Border` component template. Here is what we want to see when the application is rendered on the **AddCelebrity** page:

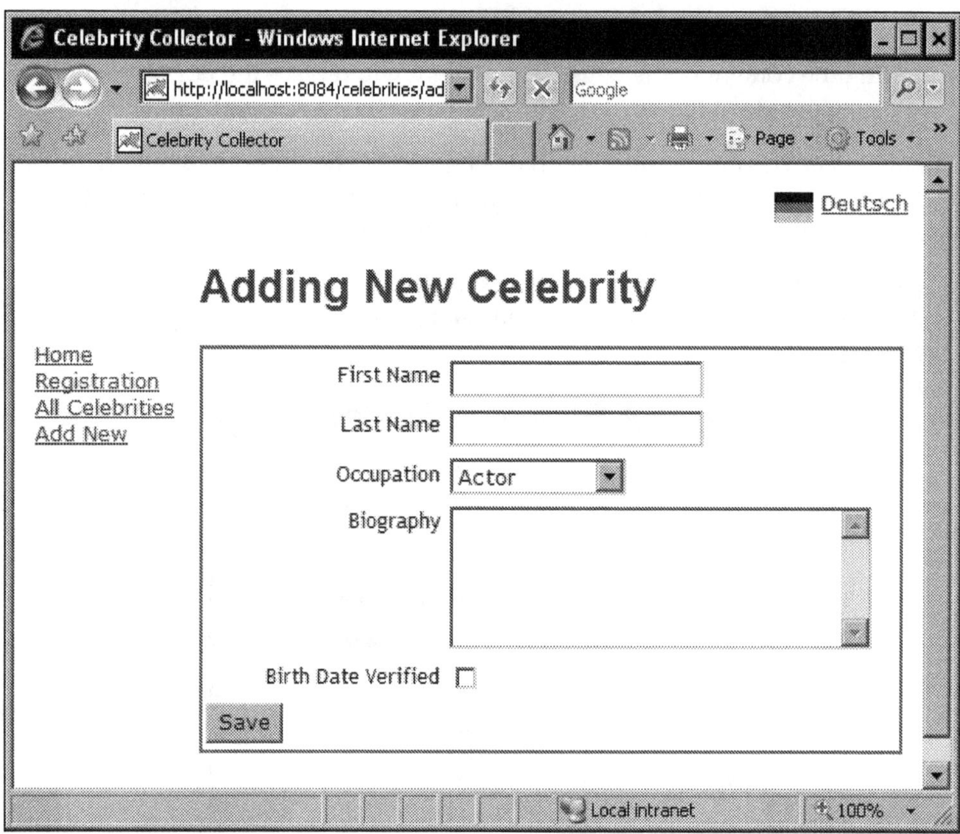

And here are the additions to the `Border.tml` template that we need to make to achieve this:

```
<html xmlns:t="http://tapestry.apache.org/schema/tapestry_5_0_0.xsd">
  <head>
    <title>Celebrity Collector</title>
    <link rel="stylesheet"
      href="${asset:context:/assets/styles.css}"
      type="text/css"/>
  </head>
  <body>
    <p align="right">
      <img src="${asset:context:/assets/flag.gif}"
          align="middle"/>
        <t:actionlinkt:id="switchlocale">
          ${localeLabel}
        </t:actionlink>
    </p>
    <table width="100%">
      <tr>
        <td width="100" valign="top">
          <br/>
          <br/>
          <br/>
          <t:pagelink t:page="Start">Home</t:pagelink><br/>
          <t:pagelink t:page="Registration">
            Registration</t:pagelink><br/>
          <t:pagelink t:page="ShowAll">
            All Celebrities</t:pagelink><br/>
          <t:pagelink t:page="AddCelebrity">
            Add New</t:pagelink>
        </td>
        <td>
          <t:body/>
        </td>
      </tr>
    </table>
  </body>
</html>
```

Now we can easily navigate from page to page, although we shall not be able to see the **ShowAll** page until we log in properly. This navigation menu however, is far from being perfect. There are at least two enhancements that we might want to add:

1. There is no need to display the navigation menu on the **Start** page, at least until the user hasn't logged in.
2. There is no need to link a page to itself, for example when we are at the **ShowAll** page, the **All Celebrities** link could be disabled.

For any of these tasks, the `Border` component will need to know which page renders it at that moment. We can easily find the class name of the page that contains the component using the already familiar `ComponentResources` class, like this:

```
@Inject
private ComponentResources resources;

private String getPageName()
{
  Component page = resources.getContainer();
  return page.getClass().getName();
}
```

We can also provide a few simple methods that will check if the current page is the **Start** page, the **Registration** and so on—as many methods as there are links in the navigation menu:

```
public boolean isNotStart()
{
  return !getPageName().equals(Start.class.getName());
}

public boolean isRegistration()
{
  return getPageName().equals(Registration.class.getName());
}

public boolean isShowAll()
{
  return getPageName().equals(ShowAll.class.getName());
}

public boolean isAddCelebrity()
{
  return getPageName().equals(AddCelebrity.class.getName());
}
```

Finally, we can surround the links with an `If` component that will hide the menu when the displayed page is the **Start** page, and add a `disabled` parameter to the `PageLink` components:

```
<t:if t:test="notStart">
  <t:pagelink t:page="Start">
    Home</t:pagelink><br/>
  <t:pagelink t:page="Registration"
      t:disabled="registration">
    Registration</t:pagelink><br/>
  <t:pagelink t:page="ShowAll" t:disabled="showAll">
    All Celebrities</t:pagelink><br/>
  <t:pagelink t:page="AddCelebrity"
      t:disabled="addCelebrity">
    Add New</t:pagelink>
</t:if>
```

When a `PageLink`'s `disabled` parameter is set to `true`, the text surrounded by the component will be rendered, but there will be no link associated with it—exactly as we wanted. Run the application and make sure that it works properly.

There is still one problem about the `Border` component however. The browser title bar displays the same title—**Celebrity Collector**—for all the pages. This might not be a big deal for human users, but search engines expect each page of a web application to have a unique title, corresponding to the page's content, and we need to ensure that.

Using a Parameter

The most natural solution for displaying a page-specific title is to pass this title to the `Border` component as a parameter, and this is very easy to do. First of all, let's prepare the component's template to display the title:

```
<head>
  <title>Celebrity Collector: ${pageTitle}</title>
  <link rel="stylesheet"
        href="${asset:context:/assets/styles.css}"
        type="text/css"/>
</head>...
```

Next, we need to define the parameter in the component class. Add the following lines of code to `Border.java`:

```
@Parameter(required = true, defaultPrefix = "literal")
private String pageTitle;

public String getPageTitle()
{
  return pageTitle;
}
```

The parameter is defined as mandatory here, which probably makes sense. If it is not provided to the component, Tapestry will throw an exception. However, we could also define it as optional and then perhaps provide a default value, like this:

```
@Parameter
private String pageTitle = "Default Title";
```

Also, we have defined that the default prefix for this parameter is literal, otherwise it will be prop.

Finally, we need to add this parameter to the `Border` component on all pages. Here is how it will look for the **ShowAll** page, as an example:

```
<t:border
  t:pageTitle="All Celebrities in Collection" xmlns:t="http://
tapestry.apache.org/schema/tapestry_5_0_0.xsd">
```

Please provide some reasonable value for the page title on the other pages too. If you run the application now, you should see that a unique title is displayed for each page, like the following screenshot shows:

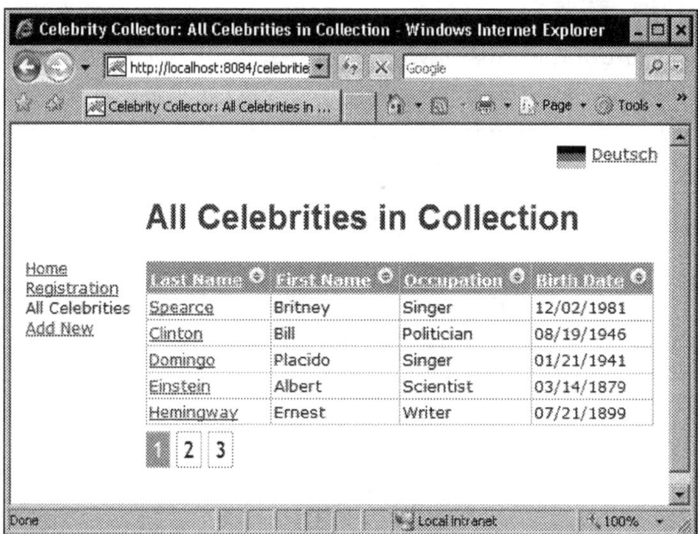

That's it, we have created our first custom component, and it was not more difficult than developing an ordinary page. Thanks to the `Border` component, we can now reuse common content and functionality in all the pages of our application. This is not the kind of component that you will want to package and give to your friends though, as it is very much application-specific. However in the next section, we shall prepare ourselves for creating a more universal component.

Unleashing the Power of Select Component

Before going further, we need to learn how to use all the capabilities that were put into the `Select` component by the creators of Tapestry. This component can be very convenient, and it will be definitely a popular constituent for all sorts of custom components, including those that we are going to create further in this chapter.

Let's remind ourselves that the `Select` component is defined on a page like this:

```
<t:select t:model="aModel" t:value="aValue"/>
```

The `model` parameter provides a number of items to display. These items can potentially be of any type—say, `Celebrity`. The model's responsibility is to explain to the component how exactly the objects should be displayed in the resulting drop-down list.

When one of the options is selected by the user and the form containing the `Select` component is submitted, the `value` parameter is used to pass the selected object to the page class. Again, we need to somehow instruct the `Select` component how exactly to retrieve a correct object based on the information available in the drop-down list.

Also, when the `Select` component is displayed by a page, it checks if the page property to which its `value` parameter is bound already has some value assigned to it, and if it does, it uses that value to decide which of the available options should be displayed as selected. Again, for a custom object, some instructions might be needed on how exactly to do this.

Since the `Select` component is designed to be very flexible, and to work with any custom class, it does require some additional instructions, as outlined above. We didn't have to provide any of them before when using the `Select` component with enumerations back in Chapter 4 because we used `EnumSelectModel`, which already contains all the information on how to deal with enumerations, but only with them.

If we want `Select` component to work with the `Celebrity` object, we need to create a model from scratch, let's name it `CelebritySelectModel`, and Tapestry expects it to be an implementation of `SelectModel` interface.

Before going into the details of constructing a custom model, it will be useful to refresh our memory by reviewing the basics of a HTML control named `SELECT`. Here is how it might look:

```
<select>
  <option value="value 1">Label 1</option>
  <option value="value 2">Label 2</option>
  <option value="value 3">Label 3</option>
</select>
```

We need to know that in HTML a drop-down list is made of a number of `<select>` elements, each corresponding to one of the displayed options. When the form surrounding a `SELECT` component is submitted, what actually gets sent to the server is the value of the selected option, the contents of its `value` attribute. The label serves only to help the user to find an appropriate option.

The Tapestry's `Select` component renders itself at runtime as an HTML `SELECT` control, and we have to explain to it, what exactly should be displayed as a label for our custom object. We need to tell it what will serve as a value and what will happen on the server when the value is submitted—how should Tapestry understand exactly which object was the user referring to.

For this we are going to extend one abstract class and use a couple of interfaces. Do not be frightened, as the amount of code we are going to write will not be overwhelming.

Creating an OptionModel

The first step in creating a custom model is to define how Tapestry should handle a single object of those to be displayed by the `Select` component. Here we shall be thinking in terms of a single `<option>` element and, fair enough, the name of the interface which we need to implement is `OptionModel`. This interface has four methods, but only two of them will be important for us:

- `String getLabel()` returns a label for the given option.
- `Object getValue()`—despite its name, this method should return not the contents for the `value` attribute but rather the object that corresponds to the option.

The other two methods, `isDisabled()` and `getAttributes()`, can be used to define whether the option should be disabled and what other attributes it should have. In many cases, they will return `false` and `null` respectively.

Here is the code for `CelebrityOptionModel`, an implementation of `OptionModel` that knows how to deal with the `Celebrity` object. Let's add this class to the `com.packtpub.celebrities.util` package:

```
package com.packtpub.celebrities.util;

import com.packtpub.celebrities.model.Celebrity;
import java.util.Map;
import org.apache.tapestry.OptionModel;
public class CelebrityOptionModel implements OptionModel
{
  private Celebrity celebrity;

  public CelebrityOptionModel(Celebrity celebrity)
  {
    this.celebrity = celebrity;
  }

  public String getLabel()
  {
    return celebrity.getFirstName() + " " +
      celebrity.getLastName();
  }

  public boolean isDisabled()
  {
    return false;
  }

  public Map<String, String> getAttributes()
  {
    return null;
  }

  public Object getValue()
  {
    return celebrity;
  }
}
```

The class is very simple, there is hardly anything worth commenting in it, so let's just proceed to the next step.

Creating a SelectModel

This is where we are going to create the model itself. The easiest way to do this is to extend the `AbstractSelectModel` class that comes with Tapestry. In this case we shall need to implement just two methods, and one of them will always return `null`.

- `List<OptionModel> getOptions()` – returns a list of options to display, using an implementation of `OptionModel` such as the one created above.
- `List<OptionGroupModel> getOptionGroups()` – used to display grouped options. Most often, only the `getOptions` method is used, and so this one should return null. And reversely, if what we want to display is a list of grouped options, the first method should return null while this one will do the job.

Here is how the class that works with Celebrity objects might look (please add it to the `com.packtpub.celebrities.util` package):

```
package com.packtpub.celebrities.util;

import com.packtpub.celebrities.model.Celebrity;
import java.util.ArrayList;
import java.util.List;
import org.apache.tapestry.OptionGroupModel;
import org.apache.tapestry.OptionModel;
import org.apache.tapestry.util.AbstractSelectModel;
public class CelebritySelectModel extends AbstractSelectModel
{
  private List<Celebrity> celebrities;

  public CelebritySelectModel(List<Celebrity> celebrities)
  {
    this.celebrities = celebrities;
  }

  public List<OptionGroupModel> getOptionGroups()
  {
    return null;
  }

  public List<OptionModel> getOptions()
  {
    List<OptionModel> list = new ArrayList<OptionModel>();
    for (Celebrity c : celebrities)
    {
      list.add(new CelebrityOptionModel(c));
    }
    return list;
  }
}
```

Again, almost nothing to comment on. We are passing a list of `Celebrity` objects to display a constructor and then create another list, wrapping each celebrity into `CelebrityOptionModel`.

We can provide this new model to a `Select` component through that component's `model` parameter, but it will not work until we provide an implementation of `ValueEncoder` for our `Celebrity` class.

Creating a ValueEncoder

The `ValueEncoder` interface has only two methods:

- `String toClient(Object obj)` that tells Tapestry what exactly should be used for the `value` attribute of `<option>`, corresponding to the given object.
- `Object toValue(String str)`, works in the opposite direction, given the contents of the `value` attribute of an option selected by the user, it should define which exactly object corresponds to this value.

Here is one possible implementation of this interface that will deal with the `Celebrity` object in our application:

```
package com.packtpub.celebrities.util;

import com.packtpub.celebrities.data.IDataSource;
import com.packtpub.celebrities.model.Celebrity;
import org.apache.tapestry.ValueEncoder;

public class CelebrityEncoder implements ValueEncoder
{
  private IDataSource source;
  public CelebrityEncoder(IDataSource source)
  {
    this.source = source;
  }

  public String toClient(Object obj)
  {
    return "" + ((Celebrity)obj).getId();
  }

  public Object toValue(String str)
  {
    return source.getCelebrityById(Integer.parseInt(str));
  }
}
```

You see that we are passing a data source as a parameter to this class' constructor. A celebrity's ID is stored in the `value` attribute, corresponding to its option, and when the form is submitted, that ID is used to retrieve the celebrity from the data source.

We have created three classes to tell the Select component how to deal with our custom class, but all the implementations were extremely simple, and we can reuse these classes whenever we want to select one of the celebrities in our application. Let's see how all this works together.

Selecting a Celebrity

Let's create a control that will allow us to use one of the available celebrities and provide a way to display exactly which celebrity was selected. I don't know what it will be used for, but it might certainly become valuable as we continue to develop the **Celebrity Collector** application. The control can be placed on any page for now, let it be `ShowAll` for example, and the end result might look like this:

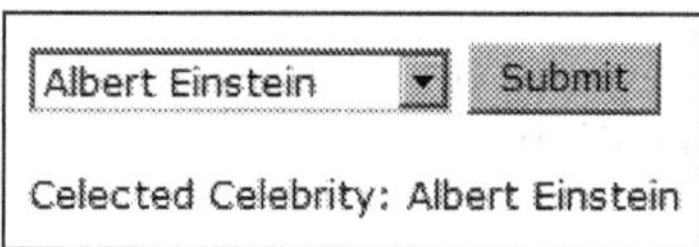

And here is how this will look in the page template:

```
<t:form>
  <t:select t:model="celebrityModel"
      t:value="selectedCelebrity"
      t:encoder="celebrityEncoder"/>
    <input type="submit" value="Submit"/>
</t:form>
<p>Selected Celebrity: ${selectedCelebrityName}</p>
```

You can see that the `Select` component has three parameters, in this case, `celebrityModel`, `selectedCelebrity` and `celebrityEncoder`. Here is how they can be provided by the page class:

```
public SelectModel getCelebrityModel()
{
  return new CelebritySelectModel(getAllCelebrities());
}

public ValueEncoder getCelebrityEncoder()
{
  return new CelebrityEncoder(dataSource);
}
```

```
@Persist
private Celebrity selectedCelebrity;

public Celebrity getSelectedCelebrity()
{
  return selectedCelebrity;
}

public void setSelectedCelebrity(Celebrity selectedCelebrity)
{
  this.selectedCelebrity = selectedCelebrity;
}
```

All the methods are one-liners! Even the method that provides the celebrity's name for the expansion looks more complex:

```
public String getSelectedCelebrityName()
{
  if (selectedCelebrity == null) return "";
  return selectedCelebrity.getFirstName() + " " +
    selectedCelebrity.getLastName();
}
```

If you run the application now, you should see a drop-down box with celebrities' names in it. If you select a celebrity and submit your selection, his or her name should appear properly underneath.

Now we know how to teach the `Select` component to do whatever we want it to do, and we are going to use this knowledge in the next sections to build some useful custom components.

DateInput Component

In Chapter 5 we became familiar with the `DateField` component. That component is implemented as a rather beautiful JavaScript-powered pop-up dialogue, and it can be very convenient and efficient in many cases.

However, there can be several reasons why we might want to have an alternative to `DatePicker`, one of them being the taste of our customers who, at least in my experience, often prefer to have a more traditional-looking control for date input. The natural alternative solution might look like three `Select` components—for days, months and years, working together as one unit. This is exactly the component we are going to create in the next sections.

This is what it is going to look like:

The size limit of this book does not allow us to fully develop the **Celebrity Collector** application, but we are going to prepare enough components for you to continue the work. For now, we are simply going to place such a component on one of the pages and make sure it works as we wish.

Before creating the component itself, we need to prepare the ground. To be able to select a day and a year, we are going to need a `Select` component that works with integers, which means that we need to create a `SelectModel` and accompanying classes that know how to deal with integers. After all that we have done with the `Celebrity` class, the code will be trivial, so let's just look at it, and I bet you will be able to figure out how it works without any help.

First of all, here is an implementation of `OptionModel`:

```
package com.packtpub.celebrities.util;

import java.util.Map;
import org.apache.tapestry.OptionModel;

public class IntegerOptionModel implements OptionModel
{
  private Number number;
  public IntegerOptionModel(Number num)
  {
    number = num;
  }

  public Map<String, String> getAttributes()
  {
    return null;
  }

  public String getLabel()
  {
    return "" + number;
  }

  public Object getValue()
  {
    return number;
  }

  public boolean isDisabled()
```

```
    {
      return false;
    }
  }
```

Next, we need to have a `SelectModel`, and this is how it could look:

```
package com.packtpub.celebrities.util;

import java.util.ArrayList;
import java.util.List;
import org.apache.tapestry.OptionGroupModel;
import org.apache.tapestry.OptionModel;
import org.apache.tapestry.util.AbstractSelectModel;

public class IntegerSelectModel extends AbstractSelectModel
{
  private List<OptionModel> options =
    new ArrayList<OptionModel>();
  public IntegerSelectModel(int numFrom, int numTo)
  {
    int increment = numTo > numFrom ? 1 : -1;
    for (int i = numFrom; i <= numTo; i += increment)
    {
      options.add(new IntegerOptionModel(i));
    }
  }
  public List<OptionGroupModel> getOptionGroups()
  {
    return null;
  }
  public List<OptionModel> getOptions()
  {
    return options;
  }
}
```

We are also going to need a `ValueEncoder`, as the current version of Tapestry 5 doesn't know how to deal with integers yet. But it will be very simple:

```
package com.packtpub.celebrities.util;
import org.apache.tapestry.ValueEncoder;
public class IntegerEncoder implements ValueEncoder
{
    public String toClient(Object i)
    {
      return i.toString();
    }
```

```
        public Object toValue(String s)
        {
          return new Integer(s);
        }
    }
```

To select a month, it will be convenient to have an appropriate enumeration and to use the already familiar `EnumSelectModel` with it. Here is a possible implementation for such an enumeration:

```
package com.packtpub.celebrities.util;
public enum Month
{
  JANUARY (0),
  FEBRUARY (1),
  MARCH (2),
  APRIL (3),
  MAY (4),
  JUNE (5),
  JULY (6),
  AUGUST (7),
  SEPTEMBER (8),
  OCTOBER (9),
  NOVEMBER (10),
  DECEMBER (11);
  private Month(int order)
  {
    this.order = order;
  }
  private int order;
  public int getOrder()
  {
    return order;
  }
}
```

Each month in this enumeration is associated with an integer number that is equal to the numeric value of the same month in the `java.util.Calendar` class.

Having all these basics ready, we can create a class and a template for the future component. They both should be placed into the `com.packtpub.celebrities.components` package, and let them be named `DateInput.java` and `DateInput.tml` correspondingly. Here is the content for the component template:

```
<html xmlns:t="http://tapestry.apache.org/schema/tapestry_5_0_0.xsd">
  <t:select t:value="day" t:model="dayModel"
      t:encoder="encoder"/>
  <t:select t:value="month" t:model="monthModel"/>
  <t:select t:value="year" t:model="yearModel"
    t:encoder="encoder"/>
</html>
```

Nothing special, as you see; just three `Select` components with their corresponding values, models, and encoders in case of day and year.

All we need now is to provide all these parameters in the component class and to handle properly any selection made by the user in the page class. Following is the code for the component class:

```
package com.packtpub.celebrities.components;
import com.packtpub.celebrities.util.IntegerEncoder;
import com.packtpub.celebrities.util.IntegerSelectModel;
import com.packtpub.celebrities.util.Month;
import java.util.Calendar;
import java.util.Date;
import org.apache.tapestry.SelectModel;
import org.apache.tapestry.ValueEncoder;
import org.apache.tapestry.annotations.Inject;
import org.apache.tapestry.annotations.Parameter;
import org.apache.tapestry.annotations.SetupRender;
import org.apache.tapestry.ioc.Messages;
import org.apache.tapestry.util.EnumSelectModel;
public class DateInput
{
  @Parameter(required = true)
  private Date date;

  @Inject
  private Messages messages;
  private Calendar c = Calendar.getInstance();

  @SetupRender
  void setupCalendar()
  {
    c.setTime(date == null ? new Date() : date);
  }

  public SelectModel getDayModel()
  {
    return new IntegerSelectModel(1, 31);
```

```
    }

    public SelectModel getYearModel()
    {
      return new IntegerSelectModel(1900, 2010);
    }

    public SelectModel getMonthModel()
    {
      return new EnumSelectModel(Month.class, messages);
    }

    public ValueEncoder getEncoder()
    {
      return new IntegerEncoder();
    }

    public int getDay()
    {
      return c.get(Calendar.DATE);
    }

    public void setDay(int day)
    {
      c.set(Calendar.DATE, day);
    }

    public Month getMonth()
    {
      return Month.values()[c.get(Calendar.MONTH)];
    }

    public void setMonth(Month month)
    {
      c.set(Calendar.MONTH, month.getOrder());
    }

    public int getYear()
    {
      return c.get(Calendar.YEAR);
    }

    public void setYear(int year)
    {
      c.set(Calendar.YEAR, year);
      date = c.getTime();
    }
  }
```

The code is pretty simple, mostly just getters and setters, and there is only one thing that might be worth commenting on—the use of `@SetupRender` annotation. It simply marks the method that we want to be invoked before the component is rendered. This gives us an opportunity to do any preparations. In this case, we are making sure that the `Calendar` instance we are using for convenience is set either to the `date` parameter or, if the parameter is null, to the current date and time.

We can now put the new `DateInput` component onto any page and see if it works. Here is how it can be declared:

```
<t:form>
  Date test: <t:dateinput t:date="theDate" t:id="testDate"/>
</t:form>
```

Don't forget to add a page property of `java.util.Date` type to provide an initial value to the component and to store the user's input.

Run the application, and you should see that the component works as expected. We had to put it inside of the `Form` component, as the `Select` components used to construct the `DateInput` will not work otherwise. But still, our new creation isn't a full member of the family of Tapestry components. Try something like this:

```
<t:form>
  <t:label for="testDate">Date test</t:label>:
    <t:dateinput t:date="theDate" t:id="testDate"/>
</t:form>
```

Providing a label like this worked fine before with other components, but it will not work with `DateInput`. Tapestry will complain that it "Could not find coercion from type com.packtpub.celebrities.components.DateInput to type org.apache.tapestry.Field". In other words, Tapestry expected that `DateInput` is an instance of `Field`, while it isn't. So let's make it to be a `Field` then!

Making DateInput a Field

To be a rightful member of the family of `Form` components that receive user input and can display validation errors, a custom component should implement the `Field` interface that contains four methods:

- `String getClientId()`—should return a unique ID for the given component.
- `String getLabel()`—naturally, should return a label.
- `String getElementName()`—should return a name that will become the content of the component's name attribute.

- `boolean isDisabled()` – should define whether the component is disabled (when it is typically greyed out and cannot accept user input).

Let's begin with the simplest. As `DateInput` doesn't have an element of its own, it doesn't have a dedicated name attribute so the `getElementName` method will be very simple:

```
public String getElementName()
{
  return null;
}
```

The `DateInput` component does contain three `Select` components, but Tapestry will take care of the names of those.

The label can be specified by the component user, but not necessarily, so we need to provide an optional property for this, and then return the value of this property in the `getLabel` method, like this:

```
@Parameter (defaultPrefix = "literal")
private String label;

public String getLabel()
{
  return label;
}
```

However, if we leave it like this and the component doesn't receive any label when defined in a page, like in the previous example, nothing will be displayed by the `Label` component associated with it. With minimal effort, we can ask Tapestry to provide a label in case it wasn't specified by the user.

Tapestry will first search for a message with the key `componentId`-label (where `componentId` is the unique ID for our component, the one returned by `getClientId` method). If such a message exists in one of the accessible message catalogs (those for the component, its page or the whole application), it will be displayed by the label. If not, Tapestry will take the component's unique ID and make a reasonable label from it. To enable all this clever functionality, all we need to do is to add the following snippet to the component class:

```
@Inject
private ComponentResources resources;

@Inject
private ComponentDefaultProvider defaultProvider;

String defaultLabel()
```

```
{
  return defaultProvider.defaultLabel(resources);
}
```

As for the `getClientId` method, the value returned by it should be unique within the page. The simplest way to ensure this is to ask Tapestry to give us this ID, like this:

```
public String getClientId()
{
  return resources.getId();
}
```

Finally, we need to provide a way to make the component disabled, which means creating a boolean property. We can then return the value of this property:

```
@Parameter
private boolean disabled;

public boolean isDisabled()
{
  return disabled;
}
```

But this is not enough. When the `DateInput` component is disabled, the `Select` components that it is made of should be disabled too, but this is easy. Modify the `DateInput.tml` template to look like this:

```
<html xmlns:t="http://tapestry.apache.org/schema/tapestry_5_0_0.xsd">
  <t:select t:value="day" t:model="dayModel"
    t:encoder="encoder" t:disabled="disabled"/>
  <t:select t:value="month" t:model="monthModel"
    t:disabled="disabled"/>
  <t:select t:value="year" t:model="yearModel"
    t:encoder="encoder" t:disabled="disabled"/>
</html>
```

Finally, don't forget to declare that the `DateInput` component implements the `Field` interface:

```
public class DateInput implements Field
```

Now, having the `DateInput` component declared like this:

```
<t:form>
  <t:label for="testDate">Date test</t:label>:
  <t:dateinput t:date="theDate" t:id="testDate"/>
</t:form>
```

you will see that it displays properly, and the value for its label is taken from the component's ID:

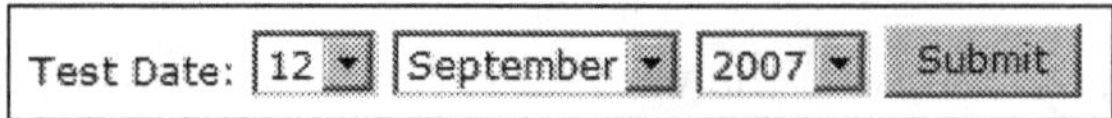

Having the component's label displayed properly is one of the benefits of making it an implementation of `Field`. Another benefit is having an opportunity to add validation to the component with minimal efforts. The next section will show how this can be done.

Adding Simple Validation

What we are going to do here is not a robust and universal example of user input validation. However, the benefit of this approach is its extreme simplicity. You can always take it as a starting point and go further, but as for me, the approach is good enough to use it as it is.

Let's say we want the date accepted by the component to be no earlier than a certain limit. Let's add the appropriate parameter to the component's class:

```
@Parameter
private Date dateFrom;
```

We can add this parameter in the component's declaration in the page template:

```
<t:dateinput t:date="theDate" t:id="testDate"
  t:dateFrom="lowerLimit"/>
```

We shall also provide a value for this parameter in the page class, like this:

```
public Date getLowerLimit()
{
  return new Date();
}
```

We are going to check if the date submitted by the user is no earlier than the current date, and if there is a problem, we are going to ask Tapestry to take appropriate measures. For this, we need to inject a `ValidationTracker` which is achieved like this:

```
@Environmental
private ValidationTracker tracker;
```

But where do we put the code to do the check? `DateInput` contains three `Select` components, the values selected in those components are being stored in the `DateInput` class by using appropriate setter methods, for day, month, and year. The year is handled last simply because the `Select` for it goes last in the template, so at the time the `setYear` method is invoked, the date selected by the user is already fully known to the component.

This means that one possible answer to where to handle validation is the `setYear` method of the `DateInput` class:

```
public void setYear(int year)
{
  c.set(Calendar.YEAR, year);
  date = c.getTime();
  if (dateFrom != null && date.before(dateFrom))
  {
    tracker.recordError(this, messages.get("too-early"));
  }
}
```

The `recordError` method of `ValidationTracker` has two versions. The simpler version takes only one parameter, a `String` for an error message. The other version, which is used here, takes one additional parameter, a `Field`, and as you will see soon, Tapestry will decorate the label of the field in error. Since our component is a `Field`, we simply pass a reference to it as the first parameter.

Finally, we do not simply provide some `String` for an error message, but we do it properly, using a reference to message catalogs, so that the error message is displayed in a currently preferred locale. The last step of this experiment is to add component-specific message catalogs (we could also put the error message into either of the page's or root message catalogs too, if we considered that as a better solution).

In the IDE, right-click on the `com.packtpub.celebrities.components` package and add to it two message catalogs, `DateInput.properties` and `DateInput_de.properties`. Put an error message into them, like this:

```
too-early=The date is too early!
```

Also add an `Errors` component and a **Submit** button to the form containing the `DateInput` component:

```
<t:form>
  <t:errors/>
    <t:label for="testDate">Date test</t:label>:
    <t:dateinput t:date="theDate" t:id="testDate"
      t:dateFrom="lowerLimit"/>
    <input type="submit" value="Submit"/>
</t:form>
```

Now we are ready to see how our simple validation works. Run the application, navigate to the page where you have placed the `DateInput` component and try to submit some date from the past. This is what you should see:

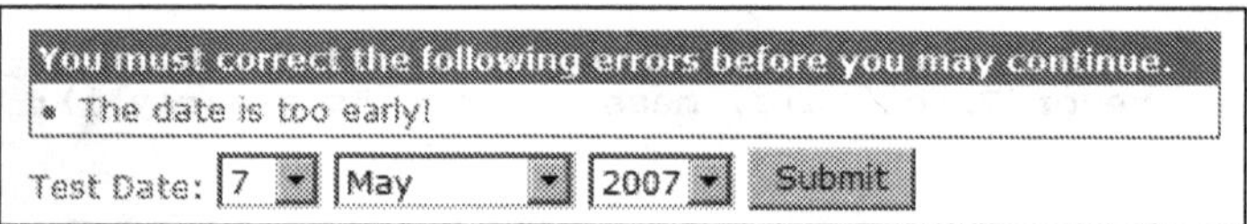

We were able to successfully plug our custom validation into the existing Tapestry infrastructure, and so with minimal efforts we have achieved quite a substantial result. We have also built a decent custom component in the last few sections, and if you think it could be better, you can always use it as a basis for your own powerful, feature-rich solution for date input.

Now let's try creating another useful component.

Creating a Universal Locale Switcher

Every internationalized application needs to have some solution for switching the current locale, and it would be nice to have a universal component for this purpose. Let's try to define what such a component should do:

- It should find out which locales are supported by the application.
- It should display a drop-down box with an option for each supported locale.
- It should also display a flag image for the currently selected locale.

In a way, the logic of this component will be opposite of the logic of the English/German locale switcher we created in the previous chapter, because it will display the flag and the label for the currently selected locale, not for the alternative one (as there potentially can be more than one alternative locale). The following is what we want to achieve:

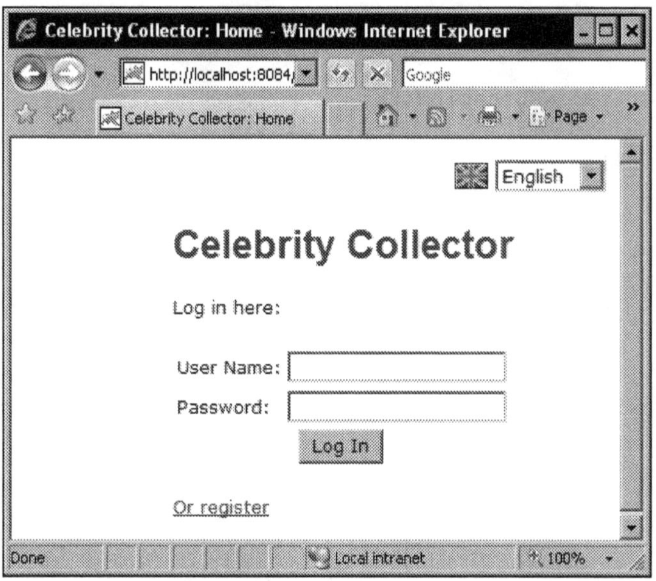

At the first stage, let us simplify our task and pass a list of supported locales to the new component as a parameter. Later we shall see what it will take to obtain this list from the application automatically.

First of all, as we are going to have a `Select` component working with locale objects, we need to provide an appropriate `SelectModel` implementation. We already have had significant experience with custom models, so I will simply show the code for all the necessary classes, and you should be able to easily figure out how all this works.

Here is the `OptionModel` implementation:

```
package com.packtpub.celebrities.util;

import java.util.Locale;
import java.util.Map;
import org.apache.tapestry.OptionModel;

public class LocaleOptionModel implements OptionModel
{
  private Locale locale;
  public LocaleOptionModel(Locale locale)
  {
    this.locale = locale;
  }

  public String getLabel()
  {
```

```
        return locale.getDisplayName(locale);
    }

    public boolean isDisabled()
    {
        return false;
    }

    public Map<String, String> getAttributes()
    {
        return null;
    }

    public Object getValue()
    {
        return locale;
    }
}
```

The next implementation is that of the custom `SelectModel` itself:

```
package com.packtpub.celebrities.util;

import java.util.ArrayList;
import java.util.List;
import java.util.Locale;
import org.apache.tapestry.OptionGroupModel;
import org.apache.tapestry.OptionModel;
import org.apache.tapestry.util.AbstractSelectModel;

public class LocaleSelectModel extends AbstractSelectModel
{
  private String locales;
  public LocaleSelectModel(String locales)
  {
    this.locales = locales;
  }

  public List<OptionGroupModel> getOptionGroups()
  {
    return null;
  }

  public List<OptionModel> getOptions()
  {
    if (locales != null)
    {
      List<OptionModel> locList =
```

```
        new ArrayList<OptionModel>();
        String[] locs = locales.split(",");
        for (String str : locs)
        {
          locList.add(new LocaleOptionModel(
                      new Locale(str)));
        }
        return locList;
      }
      return null;
    }
  }
```

When creating the `LocaleSelectModel`, we suppose that the list of supported locales, passed as a parameter for the constructor, is a string containing language abbreviations separated by commas, like "en,de". Finally, here is an implementation of `ValueEncoder` for `Locale`:

```
package com.packtpub.celebrities.util;

import java.util.Locale;
import org.apache.tapestry.ValueEncoder;

public class LocaleEncoder implements ValueEncoder
{
  public String toClient(Object obj)
  {
    Locale loc = (Locale) obj;
    return loc.getLanguage();
  }

  public Object toValue(String str)
  {
    return new Locale(str);
  }
}
```

Now let's create the component's template, `LocaleSwitcher.tml`. It might look like this:

```
<html xmlns:t="http://tapestry.apache.org/schema/tapestry_5_0_0.xsd">
  <t:form t:id="switcher">
    <img src="${asset:images/flag.gif}" align="absmiddle"/>
    <t:select t:value="selectedLocale" t:model="localeModel"
      t:encoder="localeEncoder"
      onchange="this.form.submit()"/>
  </t:form>
</html>
```

As for the `Select` component, almost everything should be familiar to you. One new addition is the use of the `onchange` attribute and a tiny bit of JavaScript for its value. This will ensure that whenever a new option is selected in the resulting drop-down list, the form surrounding the component will get submitted automatically (in this case initiating the change of the application's locale).

But if you look closely at how the image is obtained to display a flag, you will notice something different. This is how the image is provided now:

```
${asset:images/flag.gif}
```

And here is how a similar image was obtained in the previous chapter:

```
${asset:context:/assets/flag.gif}
```

The main difference is the `context:` bit. When the context is mentioned while providing an asset, Tapestry will be looking for that asset relative to the context of the web application. This means that if the application is deployed on some server, and its URL is `www.someserver.com/celebrities`, then anything that goes after this URL will be the path relative to the application's context. In practical terms, we can think that the **Web Pages** folder in a NetBeans project or the **WebContent** folder in Eclipse represents the application context.

In the latter example, if someone wanted to see the `flag.gif` image, they could do so by navigating to the URL, `www.someserver.com/celebrities/assets/flag.gif`.

If, however, `context` is not mentioned when obtaining an asset, Tapestry will understand the path to that asset relative to the component class that is requesting it. In case of our new component, Tapestry will be looking for the image in the `images` subfolder located next to the `LocaleSwitcher` class. So let's first create such a class in the `com.packtpub.celebrities.components` package. Here is the code for it, and it is so simple that no comments are needed:

```
package com.packtpub.celebrities.components;

import com.packtpub.celebrities.util.LocaleEncoder;
import com.packtpub.celebrities.util.LocaleSelectModel;
import java.util.Locale;
import org.apache.tapestry.SelectModel;
import org.apache.tapestry.ValueEncoder;
import org.apache.tapestry.annotations.Inject;
import org.apache.tapestry.annotations.OnEvent;
import org.apache.tapestry.annotations.Parameter;
import org.apache.tapestry.services.PersistentLocale;

public class LocaleSwitcher
{
```

```
    @Parameter(defaultPrefix = "literal", required = true)
    private String supportedLocales;
    @Inject
    private PersistentLocale persistentLocale;
    public Locale getSelectedLocale()
    {
      return persistentLocale.get();
    }

      public void setSelectedLocale(Locale selectedLocale)
      {
          persistentLocale.set(selectedLocale);
      }

    public SelectModel getLocaleModel()
    {
    return new LocaleSelectModel(supportedLocales);
    }

    public ValueEncoder getLocaleEncoder()
    {
      return new LocaleEncoder();
    }
  }
```

To complete the work on the component, we now need to take care of the flag images. Create a new package named `com.packtpub.celebrities.components.images`. This will basically create an `images` subfolder in the directory structure where the component class was created. Put as many flag images into this package as you wish, making sure that the default one is named `flag.gif`, while all the others have an appropriate suffix in their file name, like `flag_de.gif`, `flag_es.gif` and so on. In the code package for this chapter you will find two flags—British and German.

In Eclipse, you can simply copy these images and paste them into the package straight in the IDE. NetBeans, however, will not allow you to do this, so you will have to navigate to the `\celebrities\src\main\java\com\packtpub\celebrities\components\images` (phew!) subfolder in the directory structure generated by Maven at very beginning and copy the images to it.

Now the component is ready, and all we need to do to use it is to place it onto a page. Or, indeed, we can use it in the `Border` component in place of that `ActionLink`-based locale switcher created in the previous chapter.

Please remove the old switcher from `Border.tml` and any code related to it from the `Border.java` file, and then put the following fragment of code where you want the new locale switcher to be:

```
<div align="right">
  <t:localeswitcher t:supportedLocales="en,de"/>
</div>
```

Run the application and, while at the **Start** page, try to switch the locale. This will not work right now, and validation system will complain that you haven't logged in properly. This is because in the `Start` class we have two generic event handlers—`onSuccess()` and `onValidate()`—that react to submission of any form on the page. We have two forms now—one surrounding the locale switcher and another one for logging in. The first form is submitted when the locale is changed, and we don't want the validation logic to run in that case.

To solve this problem, let's use the `@OnEvent` annotation to run the event handlers only when the login form is submitted. The two mentioned methods might look similar to this:

```
@OnEvent(value = "success", component = "loginForm")
Object showCollection()
{
  return ShowAll.class;
}
@OnEvent(value = "validate", component = "loginForm")
void validateInput()
{
  User authenticatedUser =
      Security.authenticate(userName, password);
  if (authenticatedUser != null)
  {
     user = authenticatedUser;
  }
  else
  {
    loginForm.recordError(
        messages.get("authentication-failed"));
  }
}
```

Now everything should work fine, but our component still has one deficiency. It obtains the supported locales as a parameter. They are configured exactly in the same way in the `AppModule` file:

```
configuration.add("tapestry.supported-locales", "en,de");
```

So why don't we just ask Tapestry to give us this information? Well, there is good news and bad news related to this. The bad news is that at the moment there is no simple way to obtain the information on the supported locales. Such a way should appear very soon—maybe it will be available by the time you be read this book—but right now we need to create a custom service to get access to this information.

The good news, however, is that creating a custom service is very easy in Tapestry 5, and we now have a good reason to create one and see how this is done.

Creating a Custom Service

A service is more or less like a standalone piece of functionality that can do something useful for our application and is usually not page-specific. It can be injected into any page where it might be needed. One example is a service that sends email messages. Another example is the service we are going to create here—it will provide information on the locales supported by the application.

To create a custom service in Tapestry 5, first of all we need to formulate what exactly that service is going to do—and to create an appropriate service interface. This is how it could look in our case:

```
package com.packtpub.celebrities.services;

public interface SupportedLocales
{
  public String getSupportedLocales();
}
```

Next, we need to create an implementation of this interface, like this one:

```
package com.packtpub.celebrities.services;

import org.apache.tapestry.ioc.annotations.Inject;
import org.apache.tapestry.ioc.annotations.Symbol;

public class SupportedLocalesImpl implements SupportedLocales
{
  private String supportedLocales;
  public SupportedLocalesImpl(
            @Inject
            @Symbol("tapestry.supported-locales")
            String locales)
  {
    supportedLocales = locales;
  }
```

```
    public String getSupportedLocales()
    {
      return supportedLocales;
    }
  }
```

One unusual detail here is the tricky looking parameter accepted by the constructor. Let's look at this parameter closely:

```
@Inject
@Symbol("tapestry.supported-locales")
String locales
```

Here, we are using the Tapestry Inversion of Control system and asking it to provide a parameter (inject into it some String value) to its constructor, when an instance of the `SupportedLocalesImpl` class is created. That value can be obtained by following a symbol (a kind of reference) like `tapestry.supported-locales`—and we have provided the value, `en,de` ourselves, by configuring the application earlier. Finally, the service simply returns whatever was provided by the Tapestry IoC.

The next step is to tell Tapestry about the new service by binding together its interface and implementation. Please have a look at the `AppModule` class again. You will find a method named `bind` which is initially empty, except for the comment that explains how to use this method. We are going to add just one line of code to it, so that the method looks like this (the original comment was removed to save space):

```
public static void bind(ServiceBinder binder)
{
  binder.bind(SupportedLocales.class,
      SupportedLocalesImpl.class);
}
```

That's it! The service is ready, and we can now inject it into any page or component. Remove the `supportedLocales` parameter from the `LocaleSwitcher` class and add the following two lines of code instead:

```
@Inject
private SupportedLocales supportedLocales;
```

We shall also need to modify the `getLocaleModel` method:

```
public SelectModel getLocaleModel()
{
  return new LocaleSelectModel(
      supportedLocales.getSupportedLocales());
}
```

Finally, remove the `supportedLocales` parameter from the component declaration in the `Border.tml` template:

```
<div align="right">
  <t:localeswitcher/>
</div>
```

Run the application, and it should work exactly as before, with the only difference being that the list of supported locales are now provided by our new custom service. Isn't it great that we can drop this simple tag whenever we want in an internalized application and the component will automatically define which locales are supported by the application and provide the functionality for switching between them?

It would be even more impressive if we could package our custom components into a library and share it with friends. Let's try to do this then!

Creating a Library of Custom Components

We have created two custom components that can be useful for many other web applications, and the natural desire is to use them to create a library and use it whenever it might become needed. Fortunately, it is very easy to add a library of custom components to a Tapestry 5 application—all we need is to put the library into the `WEB-INF/lib` directory of that application. Tapestry will automatically discover the available components, and our task will be simply to use these components whenever we need them.

It is not too difficult to create a library of custom components. All we need to do is to package all the appropriate classes into a JAR file, add one Tapestry-specific line to the manifest of that file, and create a module class that will serve as a kind of anchor for the library. Tapestry will find and load this module. From it, Tapestry will find out where exactly to look for the library's components. The Library module should be packaged into the JAR along with all the other classes, and that Tapestry-specific line in the manifest should be pointing to the module. Such concentrated description looks perhaps too complicated, but its practical application is not that difficult.

To begin with, let's create a list of everything we need to package into the library JAR for both components.

Here is the list for `DateInput`:

- `com.packtpub.celebrities.components.DateInput`
- `com\packtpub\celebrities\components\DateInput.tml`
- `com\packtpub\celebrities\components\DateInput.properties`
- `com\packtpub\celebrities\components\DateInput_de.properties`
- `com.packtpub.celebrities.util.IntegerEncoder`
- `com.packtpub.celebrities.util.IntegerOptionModel`
- `com.packtpub.celebrities.util.IntegerSelectModel`
- `com.packtpub.celebrities.util.Month`

And this is the list for `LocaleSwitcher`:

- `com.packtpub.celebrities.components.LocaleSwitcher`
- `com\packtpub\celebrities\components\LocaleSwitcher.tml`
- `com\packtpub\celebrities\components\images\flag.gif`
- `com\packtpub\celebrities\components\images\flag_de.gif`
- `com.packtpub.celebrities.services.SupportedLocales`
- `com.packtpub.celebrities.services.SupportedLocalesImpl`
- `com.packtpub.celebrities.util.LocaleEncoder`
- `com.packtpub.celebrities.util.LocaleOptionModel`
- `com.packtpub.celebrities.util.LocaleSelectModel`

For `LocaleSwitcher`, we shall also need to make sure that the interface and the implementation for the `SupportedLocales` service are bound in the library's module.

Additionally, more flag images should be added for different languages. Right now, if the preferred locale is not German, the default British flag will be displayed by the component, which means, it will be displayed for any language other than German. Let me leave this task to you. You can add as many flags as you wish, and as soon as you use an appropriate suffix for the file name, Tapestry will pick up the required flag for the selected locale automatically.

I would recommend the you create a separate project for working with the new library. In NetBeans, when creating this project you might select **General** in **Categories** and **Java Class Library** in **Projects**. In Eclipse, simply create a new Java Project. The name for the new project can be something like `MyLib`.

Make sure the compiler compliance level is set to at least Java 5. Both in Eclipse and NetBeans you can do this in the project's properties dialogue. The following screen shot demonstrates such a dialogue in Eclipse:

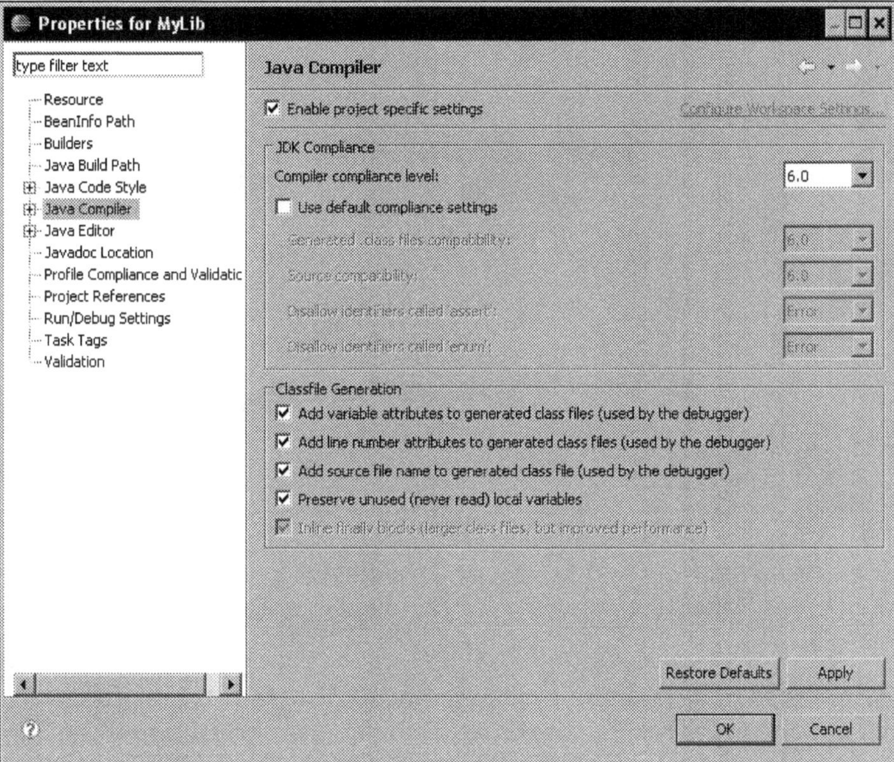

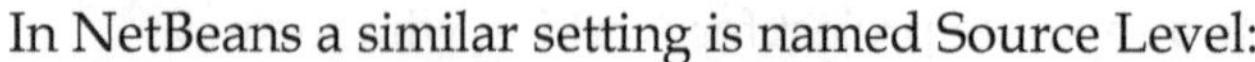

In NetBeans a similar setting is named Source Level:

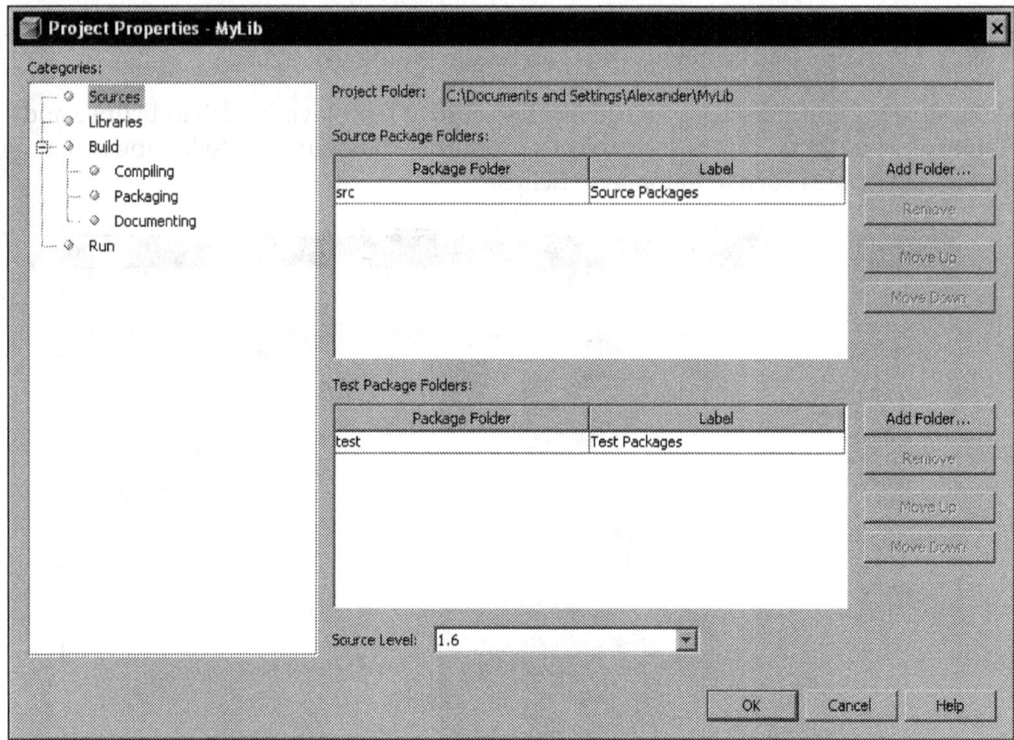

The next step is to copy all the files listed above into the `src` subdirectory of the new project (you will find all the required files packaged together in the code package for this chapter).

We will also need to make Tapestry libraries available to the **MyLib** project. To do this in Eclipse open the **Project Properties** dialogue again, select **Java Build Path** in the left pane, the **Libraries** tab in the right pane, click on the **Add JARs...** button and then add two libraries, `tapestry-core-5.0.6.jar` and `tapestry-ioc-5.0.6.jar` from some other Tapestry 5 project in the workspace.

To add the same libraries in NetBeans, right-click on the **Libraries** subfolder in the project, select **Add JAR/Folder...**, then find the libraries on the hard drive and select them.

The next step is to add the library module. Let's put it into `com.packtpub.celebrities` package, and here is the code for it:

```
package com.packtpub.celebrities;

import com.packtpub.celebrities.services.SupportedLocales;
import com.packtpub.celebrities.services.SupportedLocalesImpl;
import org.apache.tapestry.ioc.Configuration;
import org.apache.tapestry.ioc.ServiceBinder;
import org.apache.tapestry.services.LibraryMapping;

public class LibraryModule
{
  public static void bind(ServiceBinder binder)
  {
    binder.bind(SupportedLocales.class,
        SupportedLocalesImpl.class);
  }

  public static void contributeComponentClassResolver(
                       Configuration<LibraryMapping> configuration)
  {
    configuration.add(new LibraryMapping("mylib",
        "com.packtpub.celebrities"));
  }
}
```

You are already familiar with the `bind` method of this module—it tells Tapestry how to instantiate our custom service. The other method, `contributeComponentClassResolver()`, serves to tell Tapestry that if any component on a page is defined using the **MyLib** prefix (you will see how this is done soon), it will find this component in the `com.packtpub.celebrities` package.

With all the source files and resources in place, you should have the following structure of packages in your project:

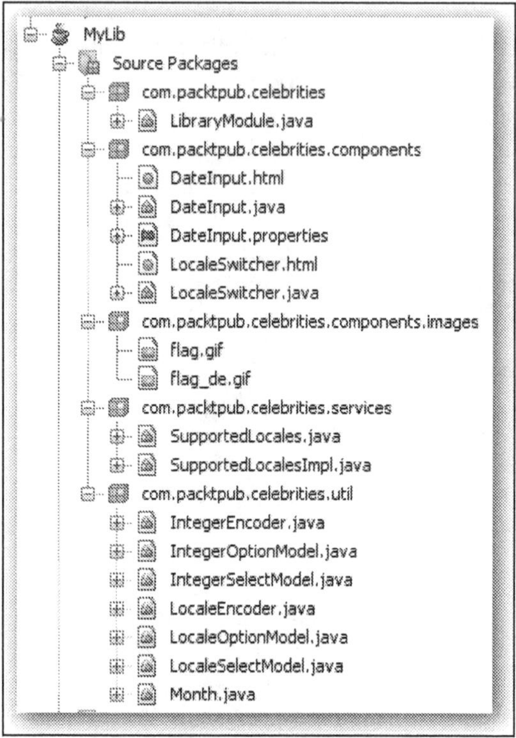

The final step is to make sure that Tapestry knows how to locate the library module we have recently created. For this, we need to put the following entry into the manifest of the JAR file containing our library:

```
Tapestry-Module-Classes: com.packtpub.celebrities.LibraryModule
```

The Manifest is a standard part of any JAR file. It is named `MANIFEST.MF` and placed in the `META-INF` directory of the package. Often, we do not care about what this file contains and it is generated for us automatically. This time, however, we need to ensure that the path to our library module is added to the manifest. The way we do this will depend on the IDE, but first of all, let's decide what our manifest will contain. One possible approach is to take the contents of some automatically generated manifest and just add the desired entry to it:

```
Manifest-Version: 1.0
Ant-Version: Apache Ant 1.6.5
Created-By: 1.6.0_02-b06 (Sun Microsystems Inc.)
Tapestry-Module-Classes: com.packtpub.celebrities.LibraryModule
```

This is important: Make sure that the last line of your manifest ends with a new line or a carriage return. In other words, place the cursor at the end of the last line and press *Enter*—otherwise the notorious Java bug will prevent the manifest from being parsed properly.

If you are using Eclipse, right-click on the **MyLib** project in the **Project Explorer**, and create a new file named `MANIFEST.MF`. Make sure it has the contents shown above. Again right-click on the **MyLib** project in the **Project Explorer** and select **Export...** In the dialogue that appears select **JAR file**:

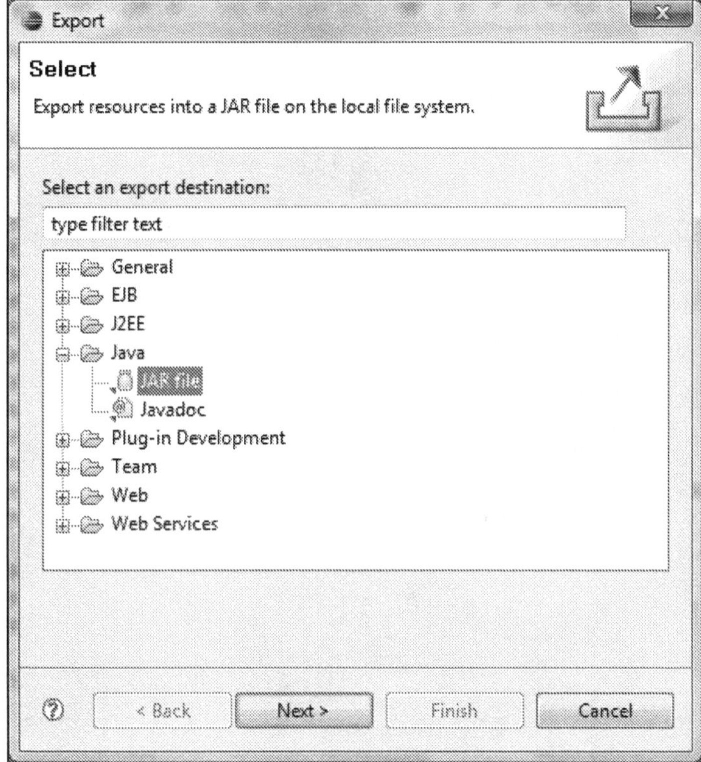

Click on the **Next** button, and in the next dialogue make sure that the new JAR file will contain only those files that we really need (do not select **MANIFEST.MF** here). Also, specify where it should be placed:

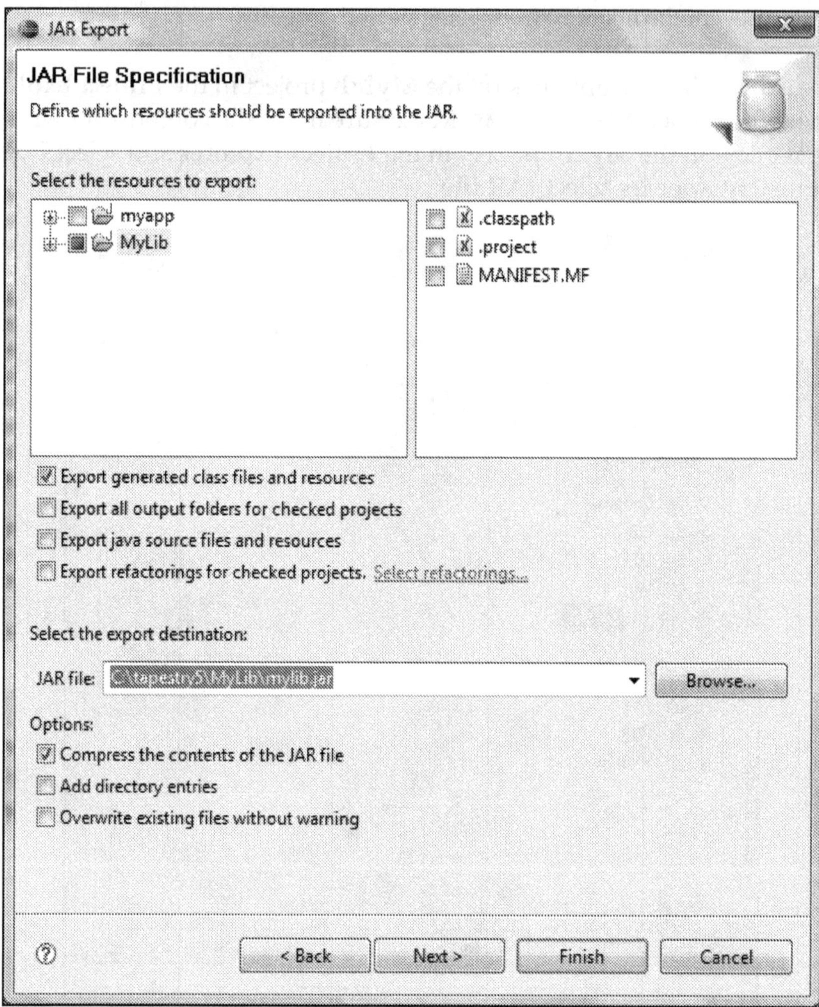

Click on **Next** again and make sure the next dialogue looks like this:

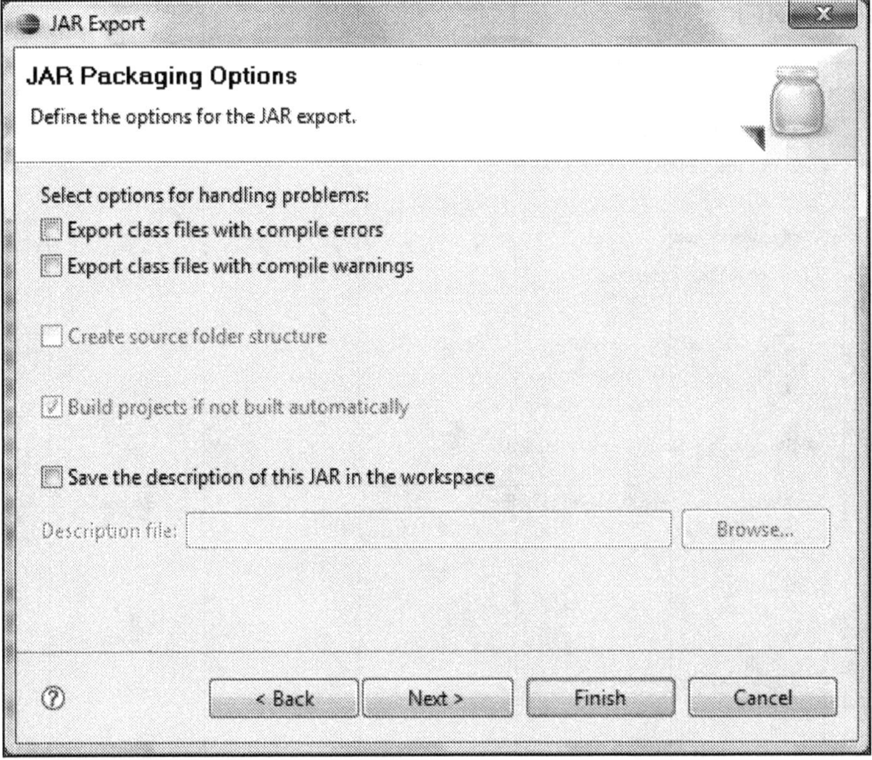

Click on the **Next** button again, and in the next dialogue, select the **Use existing manifest from workspace** radio button, then select the recently created **MANIFEST.MF** file:

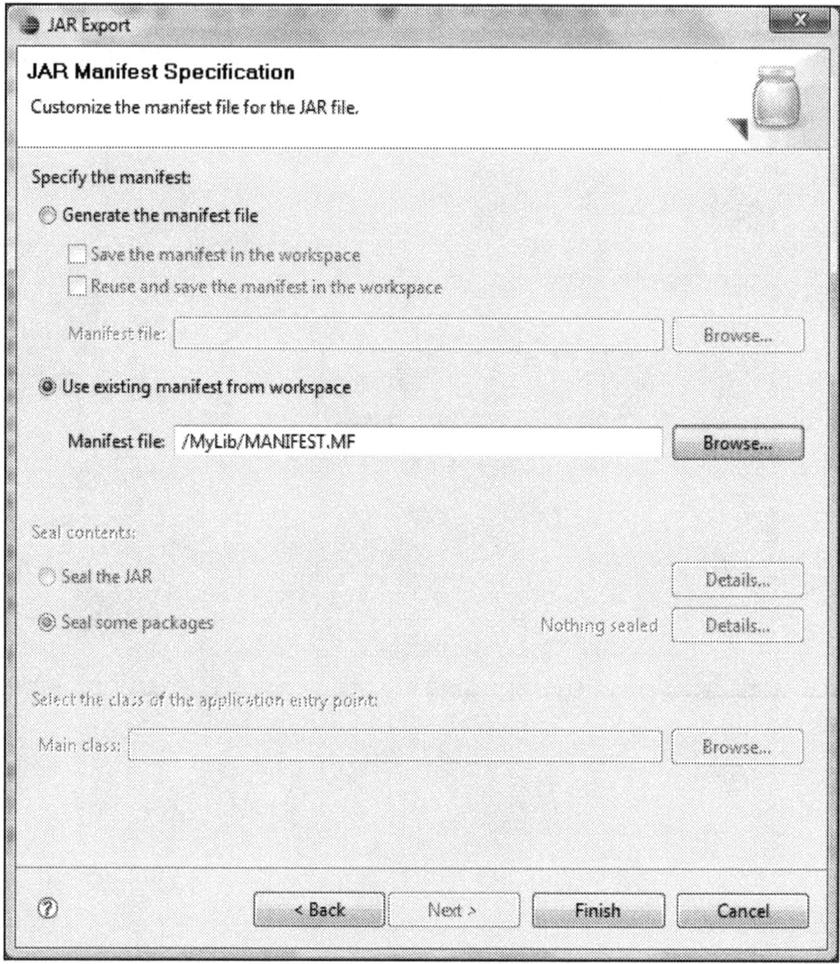

Finally, click on **Finish**, and your brand new custom library will be created at the location that you have specified.

In NetBeans, creating a custom library requires somewhat different steps. First of all, open the **Files** view instead of the usual **Projects** (by clicking on the **Files** tab on the left hand pane). Here, right-click the **MyLib** project and create **MANIFEST.MF** file with contents shown previously. Make sure this file is saved directly in the **MyLib** folder:

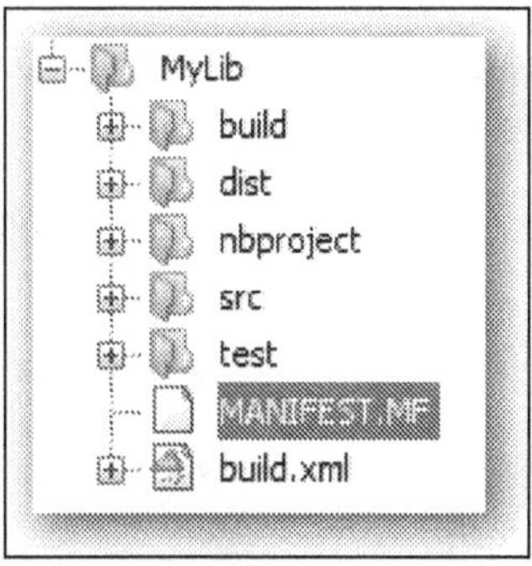

Now in the **Files** view, open the **nbproject** folder and locate in it the **project.properties** file. Open this file and add the following line at the end:

```
manifest.file=MANIFEST.MF
```

Save the file and go back to the **Projects** view. Right-click on the **MyLib** project and select **Build Project**. In a few seconds, the JAR file will be created. You can locate it in the **Files** view in the **dist** subfolder:

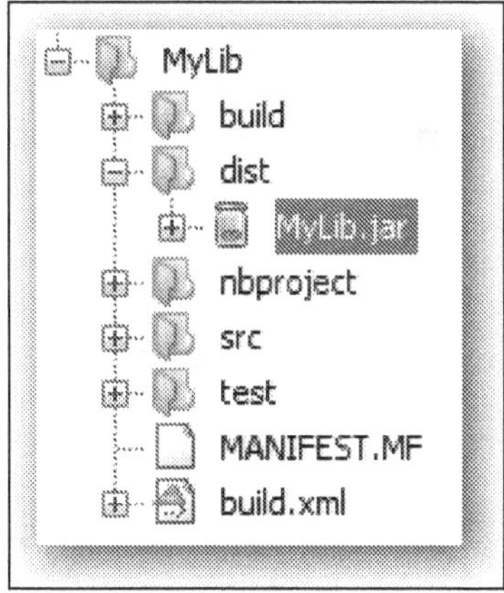

Whichever way you have created the custom library, it can be easily used now in any Tapestry 5 project. For example, you might want to test it in the **t5first** project we created back in Chapter 2. Just put the library JAR file into the `WEB-INF/lib` subfolder in the host project's structure and then define components on any page where you need them using the library's prefix (defined in its module). One way to do this is as follows:

```
<t:mylib.DateInput t:date="theDate"/>
<t:mylib.LocaleSwitcher/>
```

Alternatively, you can do the same inside the `<span>` element, but the syntax will be slightly different:

```
<span t:type="mylib/DateInput" t:date="theDate"/>
<span t:type="mylib/LocaleSwitcher"/>
```

Do not forget that `DateInput` will expect to find an appropriately named page property and that it should be placed inside of a Form component.

Test the project with custom components used on its pages, and everything should work fine.

Congratulations! We have just created our first library of custom components. You can now send it to your friends so that they can enjoy the results of your work!

Summary

One book like this cannot cover everything that comes with Tapestry 5. To discover the power of AJAX and how easily it can be used from a Tapestry web application, to learn how to integrate Tapestry with popular back end frameworks like Spring or Hibernate, to see how readily Tapestry can be configured and extended to deliver exactly what you want from the framework, another book would be needed, or even more than one book.

However, we were able to cover quite a lot here. In particular, we have learned:

- What Tapestry is, why it is special and how Tapestry 5 relates to the previous versions.
- How to create a Tapestry project skeleton using Maven and then work with it using both Eclipse and NetBeans IDE.
- The core concepts of Tapestry, including pages and how they are handled by the framework, how to navigate from page to page and how to pass information between pages.

- What are expansions, components, and how components can be defined in different ways.
- How to structure a Tapestry web application by placing its pages into different subfolders.
- How to use Application State Objects.
- How to use many of the components that come with Tapestry—both the simple ones that map directly to an HTML control and those sophisticated ones that bring with them a lot of powerful functionality.
- How to use the validation subsystem of Tapestry, so that with minimal efforts we are able to check whether user input is acceptable, and if not, display an appropriate message.
- How to display web applications in different languages, how to change its current locale and also how to store localized messages in both root and page-specific message catalogs.
- How to create custom components that can be reused within the same application or across various applications, and how to package them into a library.

We have developed a significant part of **Celebrity Collector**—a web application that can be easily extended and deployed on the Internet to provide a useful service.

I hope this book gives you a good impulse towards creating a web application of your own, and it teaches you, hopefully, everything you will need for your first Tapestry 5 application. However, as you gain experience, you will want to solve more and more complex tasks, and you will have many questions.

A
The Basics of Java for the Web

The laws that govern the life of Java code on a web server are laid out in the Servlet Specification (can be downloaded from `http://java.sun.com/products/servlet/download.html`). A Servlet is basically a standardized way of writing Java code so that it can be used with any *servlet container*, and benefit from the services provided by it.

A servlet container is a piece of software that collaborates with a web server. Requests from the Internet come to the web server first, and if it decides that those requests are for functionality provided by a Java application, it passes them to the servlet container.

Servlet containers manage low-level issues like networking, maintaining special kinds of memory to be used by the applications or making sure that proper initialization was made as required. This way it frees servlet developers to write code specific only to their application.

However, writing Java code at the level of servlets is still rather low-level work, and many Java web frameworks appeared to provide ready-to-use solutions for common, repeating tasks. Frameworks are ultimately based on the Servlet API, but building web applications with them is much easier, and more efficient, than working on the level of servlets.

Tapestry 5 is perhaps the most advanced and the most developer-friendly of the Java web frameworks, and so it shields us very efficiently from the nitty-gritty of servlet specification. However, there are a few pieces of servlet-related information that will be useful for us, such as:

1. The standard structure of a Java web application.
2. The basics of a deployment descriptor.
3. The basics of a WAR file.

It might also be useful to mention different kinds of Java-enabled servers so that you can decide which one of them to use.

The Standard Structure of a Java Web Application

A Servlet container requires every Java web application to have a certain structure so that it can manage the application properly. Here is the outline of such a structure:

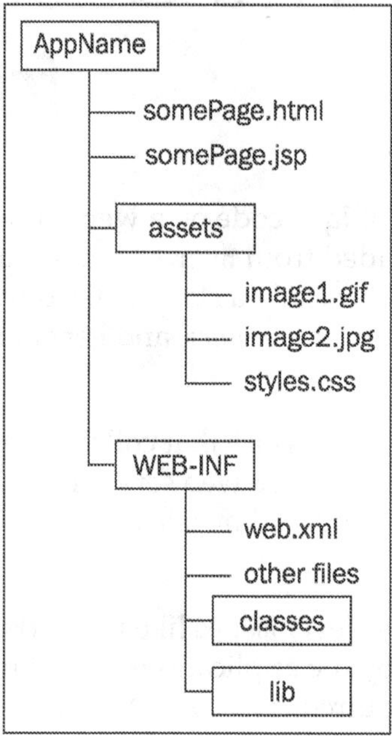

Perhaps the most important part of it is the `WEB-INF` directory. It is the brain and heart of a Java web application. The contents of this directory are protected by the servlet container—it prevents anyone from navigating to, say, `http://www.someserver.com/myapp/WEB-INF/` and seeing what this directory contains.

The `WEB-INF/classes` subdirectory is where the compiled Java classes go—those classes that we create for our application, such as page classes.

The `WEB-INF/lib` subdirectory is for the libraries used by the application, such as the Tapestry framework libraries. Any class or resource stored here should normally be packaged in a JAR file.

The `web.xml` file which must be present inside the `WEB-INF` directory is a deployment descriptor—it is described in the next section. Also, the `WEB-INF` directory can contain other files as needed by the application.

There can be another hidden directory in a Java web application, `META-INF`. It can contain other useful information about the application.

All the other files and directories, those outside `WEB-INF` and `META-INF`, are accessible from the Web. This means that if we have have a JSP page named `somePage.jsp`, it can be seen by anyone by navigating to something like `http://www.someserver.com/myapp/somePage.jsp`. Typically you will find here HTML and JSP pages as well as images and stylesheets. Naturally, they all can be put into as many different directories as is convenient.

Returning to the `web.xml` file, we never had any need to look into it in the course of the book, so it is actually not necessary to know its contents. But sometimes such knowledge can be useful, so let's have a look into deployment descriptor.

The Basics of the Deployment Descriptor

The Deployment descriptor, which is a `web.xml` file, serves to tell a servlet container important details about a Java web application. Most commonly, it defines the servlets of the application and associates them with certain URL patterns, so that the servlet container knows which request should be passed to which servlet. Here is an example of a deployment descriptor, the one that would be typically be used in a Tapestry 4 application:

```
<?xml version="1.0" encoding="UTF-8"?>
  <web-app version="2.4"
    xmlns="http://java.sun.com/xml/ns/j2ee"
    xmlns:xsi="http://www.w3.org/2001/XMLSchema-instance"
    xsi:schemaLocation="http://java.sun.com/xml/ns/j2ee
      http://java.sun.com/xml/ns/j2ee/web-app_2_4.xsd">
  <display-name>Celebrity Collector</display-name>
  <servlet>
    <servlet-name>CelebrityCollector</servlet-name>
    <servlet-class>
      org.apache.tapestry.ApplicationServlet
    </servlet-class>
  </servlet>
  <servlet-mapping>
    <servlet-name>CelebrityCollector</servlet-name>
    <url-pattern>/app</url-pattern>
  </servlet-mapping>
```

```
  <session-config>
    <session-timeout>30</session-timeout>
  </session-config>
  <welcome-file-list>
    <welcome-file>index.html</welcome-file>
  </welcome-file-list>
</web-app>
```

As you see, a Tapestry 4 application has just one servlet, named **Celebrity Collector**, and there is a Java class for it that is provided by the framework—all this is defined inside the `<servlet>` element. All requests addressed to the current application that start with `/app`, such as `http://www.someserver.com/myapp/app`, will be passed to this servlet, and then Tapestry will step in and do its job. This mapping is defined in the `<servlet-mapping>` element.

We can optionally define a session timeout—the amount of time in minutes after which the user's session will be invalidated if he or she will remain inactive. Also, a "welcome file" can be specified, which means a page that will be displayed if no specific page is requested by the user (for example, when navigating to `http://www.someserver.com/myapp/`).

In Tapestry 5, the deployment descriptor is somewhat unusual. This is what you will see if you look into the `web.xml` file of one of the applications created in this book:

```
<?xml version="1.0" encoding="UTF-8"?>
<!DOCTYPE web-app PUBLIC
    "-//Sun Microsystems, Inc.//DTD Web Application 2.3//EN"
    "http://java.sun.com/dtd/web-app_2_3.dtd">
  <web-app>
    <display-name>myapp Tapestry 5 Application</display-name>
    <context-param>
      <param-name>tapestry.app-package</param-name>
      <param-value>org.example.myapp</param-value>
    </context-param>
    <filter>
      <filter-name>app</filter-name>
      <filter-class>
        org.apache.tapestry.TapestryFilter
      </filter-class>
    </filter>
    <filter-mapping>
      <filter-name>app</filter-name>
      <url-pattern>/*</url-pattern>
    </filter-mapping>
  </web-app>
```

You can see that no servlets are defined in the Tapestry 5 deployment descriptor, and this is unusual. Instead, there is a filter, which is configured and associated with a URL pattern similarly to a servlet. Filters are normally used to do something before or after a servlet is invoked. In Tapestry 5, however, the whole framework looks to a servlet container as one complicated filter that intercepts all the requests and does with them whatever it thinks to be appropriate.

In the previous example, you can also see how certain values—in this case the package name of the application—can be provided in the deployment descriptor to be stored in application context—a special piece of memory where these values can be read later by the application.

This was a very brief overview of what a deployment descriptor is and what sort of information it can contain. If you are curious to know more, or if you need to know more to achieve the goals you are aiming for, please consult the Servlet Specification. It is perfectly readable, unlike some other specifications, and very useful.

WAR Files Basics

The same Servlet Specification defines a very convenient way to package Java web applications—a Web Archive (WAR) file. This is basically the same as a JAR file, which is an archived collection of files, The difference is that the WAR file contains the whole web application's structure.

A WAR file can be distributed conveniently, and when it comes to deployment, this file can be simply uploaded to a servlet container, and the latter will either automatically unpack the contained web application or run it straight from the WAR file.

About Java-Enabled Servers

There are a significant number of different servers that were specifically created to run Java applications on them. This section will provide a brief orientation on them so that you can more easily choose which server to use for your application.

All Java servers can be roughly classified into two groups:

1. Java Web Servers.
2. Full Java EE Application Servers.

The main component of the first group of servers is the servlet container. They can have other specifications and services implemented too, but all their functionality is centered upon hosting Java web applications.

The most famous and widely used representative of the first group is Apache Tomcat. The other free server, especially popular among Tapestry developers is Jetty. Gaucho Resin, yet another representative of the first group, is not free but has a very good reputation.

If all you need is a web application, even if it uses popular frameworks like Spring or Hibernate and a database to store its information, any Java web server should be fine for you. If, however, you decide one day to use Enterprise JavaBeans or Java Message Service, you will most probably need a full Java EE application server.

The second group implements a wide range of Java EE specifications which means that the purpose of these servers is to host multi-tier, distributed enterprise-level applications that communicate across the network, coordinate the work of their parts and can withstand a significant workload.

A few representatives of the second group are JBoss, Apache Geronimo, IBM WebSphere or BEA WebLogic. Some of them are free, others are very expensive, but in any case I would suggest that these servers should not be used unless you really need the functionality provided by them. As a side note, several full Java EE servers, like JBoss and Geronimo, use Tomcat for their servlet container.

This completes a brief overview of Java EE-related terminology. I hope you found it useful, especially if you are new to Java web development.

B

Creating a Real Data Source with db4o

Throughout this book we have used a mock data source—a simple Java class which only imitated storing and retrieving data. This wasn't very exciting, but dealing with a real database normally means a lot of distractions. We would have to download such a database, install and configure it, and create the necessary tables in one or another way.

In order to work in a contemporary way, we might also wish to use some object-relational mapping solution like Hibernate. That would mean downloading, installing, configuring, and then writing a lot of XML, all from scratch to achieve what we want.

I would not dare to explain how to do all this in an appendix. Fortunately, there is a fantastic alternative—to use an object database named **db4o**. All you need to do to get this database is to download the most recent version from the project's website (`http://www.db4o.com`), extract an appropriate JAR file from the package and drop it into the `WEB-INF/lib` subdirectory of your Java web application. That's it; your new database is ready!

But what is most amazing is that db4o is not just a toy to play with in an example project. It can be easily used in a real life web application. Here is what the creators of db4o write about it:

> ...it allows you to store even the most complex object structures with ease, while achieving highest level of performance. Database benchmarks show db4o to be up to 55 times faster than Hibernate and MySQL, a popular object-relational mapper and relational SQL database stack.

For further information please refer to `http://www.db4o.com/about/productinformation/`.

As an additional bonus for us, db4o comes with an excellent interactive tutorial that you will find inside the downloaded package. I wholeheartedly recommend that you read this tutorial—you will understand how to deal with this unbelievable database in no time.

Here, you will find a demonstration of how db4o can be used to create a real data source for our **Celebrity Collector** application.

Preparing the Database

The package you download from the previously mentioned website will be named something like `db40-6.3-java.zip`, although the version number might be different. In its `lib` subfolder, you will find a number of JAR files—for different versions of Java. We need the one that works with Java 5, it will be named like `db4o-6.3-java5.jar`. Copy this file to the `WEB-INF/lib` subdirectory of the **Celebrity Collector** project.

The last piece of "configuration" is to decide where you are going to store the database file on your hard drive. You can name it whatever you wish and you will be able to copy, distribute, or back it up like any other file. Let's say our file will be at `C:\tapestry5\data\celebrities.dat`.

The Main Operations

To create the database, we use the following line of code:

```
ObjectContainer db =
    Db4o.openFile("C:\tapestry5\data\celebrities.dat");
```

If such a file already exists, db4o will just open it, otherwise it will create a new file.

Perhaps the simplest thing we can do is to retrieve all the celebrities stored in the database. Here is how the `getAllCelebrities` method of the new data source will look:

```
public List<Celebrity> getAllCelebrities()
{
  return db.query(Celebrity.class);
}
```

We just tell the database the representatives of which class we want to retrieve, and it returns a list, returning all the available objects of that class.

If however we want to retrieve a specific object, we'll need to do a little more work. First of all, we need to select one of the two main approaches to querying a db4o database—Query by Example (QBE) or Native Query. QBE is a very simple approach, but it is limited in a few ways (read the tutorial for details). Anyway, let's use QBE for the `getCelebrityById` method. Here is how this method will look:

```
public Celebrity getCelebrityById(long id)
{
  Celebrity proto = new Celebrity();
  proto.setId(id);
  ObjectSet result = db.get(proto);
  if (result.hasNext()) return (Celebrity)result.next();
  return null;
}
```

First of all, we need to create a prototype object of the same type as the object, or objects we are going to retrieve:

```
Celebrity proto = new Celebrity();
```

Next, we need to set some of the properties of the prototype to the values we want to see in the returned objects. The database will return all the objects that match all non-default values of the prototype's properties. In our example we want to find a celebrity with a certain ID, so we set the `ID` property of the prototype to the desired value:

```
proto.setId(id);
```

Then we pass the prototype to the `get` method, and the result will be provided as an `ObjectSet`:

```
ObjectSet result = db.get(proto);
```

We can then check whether there is something in the result by using the `hasNext` method and retrieving that next object as the example shows.

Storing an object in the database is also quite simple. This is how `addCelebrity` method looks:

```
public void addCelebrity(Celebrity c)
{
  db.set(c);
}
```

However, there is one potential problem with such an implementation. Say we have just saved a `Celebrity` object containing the data for Bill Clinton. Then we created another object with exactly the same data and saved it too. For db4o, as this database operates with objects, any two distinct objects are different, so it will just save the second Bill Clinton object without any doubt, and we shall have two objects with the same data, which is probably not what we really want.

To avoid such a problem, we need to check whether an object with exactly the same values already exists before saving an object to the database. So here is a more robust implementation of the `addCelebrity` method:

```
public void addCelebrity(Celebrity c)
{
  ObjectSet result = db.get(c);
  if (!result.hasNext())
  {
    db.set(c);
  }
}
```

I cannot finish this demonstration of db4o without showing you an example of a Native Query—the approach we are most often going to use in real life applications. This approach isn't much more complex than QBE, by the way, but more efficient and powerful.

Let us, just for the purposes of this appendix, implement the `getRange(int indexFrom, int indexTo)` method in a way slightly different from how it was dealt with in the main body of the book. Say we want this method to return a list of `Celebrity` objects whose ID property is greater than or equal to the `indexFrom` parameter and less than or equal to the `indexTo` parameter. This is how we can define such a condition in Java:

```
celebrity.getId() >= indexFrom &&
  celebrity.getId() <= indexTo
```

For this condition to work in our native query, we need to put it into the `match` method of an implementation of the `Predicate` interface. Then we pass this `Predicate` to the `query` method of our database. To do all this, the tutorial that comes with db4o uses the "anonymous inner class" feature of the Java language that allows creating an implementation of an interface "on-the-fly". Let's follow the same approach:

```
public List<Celebrity> getRange(final int indexFrom,
    final int indexTo)
{
  List<Celebrity> result =
```

```
      db.query(new Predicate<Celebrity>()
    {
        public boolean match(Celebrity celebrity)
        {
          return celebrity.getId() >= indexFrom &&
                        celebrity.getId() <= indexTo;
        }
      });
    return result;
  }
```

This way, in pure Java, we can define any kind of condition, and there is no need to resort to any specialized query languages. By the way, we had to make method parameters final here since otherwise Java would not allow us to use them in an inner class.

The Final Strokes

Finally, here is the complete source code of the new `ObjectDataSource`:

```
package com.packtpub.celebrities.data;

import com.db4o.Db4o;
import com.db4o.ObjectContainer;
import com.db4o.ObjectSet;
import com.db4o.query.Predicate;
import java.util.List;
import org.example.myapp.model.Celebrity;
import org.example.myapp.model.Occupation;
import org.example.myapp.util.Formats;

public class ObjectDataSource implements IDataSource
{
  private ObjectContainer db;

  public ObjectDataSource()
  {
    db = Db4o.openFile("C:\\t5\\data\\celebrities.dat");
    addCelebrity(new Celebrity("Britney", "Spearce",
      Formats.parseDate("12/02/1981"), Occupation.SINGER));
    addCelebrity(new Celebrity("Bill", "Clinton",
      Formats.parseDate("08/19/1946"),
      Occupation.POLITICIAN));
  }
```

```
  public List<Celebrity> getAllCelebrities()
{
    return db.query(Celebrity.class);
  }

  public Celebrity getCelebrityById(long id)
  {
    Celebrity proto = new Celebrity();
    proto.setId(id);
    ObjectSet result = db.get(proto);
    if (result.hasNext()) return (Celebrity)result.next();
    return null;
  }

  public void addCelebrity(Celebrity c)
  {
    ObjectSet result = db.get(c);
    if (!result.hasNext())
    {
      db.set(c);
    }
  }

  public List<Celebrity> getRange(final int indexFrom,
                                  final int indexTo)
  {
    List<Celebrity> result = db.query(
      new Predicate<Celebrity>()
      {
        public boolean match(Celebrity celebrity)
        {
          return celebrity.getId() >= indexFrom &&
                 celebrity.getId() <= indexTo;
        }
      });
    return result;
  }
}
```

To make sure our application uses the new data source, not the mock one, we need to modify the `AppModule` class like this:

```
public void contributeApplicationStateManager(
    MappedConfiguration<Class, ApplicationStateContribution>
    configuration)
{
  ApplicationStateCreator<IDataSource> creator =
          new ApplicationStateCreator<IDataSource>()
          {
            public IDataSource create()
            {
      return new ObjectDataSource();
            }
          };
  configuration.add(IDataSource.class,
      new ApplicationStateContribution("session", creator));

}
```

The new data source is ready, and now the newly added celebrities will not disappear after the application's restart—this is a proper database, after all!

Of course, such a brief demonstration could not cover all, or even the most significant features of db4o. This database, with its transactions management and client/server mode of operation, is perfectly able to serve the needs of a real-life, enterprise-scale application. I encourage you to read the documentation that comes with db4o.

I am not sure how quickly db4o will find its place in the world that's got used to Oracle and SQL Server, but as for me, I am going to use this fantastic database for all my personal projects from now on.

To make sure our application uses the new data source and not the mock one, we need to modify the ApplicationClass like this:

[illegible]

C
Where to Go Next

An invaluable source of information on different versions of Tapestry is the Tapestry website (`http://tapestry.apache.org/`). Visit its Tapestry 5 (`http://tapestry.apache.org/tapestry5/`) section to find links to different resources related directly to the version discussed in this book.

Of special importance are the User Guides for Tapestry Core (`http://tapestry.apache.org/tapestry5/tapestry-core/`) and the Tapestry IOC (`http://tapestry.apache.org/tapestry5/tapestry-ioc/`).

The invaluable source of the latest of the latest news and advice is the Tapestry User List (`http://tapestry.apache.org/tapestry5/mail-lists.html`). It is quite active, and if you subscribe to it, you should be ready to receive a significant number of messages. If you are stuck with some problem, send a message to the list and chances are that someone more experienced will help you out.

Another valuable resource of knowledge is the Tapestry Wiki (`http://wiki.apache.org/tapestry/`). Here you will find many solutions for common problems—and you can share your experience too.

All that is left is to wish you creativity and inspiration that will help you to create many exciting web applications, and also patience and persistence that will help you to overcome difficulties when they arise.

Index

D

E

F

G

I

J

V

W

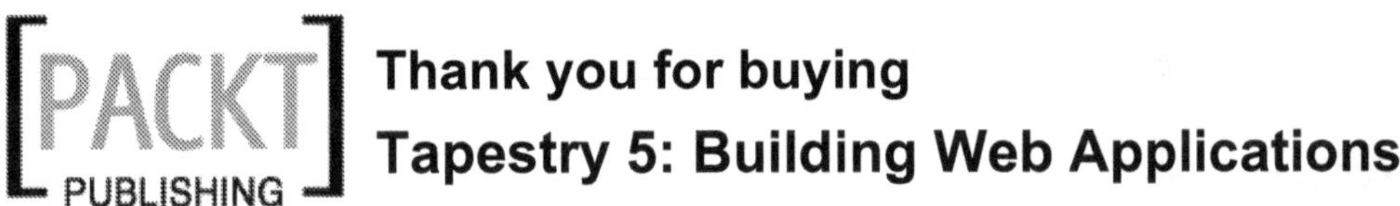

Thank you for buying
Tapestry 5: Building Web Applications

Packt Open Source Project Royalties

When we sell a book written on an Open Source project, we pay a royalty directly to that project. Therefore by purchasing Tapestry 5: Building Web Applications, Packt will have given some of the money received to the Apache Tapestry project.

In the long term, we see ourselves and you—customers and readers of our books—as part of the Open Source ecosystem, providing sustainable revenue for the projects we publish on. Our aim at Packt is to establish publishing royalties as an essential part of the service and support a business model that sustains Open Source.

If you're working with an Open Source project that you would like us to publish on, and subsequently pay royalties to, please get in touch with us.

Writing for Packt

We welcome all inquiries from people who are interested in authoring. Book proposals should be sent to `authors@packtpub.com`. If your book idea is still at an early stage and you would like to discuss it first before writing a formal book proposal, contact us; one of our commissioning editors will get in touch with you.

We're not just looking for published authors; if you have strong technical skills but no writing experience, our experienced editors can help you develop a writing career, or simply get some additional reward for your expertise.

About Packt Publishing

Packt, pronounced 'packed', published its first book "Mastering phpMyAdmin for Effective MySQL Management" in April 2004 and subsequently continued to specialize in publishing highly focused books on specific technologies and solutions.

Our books and publications share the experiences of your fellow IT professionals in adapting and customizing today's systems, applications, and frameworks. Our solution-based books give you the knowledge and power to customize the software and technologies you're using to get the job done. Packt books are more specific and less general than the IT books you have seen in the past. Our unique business model allows us to bring you more focused information, giving you more of what you need to know, and less of what you don't.

Packt is a modern, yet unique publishing company, which focuses on producing quality, cutting-edge books for communities of developers, administrators, and newbies alike. For more information, please visit our website: `www.PacktPub.com`.

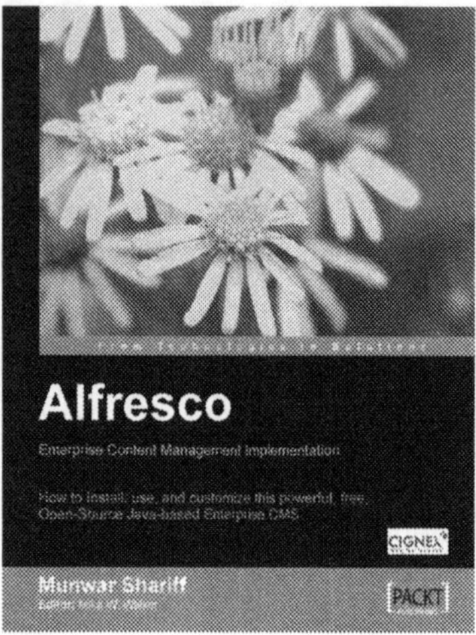

Alfresco Enterprise Content Management Implementation

ISBN: 1-904811-11-6 Paperback: 350 pages

How to Install, use, and customize this powerful, free, Open Source Java-based Enterprise CMS

1. **Manage your business documents:** version control, library services, content organization, and search
2. **Workflows and business rules:** move and manipulate content automatically when events occur
3. **Maintain, extend, and customize Alfresco:** backups and other admin tasks, customizing and extending the content model, creating your own look and feel

---

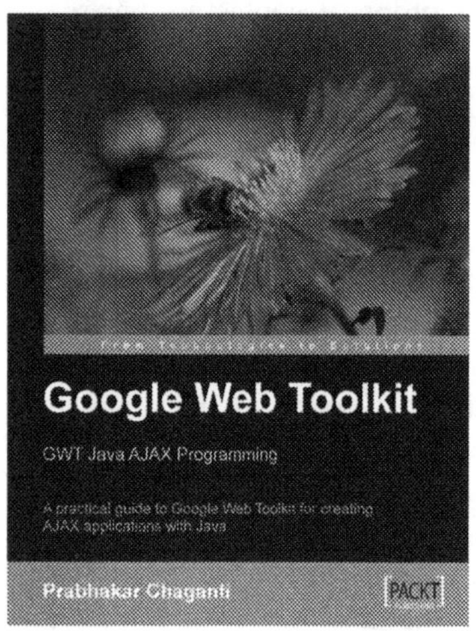

Google Web Toolkit GWT Java AJAX Programming

ISBN: 978-1-847191-00-7 Paperback: 240 pages

A step-by-step to Google Web Toolkit for creating Ajax applications fast

1. **Create rich Ajax applications** in the style of Gmail, Google Maps, and Google Calendar
2. **Interface with Web APIs** create GWT applications that consume web services
3. **Completely practical** with hands on examples and complete tutorials right from the first chapter

Please check **www.PacktPub.com** for information on our titles

Java EE 5 Development using GlassFish Application Server

ISBN: 978-1-847192-60-8 Paperback: 400 pages

The complete guide to installing and configuring the GlassFish Application Server and developing Java EE 5 applications to be deployed to this server

1. Concise guide covering all major aspects of Java EE 5 development
2. Uses the enterprise open-source GlassFish application server
3. Explains GlassFish installation and configuration
4. Covers all major Java EE 5 APIs

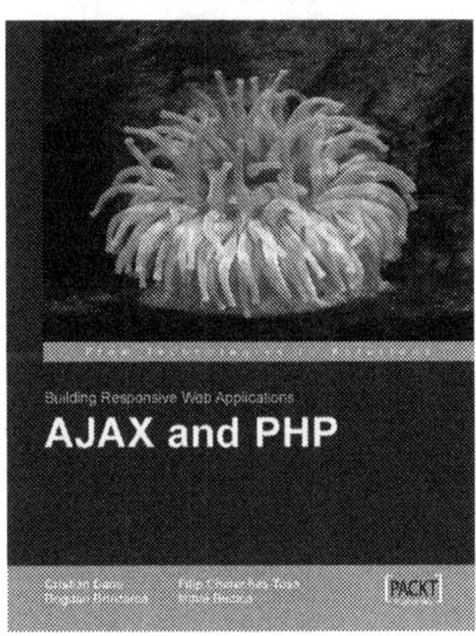

AJAX and PHP

ISBN: 1-904811-82-5 Paperback: 275 pages

Enhance the user experience of your PHP website using AJAX with this practical tutorial featuring detailed case studies

1. Build a solid foundation for your next generation of web applications
2. Use better JavaScript code to enable powerful web features
3. Leverage the power of PHP and MySQL to create powerful back-end functionality and make it work in harmony with the smart AJAX client

Please check **www.PacktPub.com** for information on our titles

www.ingramcontent.com/pod-product-compliance
Lightning Source LLC
Chambersburg PA
CBHW060527060326
40690CB00017B/3410

* 9 7 8 1 8 4 7 1 9 3 0 7 0 *